PETER FIVE

By

Freddie Clark

Published in 1993 by
Independent Books
3, Leaves Green Crescent
Keston
Bromley BR2 6DN
Great Britain

First published 1993 by Independent Books

Printed in Great Britain by
Bookcraft, Midsomer Norton, Avon.

A catalogue record for this book is available from the British Library

ISBN 1 872836 04 6

CONTENTS

PHOTOGRAPHS & ILLUSTRATIONS

For my son Paul Frederick

PREFACE

I was clearing out the attic and up there I found a trunk full of memorabilia. When I rummaged through it a manuscript typed on pink paper came to light. It had been written soon after I left the RAF in September 1947, following extended service in the hope I would continue flying - it was time wasted, I was pleased to go. My flying career would not have lasted long had it come about since when I left the service, unbeknown to myself, I was going completely deaf!

I re-read those pink pages, and relived long forgotten memories - abandoning this effort because of the hurt it gave me, remembering so many young friends who had died. At the same time I abandoned the manuscript I decided to bury those memories for ever. However, also in that trunk, I found a bundle of letters I had written home to my parents, and to Dorothy, my wife to be, and every letter that had been written to me. It was a joy reading them. I returned them reverently to the trunk, but my curiosity had been aroused.

Nearly fifty years earlier I had found myself on a 'Special Duty' Squadron, dropping supplies to the Resistance from Halifaxes. I thought it would be interesting to research what became of our exhausting and extremely dangerous efforts. I cannot say I enjoyed this research, it was a heart-aching experience with so many familiar names, long since dead, appearing like ghosts. I was nauseated with the knowledge that Lt-Col Sir Claude Edward Marjoribanks Dansey KCMG, deputy head of MI6, thought the SOE (Special Operations Executive) were amateurs interfering with his so called professional SIS (Secret or Special Intelligence Service i.e. MI6) operations. He was reputed to have been dedicated to the destruction of SOE[1] on the ground when we, poor bastards, were fighting and dying to keep it alive from the air. It was a bitter pill to swallow when I realised that he was probably acting with the knowledge of Winston Churchill[2] and we were helping to engage in the intrigue and subterfuge that went on - not all of which, lamentably, was to confuse the enemy as to the actual date and venue for 'D-Day'. Unhappily the truth will never be known since most, if not all, of the SOE files have been destroyed. Why so? If there was nothing to hide

---

[1] *'All The Kings Men' - Robert Marshall - Collins 1988*

[2] *Winston Churchill was certainly aware of the inter-departmental rivalry. He is reported to have said to General Ismay on the 10th February 1944, 'The warfare between SOE and SIS... is a lamentable but perhaps inevitable feature of our affairs.' I ask myself, if he knew about it, why didn't he stop it!?*

they should still be available. I also learned that the AOC Bomber Command, Air Chief Marshal A.T. Harris GCB, OBE, AFC was none to happy with the resources we were taking from him, and slighted us.

Most of the books I read on SOE flying dwelt largely on Lysander and Hudson flights landing in enemy occupied territory, I see no reason why this should not be so. In my opinion the pilots who flew these operations were amongst the most skilled in the Royal Air Force, but few books dwelt on the less glamorous efforts of the night to night work-horse activities of the Halifax and Stirling operations. Ken Merrick's excellent book, 'Flights of the Forgotten', published by Arms and Armour Press, is by far the best I have read on the subject of 'Special Duty' operations. However, none of the books I read told anything about how one progressed to Tempsford, what life was like there, what it was like to fly from there and, for that matter, what it was like for those who died from there.

Thus I decided to disinter those memories I had so long wished to bury and beat my way back to the attic and the pink pages which recorded my small part in affairs. With this material I thought I would try again to complete my tale. A history book, which would capture the atmosphere of the time. A story of a 'Duration of Hostilities' pilot, one of the many that went down the same path as I, made the same mistakes, and became another casualty statistic. Cemeteries and Air Force monuments are full of the names of those who served in the RAFVR, we were many, the overwhelming flood that followed *'The Few'*. I still cannot believe my luck that I survived. Someone undoubtedly guided me through to still waters, without which my name must have surely been chiselled on stone.

You may ask why I included the prologue and, for that matter, the epilogue in this book. Well, so much has been written of the 75th anniversary of the RAF I thought I would make my contribution, based on the personal story of Albert Stanley, a relative by marriage. He flew with the RFC, before the inception of the RAF, and his career represented a not untypical one of an early airforce pilot. I thought it would epitomize the vast difference in the acquired skills and living conditions of operational aircrew during the First World War, compared with that of the second, and then on to today.

The training of the RFC pilot was appallingly inadequate and he was thrown into the 'deep end' in France with little or no knowledge of what to expect. An observer in the early days of the first World War had no training at all! I suppose aircrew of the RFC and, later, the embryonic RAF were an elite Corps, the so called 'cream'. What that young generation did not realise was the more elite and the creamier you were the more expendable you became!

The first prologue would not have been possible without the generosity of

Mr J.R.Bailey, Managing Director of Bailey Bros & Swinfen Ltd, who gave me permission to use extracts of Lt. Col. Harold Hartney's book *'Wings Over France'* published by Bailey Bros & Swinfen in 1974. By the time Albert Stanley's log books came into my possession, those who could have told me much more about him had gone. I was eventually able to contact Cecil Lewis, (as the copyright had passed back to him) for permission to quote from his most wonderful book *'Sagittarius Rising'* published by Heinemann; Peter Davies. I was delighted when he wrote and said it would be in order. Unfortunately I now only have the re-issue of 1982, my first edition of 1936 was never returned when I was stupid enough to loan it out.

My thanks must go to lifelong friend 'Pip' Hagues for the occasional loan of his memory. Also to Jack Beaumont, old friend, ancient RAF pilot and ex-aviation bookseller, who said 'People (in the story) come and go like ghosts!'. I apologise for that but most of my story is about ghosts. Also to P.J.V Elliot, the librarian, and Mungo Chapman of the RAF Museum, Commandant A.E.Smit of the SAAF Museum, Pretoria, Air Commodore A.J.Bell OBE (who navigated me through 1993 pilot training!), and the Public Records Office at Kew from where I discovered so much from Operation Reports and Unit ORB's (Operational Record Books); the Air Historical Branch 5 (RAF) of the Ministry of Defence who were so patient with my questions and so helpful with their answers. My thanks also to R. Piper GMBH & CO KG of Munich - the publishers of a delightful book of poems, Morgenstern's *'Galgenlieder und Andere Gedichte'* (Gallows songs and other poems) - and allowing me to quote excerpts from them.

I found a wealth of information about the RFC and the RAF in the hands of private individuals, both authors and collectors and thank them for their willingness to impart their knowledge. Among them were: Chaz Bowyer, author and air historian, for information, the loan of photographs and 'why don't you try him,' advice. Norman Franks, another author and air historian, for valuable WW1 photographs and information. Ken Merrick, author of *'Flights of the Forgotten',* whose opening line in his letter said, 'I was very pleased to read that F/O Clark survived!' and Jonathan Falconer for 'putting me in touch'.

Finally I must sincerely thank Dorothy, my wife, who kept me going with tireless enthusiasm when so many times I flagged in sorrow or in doubt.

FBC, Keston, 1993.

In memory also of Norman Lowes, a good friend, without whose help and enthusiasm I would not have met my publishers.

PROLOGUE PART ONE

LITTLE BROWN JUG

Ha! Ha! Ha! Hee! Hee! Hee!
Little Brown Jug don't I love thee!
Ha! Ha! Ha! You and me!
Little Brown Jug don't I love thee!

'War proceeds by slaughter and manoeuvre'
(Extract from a paper by Mr Winston S. Churchill, Minister of Munitions
dated 21st October 1917.)

There stood on a sideboard in my father-in-law's house a picture of his brother. It was framed in the tip of a first World War propeller blade, probably salvaged from the wreck of a B.E.2c. The photograph shows an oval faced young man, with laughing eyes and a trace of a smile on his thin lips. He wears a forage cap at an angle on his head and a pilot's badge is proudly worn on his left breast. On his left arm below a flash declaring ROYAL FLYING CORPS is a four bladed propeller and the stripes of a Sergeant. This was Sergeant Albert Oscar Stanley - my wife's uncle Bert. I am now the proud owner of this photograph and its frame[1].

I had once seen his flying log book and noted his rank and service number and went to the RAF Museum at Hendon to see what I could find out about him. It was precious little. They then had a casualty card which, by the look of it, had been trodden into the Flander's mud. Cryptic information on it stated that some time prior to his death, as a 2nd Class Air Mechanic, he had been wounded. I remember thinking at the time it was strange that someone of that rank should have had a gunshot wound and assumed it was the result of a bullet fired from a ground-strafing German aeroplane.

On the death of her mother my wife inherited a small cardboard box. In it was Bert's 'Soldier's Small Book' (Form B30 a record of service), two flying log books or rather one he called a 'Flying Diary' and the other an Army Book 425 (a pilot's Flying Log Book) also a talisman, a tiny brown jug the size of a thumb-nail.

[1] - *See page 49.*

There was also a photograph of him as a sergeant, wearing an observer's brevet. This was a complete surprise - I knew nothing of this. His 'Small Book' informed me he had enlisted in the RFC on the 2nd July 1915, at the age of 22 years, as a Motor Driver. He was attested Air Mechanic 2nd Class at Farnborough. McCudden says in his book, *Five Years in the RFC'*, that his first month at Farnborough was spent, '...alternatively doing cook's mate or scraping the carbon off Gnome exhaust valves.' I cannot think that Albert did anything different!

After his induction at Farnborough he was posted to Netheraven on Salisbury Plain. In September 1915, No 20 Squadron was forming at Netheraven and I presume this is when he joined this squadron. However, soon after his arrival at Netheraven he was sent to Bristol. Looking at a photograph I have of him proudly standing in front of a Crossley Tender I suspect he went there for a course of instruction on this vehicle. The picture itself was published by Vine & Co., Bath.

Air Mechanic 2nd Class A.O. Stanley standing in front of a
Crossley Tender circa September 1915.

He returned to Netheraven on Sunday 16th January 1916 and went to France, probably as part of the advance party of No 20 Squadron who arrived a week later, on 23rd January. They were the first Squadron to arrive in France completely equipped with F.E.'s - Major G.J.Malcolm, in command, brought with him from *Blighty* thirteen F.E.2b's. As a 2nd Lieutenant, Royal Artillery, Malcolm first flew a B.E.2 from Montrose to Amiens with No 2 Squadron on the mobilisation of the RFC in August 1914.

There is a superb description in Cecil Lewis's book *'Sagittarius Rising'* (Heinemann & Peter Davies) of the preparation at Gosport of a F.E. squadron and its later departure to France (No 25 Squadron, the second F.E. Squadron to go). He says, 'The F.E.2b was a pusher (the engine was behind the pilot), a development of the Vickers Fighter, made by the Royal Aircraft Factory. It had a 160-h.p. Beardmore engine and an Oleo telescopic undercarriage. This, in the air, hung down like a pair of stilts on wheels; but when you touched the ground, it shut up, taking the weight and the shock of uneven landings and settling the machine on the ground in a long comfortable rumble. It was a fine machine, slow, but very sturdy, and carried a pilot, with an observer for'ard in a boot which stuck out in front of the machine (in the manner of the Shorthorn).

Forward, therefore, it had a fine arc of fire and if attacked head on, was extremely formidable. However when attacked from the rear it was necessary for the pilot to stand up in his seat, hold the stick with his knees and use his own gun, which fired backwards over the top plane - not an easy job, but frequently resorted to in a dog-fight (presumably hanging on by his teeth with neither monkey chain nor harness to secure him to his machine!). With good battle tactics, a flight of these machines was very deadly, even to an enemy with far greater speed and manoeuvrability. F.E.'s were used for bombing raids and long reconnaissances and time and time again they would fight their way home from twenty miles beyond the lines, continually circling to protect each other's tails, surrounded by enemy scouts. It's no joke to be shot up by a dozen machine guns for half an hour, engaged in a running fight in which the enemy can outpace you, outclimb you and out-turn you. It needs a lot of guts and a cool head; but the F.E.'s were manned by stout fellows.' (There were at least 5 squadrons of F.E.2bs on the Western front in November 1918 used for night bombing).

This is a great tribute to the crews of the F.E.'s but at the insistence of High Command all RFC pilot's were expected to fly and fight beyond the enemy lines deep into the occupied territories. Then to return home almost motionless in the teeth of the prevailing winds which had forced them even further over enemy territory making the stragglers easy prey for the *Jagdgeschwaders* and sitting ducks for the anti-aircraft guns.

The 'seek and destroy' and 'offensive patrol' policies of High Command undoubtedly dated back to Nelson's times and cost us numerous unnecessary casualties; as did their attitude forbidding the wearing of parachutes. When you think of the sufferings and casualties of the infantry in the hands of their Generals one wonders if they really cared about casualties other than in huge numbers recording brutal gains of few hundred yards.

At this time the F.E. was the last word in fighting aircraft. It was said, as a plus, the rear engine gave certain protection to the pilot when attacked from the rear. As a minus it was said that the same protective engine would come hurtling forward in the event of a crash and crush him! (In those days a F.E.2b airframe without an engine, guns and instruments cost £1512, the F.E.2d £1540. The engines; 120 h.p. Beardmore cost £825, the 160 h.p. version £1045 and the Rolls-Royce Eagle III £1430 !)

Cecil Lewis continued to describe the departure of No. 24 Squadron saying, 'The mechanics kicked the chocks more firmly against the wheels and sucked in the engines. Contact! The pilots spun their starting magnetos, and one by one the engines sprang to life.' I found it difficult to believe that an F.E. would start as easily as this. The 160 h.p. Beardmore engine looks as if it drove an enormous four bladed air-screw. I imagined an air mechanic ducking beneath the booms that held the tailplane to the rest of the aeroplane, where he was like a bird in a cage with little room to move about, first turning over the Beardmore engine by the air-screw and then swinging the four blades, hoping and praying that the engine would start first time. Then, once the engine fired up, the slip-stream and the acrid exhaust gasses hitting him fairly and squarely in the chest.

It intrigued me, 'How did they do it as Cecil Lewis described,' I asked ? Then I found a 1923 Royal Air Force flying training manual and in it a paragraph, 'Drill For Swinging Air-screws, para III - Engine with self starter, where swinging is NOT necessary.' It was easy. 'With switches off the air-screw is swung to suck in. The mechanic stands clear and tells pilot "All clear contact". The pilot manipulates the starting magneto (as Cecil Lewis says "Spins their starting magnetos") and the engine starts! If the engine fails to start the air-screw is moved to another position and the procedure is recommenced.' Easy!!

Cecil Lewis continues, 'Three minutes to warm them up and then a heavy roar, which rose and fell as pilot after pilot ran up his engine and tested his magnetos, and then, satisfied, throttled down again. At last they were all ready, engines ticking over, and a deep thrumming of the planes and wires vibrating filled the air. The Major dropped his hand, and 'A' Flight Commander opened his engine up, turned and taxied his way down the aerodrome. The others followed him, single file, and one by one they headed into the wind, pushed their throttles open, rose, swaying in the ground gusts, and sailed up towards the sheds.

We stood on the tarmac watching them go. And still, after twenty years, my heart swells at the memory of the sight. I can hear the strong engines and smell the tang of the burnt oil. I can see them as they came hurtling up, their goggled pilots and observers leaning down to wave a last farewell before they passed in a deafening flash of speed and smoke fifty feet overhead. One by one they came at us as if saluting us - drumroll crescendo, cymbal crash, rapid diminuendo. One by one they disappeared behind the sheds.'

The circumstances described here by Cecil Lewis must have been identical for the departure from Netheravon for France by No.20 Squadron a month earlier.

It was Bert Stanley's 'Flying Diary' written with an indelible pencil in a firm hand and in very readable English that aroused my curiosity. It was a joy to read. I had not known he had been an observer. I had been interested in the RFC since my school days and I dug out those old aviation books which I had collected at that time and began to read them again. I borrowed a book from the library called *'The First Great Air War'* by Richard Townshend Bickers and published by Hodder & Stoughton. It was in this book, to my astonishment, I read an air mechanic named Stanley was mentioned. In the bibliography there was a book called. *'Wings Over France'*, written by his first pilot, Harold E Hartney published by Bailey Brothers & Swinfen. Major James Thomas Byford McCudden VC DSO MC MM Croix de Guerre, in his book *'Five Years in the Flying Corps'*, published by The Aeroplane magazine told me more.

Lt. Col. Harold E. Hartney USAS who was Sergeant Stanley's first pilot (via Norman Franks).

No 20 Squadron was based at Clairmarais, near St. Omer. One can imagine the difficulty the pilots, fresh from England, had in finding it. Clairmarais was a large field, some twenty five acres, inverted saucer in shape, bordered on two sides by woods, and since partial use of it was still allowed to the local farmer, cattle continued to graze on it! To quote, '...unmindful of the of the mild excitement which they gave the pilots who were called on to avoid them!' (*Vol II War in the Air*, H.E Jones, Oxford page 185). At one end of the field, furthest from the hangars, was a small lake into which all and sundry would fire their guns (McCudden for one). It sounded a highly hazardous place to operate from, what with cows on the take-off and landing runs, invisible until you climbed the hill and aircraft from other squadrons popping off ammunition into the lake!

Albert Stanley's first flight recorded in his 'Flying Diary' took place at 06.45 hours on 12th June 1916 in an F.E.2d registration number, of all things, 'A1!' It was of five minutes duration and the pilot was Capt Maxwell, a pilot with whom he would fly many times. The duty was recorded as a 'joy ride!' I imagine that it was very thrilling to be stuck out in front of the aeroplane like the figure-head of a frigate in Nelson's days and breathtaking, in so far as having cold air forced into his lungs. Capt Maxwell was later to receive an MC and two DFC's, the bar being given in October 1921 for operations against the Turks. He retired from the RAF with the rank of Air Commodore.

F.E.2d number A1 in which Stanley took his first flight.

I have no knowledge of Bert's activities up to that time. One must assume that he'd had some sort of instruction on the Lewis gun and that he had at least fired some rounds from it either into the butts or into that lake. At this time there is no record of him having fired a gun from the air. In other words his crew training was nil. Arch Whitehouse reported to his F.E. Squadron No 22 having previously been up the line as a machine gunner. The sergeant who received him said all aerial gunners were barmy!! He was issued with a flying helmet, goggles, flying boots, gloves and a blood stained leather coat, the property of its previous wearer who had been killed! He'd had no air experience before he found himself in action over the lines! In his book, *The Fledgling*, he says the edge of the plywood nacelle, hardly reached his kneecaps and he was petrified! As a gunner he shot down 16 EA and 6 kite balloons and was awarded the MM. He later flew Camels as a pilot. His weekly pay as 2nd Class Air Mechanic was £1.18s 6d which included 4 shillings flying pay.

At the time Albert started flying with No 20 Squadron they were re-equipping with the new F.E.2d with a 250 h.p. Rolls Royce Eagle engine. The first F.E. 2d to go to France was delivered intact to the Germans. The pilot landing in poor visibility at Lille in mistake for St. Omer!

On June 16th 1916, Lt H.E.Hartney arrived on 20 Squadron, a 28 year old Canadian known as 'Yank'. Within two years he was to play an important part in the foundation of the U.S Air Service commanding the first pursuit group. He retired in 1921 with the rank of Lt Colonel, practising aviation law until he died at the age of 59 in 1947. When he joined No. 20 Squadron he had 19 hours solo flying (in his Book *'Wings Over France'* he termed himself as a 'fully fledged war aviator!') and the doubtful recommendation of having had Captain Aizelwood for his instructor; the officer who later had the misfortune of presenting the new F.E.2d to the Germans at Lille! No. 20 Squadron, he says, composed of three 'flights' of six aircraft, eight pilot officers each and an equal number of observer officers (he was in for a shock, many of the gunner/observers seem to have been air mechanics and N.C.O's!).

He goes on to say the Squadron was equipped with wooden framed, cloth covered hangars. This sounds like the Bessonneaux hangar of French design, probably the smaller version some sixty-five feet square with a light detachable wooden framework covered with canvas. It housed four to six two-seater aeroplanes, weighed eight and a half tons, requiring five or six lorries to transport it! He added that there were also several *'hastily'* constructed wooden dormitories and messes for each flight. Major Malcolm greeted him with, 'Glad to meet you, Hartney,' shook his hand and continued, 'Happy to welcome you to the best outfit (though I doubt if he used this word!) in France. You have nineteen hours solo, I see, but hours mean nothing. All you need are guts and loyalty!' At the end of his little speech Malcolm wished him 'Good luck,' which I would have thought Hartney needed more that anything else!

Two days later, on 18th June, Immelmann, one of the great German fighter pilots of that time, was shot down by a No. 25 Squadron F.E.2b, crewed by 2nd Lt G.R.McGubbin, the pilot and Cpl J.H.Waller the gunner. On 20th June, at 05.37, Lt Hartney and 2nd Class Air Mechanic Stanley took the air in the oldest F.E.2b on the Squadron which he says he inherited along with four 'ground men' to look after it. It was Hartney's first F.E. flight and Stanley's second. They were aloft for 58 minutes. Albert recorded it as a 'patrol'. Hartney did not record this flight in his book.

Hartney records the second flight they had together that day as his first ever! I will quote him from his book. 'My first flight was to make or break me. I was to take up 'A9' Rolls at 3.16 pm June 20 with AM. Stanley as gunner. It was a dizzy affair, right in front of my flight commander and the Squadron C.O. I had studied all the plane's instruments and gadgets and could have located them blindfolded. I had checked and double checked fuel, oil, temperature and other items and bumped off down that awful field for a take off (that I can imagine, what a perfect description). Rising nicely and not too abruptly I was beginning to pat myself on the back when - whang! - bang! - bang! - whang! The engine was stalling - one bank of six cylinders cut out. Down went the nose like a bullet and in the steepest bank I had ever made in my twenty-odd hours of flying I turned abruptly and glided back to the field with a dead engine and landed back on the runway (?) downwind with scarcely a bump. Any flyer today knows that such a manoeuvre is practically always fatal. It is the way Hobey Baker and countless others have been killed. Hardly anyone gets away with it, I was fortunate beyond words. I lived and was actually complimented because the last boy trying it had been killed only the week before. The order, "Land straight ahead if your motor stalls on the take-off", had not yet been written. Flying was too young.

F.E.2b number A9. referred to in the text. It was built by the Royal Aircraft Factory, Farnborough, Hants, and was presented to the RFC by the residents of the Punjab (Imp. War Museum ref: Q27644).

Within a few minutes I had made another take off and did a little overhead sightseeing around Clamarais (Clairmarais) and took a short circle over St Omer, the air depot nearby.'

Bert Stanley writes in his flying diary: '20 June, aircraft 'A8', Pilot Lt Hartney, hour 3.16, air time 12 minutes. Pilot's first time with Rolls Royce. Climbed to 4000 and engine konked out over St. Omer. Thought we were in the soft stuff but he banked around a bit and made a fine landing. Damn good pilot.' I can imagine a white-faced Bert grimly holding on to the nacelle, stuck out into the firing line so to speak looking rather like a wind swept Valkyrie.

For the next ten days Bert flew 10 sorties, 5 of which were patrols, the shortest one lasting 2 hours. On 23rd June, the day the artillery barrage intensified for the forthcoming Battle of the Somme, he flew for 2 hours and 49 minutes. Intermingled with these patrols were flights used for 'gunnery' and one imagines that he was firing his Lewis gun from the air into the lake at the end of the airfield. This appears to be his only flying training, a total flying time of 1 hour 26 minutes - an average of 17 minutes per sortie! The pilots for 9 of these sorties are not recorded, only one, 'a test', was shown to be flown with Lt Hartney.

On 30th June Bert records in his diary: 'Hour 5.34, Air Time 1 hour 54 minutes, Duty Recon. Picked up 16 B.E's with bombs at Abeele (No 6 Squadron were based there) and escorted them over Lille where they dropped their duff. This was reported in German Offs (?) as doing no damage of military importance, but killing 70 odd civvies. Archied (anti-aircraft fire) like blazes. Moral: That's the stuff to give 'em.' (I believe the target was the ammunition depot at St. Sauveur station, Lille.)

Hartney, on the other hand, was detailed for his first operational sortie. He was to fly south down the line and land on a field beside a canal, refuel, and escort thirty bombers to bomb German balloon sites. They were well received and enjoyed a 'grand luncheon'. Hartney had flown 20 hours solo at that time and had only one hour over the front. He says he kept it quiet! Each of the bombing aircraft had two 60 pound phosphorous bombs, '...on racks hastily constructed.' (85 of them complete with special carriers had arrived in France on the 16th June.) The crews of the bombers, he says, knew their targets well and the idea was at zero hour, attacks on balloon sites from the North Sea to Strasbourg would occur simultaneously.

Hartney in his book writes, 'The idea this time was a sudden surprise mass attack with phosphorous bombs. It was a good plan theoretically. Already the home defence units had discovered that the flaming bullet was the only practical missile against the lighter-than-air craft. But one lucky British flyer, Warneford, had brought down a Zepplin (his spelling) in flames over Dunkirk with a phosphorous bomb and the high command became temporarily mad on them'.[2]

They waited for the bombers to take off; the F.E.'s superior speed would soon enable them to catch up. A phosphorous bomb on the first aircraft dropped off as it was taxying and exploded, likewise a bomb dropped off the second aircraft! He says that those two aircraft were instantly in the centre of an appalling hurricane of phosphorous streaking in every direction. When the excitement died down two hangars and five aircraft had been destroyed, including one new F.E.2d belonging to No 20 Squadron! The operation continued and he said he finally got a glimpse of phosphorous bombs bursting on the ground up and down the front line, none striking their targets! On the way back he encountered a Rumpler and forgot that it had a gunner in the rear cockpit and failed to co-operate with his own gunner, a man named Hodder. He wasn't very happy with himself when he landed, but he certainly must have learnt from this encounter with the enemy, as we shall see.[3]

The following day, Saturday 1st July, the British infantry left their forward trenches to advance into no-man's-land. The Battle of the Somme had begun. (It is said there were 30,000 casualties during the first hour!) Hartney and Stanley were detailed to fly together. Hartney writes: 'July 1st, 1916, Canada's famous Dominion Day, was to mark the first real Allied offensive. Surely the war would not last long after the Allies got under way that day, in the first battle of the Somme! (How often were we to hear something similar in World War II together with that other morale booster - 'Home for Christmas!') The main theatre of operations adjoined us to the south, but to flyers in the air, naturally, there is no clean cut line anywhere. Fifteen miles

[2] - *I must comment on this! Flight Sub-Lieutenant R.A.J. Warnford of the R.N.A.S. dropped six 20lb bombs on the Zeppelin LZ.37. at an altitude of 11,000 feet from a Morane. The time was 01.50 hours on 7th June 1915 (over a year before the operation Hartney is referring to). The subsequent explosion of the airship broke a fuel line on his aircraft and he had to land in enemy territory where it took him 35 minutes to repair the damage. He finally started his engine by himself then took-off in thick fog eventually landing at Cape Gris-Nes. He was awarded the Victoria Cross for this action - the first air victory over a Zeppelin. He was killed ten days later when a Henri Farnam aeroplane in which he was flying broke up in the air near Paris.*

[3] - *I have searched for reference to this operation but can find nothing other than the arrival in France of the bomb racks and phosphorus bombs on the 16th June. I am not suggesting it did not happen but I would have thought that such a balls up would have been worthy of mention by the historians.*

or so one way or the other makes little difference. On the night of 30th June, about ten o'clock, our big Scots flight commander called us all to the officers' mess hall - combat orders for the big push had come through and we were to do our part with the whole squadron. I had done well with my Rolls that day so I was switched to another one, A3, and was to take along First "Ack Emma" Stanley, the best gunner in the outfit'. (Bert was not actually promoted First Class Air Mechanic until the coming October! He had, at the time of which Hartney writes, 14 hours flying and as far as I can make out had never fired his guns in anger at anything other than the lake at the end of the airfield. Hartney had had about 21 hours solo. They could hardly be termed 'experienced'!)

'No more patrols on our side of the lines,' continues Hartney. 'From now on it's fifteen miles over and we'll sink everything in sight. This war's got to end. We must knock the Germans out of the air, especially over a couple of aerodromes near Lille. Big doings down south and the show is over!' Hartney then goes on to deliver a heavy lecture on the obedience of orders and then continues the briefing. 'Be in your planes with the engines ticking over at 4 a.m. and be ready to push off promptly at 4.15 a.m. You will cross at Armentieres on our side, and then back over. Keep doing so. Strafe everything in sight.' (This was an unbelievably short briefing, as I am sure it was. No information on army objectives, weather, alternative landing grounds, enemy defences. It goes to show how little they knew when they took off. I wonder if the gunners/observers were present?)

Hartney continues to say that No 20 Squadron was the first to use formation flying (As far as I can make out these five aircraft flew in a loose 'card five' configuration. The flight commander in the centre, the forward two slightly higher than the flight commander and the rear two five machine lengths back and considerably higher). In Hartney's own words, 'The theory was that the gunners in the front two planes would watch the higher rear planes and transmit their signals to the leader in the lowest centre plane. With pusher-type machines this arrangement was ideal and gave plenty of gun play in every possible direction from which an attack may come and, in turn, afforded a good field of fire for us in pouring bullets from our side.' (I am not sure if I understand this!)

Hartney goes on to say, 'This was the first dawn patrol and everything worked perfectly. Thanks to fair weather, we formed up quickly over Cassel at 4,000 feet and began a steady climb to the lines east and slightly south. I shall never forget that climb in formation. My position on the left rear I knew was the one always assigned to the newest arrival in the squadron and was invariably the plane first attacked by the enemy - frequently picked off at the beginning of the battle.' (It follows, but it surely depends which way you are going and the position of the sun!) 'I did not worry whatever about that, but there was plenty of excitement in me as we roared forth into mortal combat (!!). Ahead and below me over the top wing of the left advanced plane I could see the gunner in the cockpit with his eye on me and he, in turn, was in line with the other front plane and closely watched by the flight commander in the middle ship. I felt entirely safe with such protection in addition to Sergeant Stanley, my own veteran gunner.' (Bert, hardly a veteran, is certainly getting some rapid promotion!)

They crossed the line at 4:55 at 10,000 feet; assuming they took off on time at 4:15 this meant they climbed at 250 feet a minute. As expected they were shot at by 'Archie' the nearest 'soft blossom of lethal smoke' some 400 yards away. In Hartney's own words, 'There was a slight breeze blowing from the west, a dangerous thing when your home base is in the west. (This was the prevailing wind anyway.) Presently I could make out the big industrial cites of Lille, Tourcoing, and Roubaix standing out clearly in the morning sun. I could see two enemy aerodromes and even from ten thousand feet I could discern several planes taking off to come up after us. Once in the air they seemed to disappear, but I knew we would have some fun with them. About five miles south and east of Lille, on signal we made a slow turn to the left, my machine acting as a pivot, high above the others. Back to Armentiers we sped, in perfect formation, (Without any previous practice or training keeping formation must have been extremely difficult, I know my first efforts were) climbing steadily up to 12,500 feet. (Without oxygen in those days.) We got another greeting of 'archies' falling far short, as we scurried over the lines, then freedom for a few minutes as we sailed over our own territory, then around in turn to go back at them again.'

They were turning again at 13,000 feet over Lille when in the east Hartney spotted two little specks, enemy planes circling, watching, and climbing. During the turn Hartney saw the same two little specks wheel and come in a flattish dive at Lt Callender flying the right rear aircraft. Hartney fired his Verey pistol to warn everyone they were about to be attacked. At the same time as the flare ignited '...two smoky streaks of tracer bullets' came from the German aircraft. 'The two planes zipped past Callender, almost as if they were going right through him, brave men, then turned above and behind him, I swerved for the attack - to shoot them off Callender's tail. Like all fresh pilots, I was quivering with anxiety to land my first quarry. He saw me first, however, and veered sharply away, scooting straight north. Callender, still unhit, did an Immelmann turn (In an F.E.2d! - a roll off the top of a loop, my thoughts are with the gunner hanging on by the skin of his teeth!) and was soon mastering the other plane. I was fascinated, watching my gunner on the one hand, and Callender's scrap on the other. Handling his Lewis machine guns with wonderful coolness, holding his fire when useless, giving short, quick bursts when it seemed likely to be effective, Callender's gunner literally butchered that poor single seater light rotary-engined Fokker monoplane. (The Fokker E III was at time the most deadly fighting machine in the air although the tide was just beginning to turn against it.) In a few seconds the hun was belching smoke and flame and was on its way to the ground.'

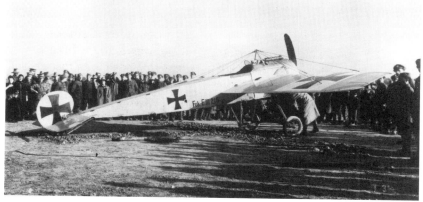

The Fokker E III the first single engined fighter to be fitted with a machine gun capable of firing forward through the airscrew. It reaped a grim harvest up to the spring of 1916 (Imp. War Museum ref:Q66596).

He now realised he had lost height to 8,500 feet and gone too far north. Stanley had signalled that both his guns were jammed and was busy clearing the stoppages. Climbing at 60 m.p.h. he was making little progress and it occurred to him that, '...things were suspiciously quiet round here!' He then undid his safety belt, grasped the radiator cap behind him, let go of the control column, and lifted himself up to peer over the tail. (This is incredible! - What nerve! Although McCudden said he sometimes did this, the F.E. being so stable, his observer never approved, more so after once, when standing up, McCudden's glove came off and knocked off a propeller blade!)

Hartley goes on to say, 'Swarms of bullets came snapping past my ears on both sides, smokers and clear ones. And as I looked up quickly there was a Fokker monoplane diving straight at me from above. To this day, all I have to do to bring that awful sight back is to close my eyes - it appears before me instantly like the black spots you see after looking at a welding torch - a simple, straight, oncoming black mid-wing monoplane with a rounded cowl hurtling through the air at me is engraved forever on my retina. Stanley, busy with his guns, did not know what was going on. He did not even look up. With safety belt still unbuckled I threw myself back into my seat.

This photograph illustrates the difficulties and dangers facing the F.E.2d gunner when under attack. He had no safety harness to anchor him to the aircraft. This particular F.E. belonged to 20 Squadron based at St. Marie Chappel, France, 1916/17. Pilot - Capt F.D. 'Inky' Stevens, the observer / gunner - W.C. Cambray (Imp. War Museum ref:Q69650).

(I bet he never did that again!) Frightened out of my wits, I leaned over and hit Stanley a vicious clout on the head...' He goes on to tell of the unlikely manoeuvres he flung the aircraft into with Bert, '...clinging tensely to the nacelle ring!' (Why both of them didn't fall out I shall never know!) After which there in front and below appeared the Fokker. The begoggled pilot quite clear in his black helmet. Bert shot him down in flames.

In Hartney's own words: 'As the poor fellow went down, Stanley turned around to me with a sickly, half-guilty but triumphant smile below his leather-rimmed face mask and goggles. With one hand he signalled 'thumbs down' for the fallen enemy - a traditional gesture with all war aviators. I banked up and looked over the side for a moment to see where the Fokker hit. Then I came to my senses. We were much farther over the enemy lines than we should have been, our fuel was running low and we had a nasty headwind. It was time to scuttle home - a mean job well done. I had killed or helped to kill, my first German. I could feel no exaltation. I could only think of that black clad flyer and his family.'

Stanley reloaded his guns and gave them a short testing burst. Hartney could see the remaining three front aircraft of his formation high above. 'High in the blue - and completely out of touch'. Stanley came to life pointing over the tail then shaking his fist madly - signifying enemy aircraft! They were at 7,000 feet then, ten miles behind the enemy lines and short of fuel! It was the aircraft that had previously turned away from them now coming into attack. Stanley touched the rear mast mount, which signified he could not bring his guns to bear, at the same time pulling his hand back into his stomach. Hartney, as instructed, pulled back on the stick and Stanley got a few shots at the Fokker as it went over the top of them. Hartney went after him. 'Stanley looked around to see me frantically shaking my fist to signal an E.A.[4] ahead. And he was shaking his fist just as furiously to tell me of an E.A. to the rear. It was two against one! Finally, on insistent signals from Stanley, I steadied out and his cool eyes and flexible guns caught one of the Boche ships in a vital spot on a pot shot as it dived away from us. It was so close we seemed about to ride on his back.'

A ground haze hid the lines from view. Hartney was thinking about spending the rest of the war in a prison camp when another attack was mounted by the same two aircraft. One appeared to be cautious and veered away. The other pressed home his attack and as he appeared in front of the F.E., Stanley gave 'a knowing, "OK",' whereupon Hartney got onto the

4 - E.A. - Enemy Aircraft.

Fokker's tail. 'A sitting shot' - Stanley gave him a burst and the Fokker, with smoke pouring from him, appeared to dive straight towards the ground. They had now recovered five miles nearer the lines, but were still too far south. Stanley again signalled 'Hun on tail' and Hartney signalled 'Hun in front'! Before Hartney could engage bullets ripped into the nacelle and into the cowling, he had no idea the man behind was so close! He describes it: 'A startled glance at my instruments, a "shove away" of Stanley's number one gun, which was completely *hors de combat* and only a few bullets left for the second, two Boche pumping bullets at us, a rough engine, spluttering, quitting, a vain call from Stanley for manoeuvres I couldn't deliver, a sudden but momentary revival of the engine, the rev counter swaying madly from 10 to 1,800, air pressure gone, the needle of the oil pressure gauge down to zero. A hell of a situation! Prepare to land, but dodge that last one if possible!' (The 1916 version of 'nothing on the clock but the maker's name!')

One Fokker was coming in from the front, Stanley signalled both guns jammed. Hartney, at 6,000 feet, turned towards Armentieres and started to stretch his dive towards the lines. At a 1,000 feet he was shocked by the pock-marked ground below, but was pleased to see the trenches appear beneath, when the engine stopped. Stalling over some tall poplar trees on the Armentieres to Bailleul Road, he touched down in a small field '...moderately full of shell holes,' ruining the kitchen garden of the troops in the support trenches.

He goes on to say, 'Stanley and I jumped out quickly, "Right-o, that'll do!" he said and came over and put his arm around me. Then we began to inspect our plane. It was in a horrible shape, riddled with bullets, how it held together is a mystery. The fabric, in places, was torn clear from the leading edge to the trailing. If we had tried to paint an Iron Cross on every hole, as we did later in the war, it would have taken all night. That motor should have been put in a museum. It saved our lives, but how it did I don't know to this day. Seven bullets were actually sticking in the water jackets and in the plumbing. The cowling was almost a sieve. And here's the gospel truth, although my word on it has often been doubted - four of the aluminium pistons, a secret Rolls-Royce innovation, had actually fused and were holding up four of the exhaust valves. There was no water whatever in the engine and practically no oil. For those last few minutes it had been doing its bit for England metal to metal - at melting temperatures. I pulled out two of the bullets and kept them as souvenirs. Stanley, much more experienced than I, (Sic!) merely shook his head, mumbling, "A miracle! A bloody miracle!"'.

They had landed among some Australians who said the war was practically over (1st July 1916! There were yet to be a million more casualties before the war finished) and that they would get in touch with their squadron. Hartney and Stanley then took a short nap under the wing of their machine in the middle of the battle of the Somme. They were woken by an enemy shell bursting four hundred yards away!

During the ninety minutes (!!) air fighting Stanley said they had been in eleven scraps, his guns being out of action during two and a half of them!. He said they could claim nine victories because in one of the scraps he knew they had got two! Hartney knew it was ridiculous to claim nine victories because up to that time two in one sortie had been the maximum.

There followed an altercation on the telephone with the Squadron Commander Major Malcolm, who was upset that one of his precious Rolls-Royce driven F.E.'s had been damaged - there were only eight in France at that time. The C.O suggested that a new engine be sent out and then they would be able to fly the machine back to base! As it was they managed to convince him that it would have to be towed back. On the way the wheel bearings of the F.E. seized up which made towing a slow job. They arrived back at camp at 5 a.m, just in time to see the dawn patrol taking off! The unsympathetic adjutant said, 'Wish you hadn't ruined that machine of yours, we need it badly!'

Bert Stanley wrote in his flying diary:- 'Date 01 Jul: Pilot Lt Hartney: Hour 4.15-6.50: Air time 2h 35m: Duty Special patrol & Strafe and Recon. We were rear left machine. We went for a Hun that attacked rear right machine (Flown by Lt Callender) and chased him for miles over their lines. Think I got him alright as he seemed to be on fire and dived to the ground like hell. Got a bad jam in gun. To cut a long story short we had nine separate scraps with Fokkers, three with two at a time and wound up again over Lille with engine shot through, both guns jammed and dropping like the very devil. Another Hun attacked us, but I sighted gun on him, as soon as he saw it he dived to earth without firing a shot. Came over Lille at 4,000 to 'Archie' galore, and passed over trenches within rifle fire and landed between Armentieres and Nieppe safely and went and had breakfast. Main oil pipe shot through, petrol tank hit, but ricocheted off, cylinder shot through and jacket, pistons melted and thrown through exhaust ports, four pressure pipes and some wires shot away and compensating wire nearly severed and plenty of shot through plane, so altogether we were damned lucky to get back at all. Absolutely certain we brought down 2 Fokkers and damaged another.

Moral: If you are born to be drowned you'll never get shot.'

Callender, the pilot who fell out of the formation, was shot down,

wounded and never returned to No 20 Squadron. Hartney, believe it or not, was later threatened with a court martial for leaving the formation! Major Malcolm and his gunner, Lieutenant Chanceller, were killed later that same day when the engine of the F.E.2d they were flying failed on take off. The aircraft stalled and they plunged into the ground. He was replaced next day by Major W.H.C.Mansfield DSO. Bert flew 5 sorties during 2nd July and the 5th, Duty 'Patrol'. He had already flown an early 55 minute patrol on 6th July when he was called upon to fly again late with Lt Henshaw in the afternoon. They took off at 6.41 on a flight lasting one hour thirty minutes. Duty was: 'Pract Recon & Scrap at Abule' This is what he wrote about it:- 'Engine conked out prior to reaching aerodrome and forced to land at Nordpeene. Landed on grass very fast & machine ran on into some high crops, where front wheel stuck into ground, under-carriage smashed up & machine turned head over heels. Pilot unhurt, badly shaken but very lucky. My seat smashed to pulp. Had a damned narrow escape, thrown out a second before & pinned to the ground by top C.S. (Centre section?) leading edge with beaucoup weight. Statement that these machines weigh about two tons absolutely incorrect. The damn things weigh at least 50. Luckily about 8 men quickly arrived on the scene just in time to prevent my proving the old schoolboy rule that: 1 into 2 will go. Luckily got off with bruises & only a smashed foot. Sent to dock at St Omer. Jolly decent show. There for 12 days. Came out at a word going to Blighty or Base. Foot not right.
Moral. 'The devil always looks after his own,' so be one of the boys!' A Court of Enquiry into the accident was held on the 7th July 1916.

The next day, 8th July, while Stanley was in hospital, Flight Sergeant J.T.B.McCudden M.M, Croix de Guerre joined No 20 Squadron. He had then already flown a considerable number of hours as a observer with No 3 Squadron, returned to the UK for training as a pilot, remained at CFS[5] and had accumulated 100 flying hours when he arrived at Clairmarais. Later, flying with No 56 Squadron, he reached the rank of Major and with 57 victories received the V.C. D.S.O and Bar and M.C. and bar. He was killed crashing on take off at Auxi-le-Chateau in July 1918. He had not, up to the time of joining No 20 Squadron, flown an F.E.2b at all. His conversion training consisted of a flight the following morning. A flight which he describes in his own words, 'I flew the next morning with great vigour, and felt very pleased with my machine. The C.O was pleased too, but I am sorry to say that he was killed the same evening.' (This must have been the death

[5] - *CFS - Central Flying School.*

of Major Malcolm referred to by Hartney.)

On July 20th Hartney was in bed with a sore throat. (He said it was the 21st). He heard from his bed the B Flight patrol go off without him. He says fog was closing down and he thought it was pretty thick for a patrol to go out. He goes on to say that the fog bank had come down to the ground and that every machine, five of them, had crashed to smithereens and only Capt Maxwell and two observers had survived. McCudden writes, 'On July 20, five machines left the aerodrome at 5.30 p.m. to do an offensive patrol. We were to rendezvous over our aerodrome at 10,000 feet; Capt Maxwell was leading. Whilst climbing I noticed a low mist blowing down from the north-west, and by the time we had manoeuvred into our correct position in the formation we could not see the ground. We flew east for about twenty minutes, and then turned east-south-east. As far as I could judge at this time we should have been somewhere over Lille, but as my observer and I could not see the ground, it was difficult to say. We flew east-south-east for about thirty minutes and then turned west. We could now occasionally see the ground, and I could see by the villages that we were over unfamiliar country. We flew west for some time and then through a gap in the mist I saw what I mistook for the town of Bailleul; so, as the formation had now dissolved, I decided to get under the mist and follow the main road to Clairmarais.

When I got down to 2,000 feet I saw that the mist was decidedly low, and I continued to go down and ran into it at 600 feet. I still went down in an endeavour to get under the mist, and then just in front of and above me loomed up a large row of trees, such as always border the Routes Nationales of France. I at once switched on, zoomed over the trees, and trusted my lucky stars that the country was fairly clear in front. Fortunately it was, and I made some pretence of landing, finally running through a small fence then stopping in the back yard of a small French farmhouse.'

The machine had sustained no damage and they walked to a nearby village and had a welcome breakfast. They had landed some forty miles south of their area and waited until mid-day for the fog to clear. They heard from a Gendarme that a machine had crashed about a mile away killing Capt Teale, who had just arrived on the Squadron, and his observer Cpl Stringer. Cpl Stringer, normally McCudden's gunner, had been showing Capt Teale the local landmarks. McCudden took off again and flew back to Clairmarais where he heard that only one more had got back, Capt Maxwell being the other. Three, including Teale, had crashed.

Stanley making his first flight after spending 12 days in hospital says in his flying diary:- '20 Jul Capt Batherwick 5.22-8.45 3h.23m Strafing Patrol Slight mist when we started out, but got worse until impossible to see ground 'til within 30 ft. Short of petrol, forced to land. We were landing straight into some trees, but pilot saved by opening up & doing terrific bank. We just shaved trees & shot over the other side into a small corn field alongside a road. As machine hit ground pilot & I were knocked unconscious, but somehow stuck to machine. From all accounts machine ran through corn, dropped down 5ft bank onto road and ran across. At other side small ft (front?) wheel stuck into ground & machine turned over down 40ft cliff struck ground at foot on undercarriage & again turned over 2 or 3 times. Machine was found in 3 heaps, remains of engine resting on ground on prop. Pilot came round first & says he pulled me from under planes (wings). We both looked pretty specimens and an ambulance quickly arrived and took us to No 5 Stat.(?) Pilot broke nose & was sent to Blighty. I was only badly knocked & shaken & rejoined squadron after 6 days. All who saw it and smash remains say it was absolutely marvellous we got out alive. I don't know how we did it, except that the pilot was one of the boys & the Devil looked after us both. Another machine that was with us smashed & pilot & observer were killed. Another landed & getting off fractured observer's spine (crashed on take off). Jolly bad luck. Had a week's rest after I left dock.'

F.E.2b crash at roadside near Ypres 9.11.17. (Imp War Museum ref:E(AUS)4616).

McCudden, in his book, tells of a sortie on 2nd August, where 6 B.E.2c's escorted by 4 Morane Biplanes went to bomb the Zeppelin sheds at Brussels. Six F.E.'s also went to meet these machines on their return. The F.E.'s crossed the lines at 12,000 feet and flew over Commines, Menin, Courtrai and when over Oudenarde they spotted the B.E.'s and Moranes coming from the east. They had been unmolested. The B.E.'s had been in the air 6 hours when the formation broke up to land. Bert's flying diary recorded, '02 Aug, 1.21-4.03, 2h 42m, Recon Brussels'!

On the 4th August Stanley was graded Qualified Observer 2nd Class Air Mechanic! His flying time was 37 hours 12 minutes! The day previously McCudden had been posted to 29 Squadron then based at Abeele. He was to fly D.H.2's in which, on 6th September, he was to score the first of his 57 victories. On 6th August, Bert was in the air at 9.44 for 1 hour 15 minutes. He took off again at 2.12 for a flight of 1 hour 37 minutes. This is what he says about the landing: 'Nearly had a bad smash as engine cut out just as about to land & nearly smashed into trees & fence. Broke engine bearers & skid & had to have new machine' He was again in the air at 6.14 pm for another 1 hour 57 minutes, making the days total 4 hour 49 minutes. Without any further flying he was sent home on leave on 18th August.

Capt. RS Maxwell MC, DFC & Bar. (S St. Martin via Norman Franks).

He next flew two uneventful sorties on 6th September, likewise on the 7th. On the 8th he was flying with Capt R.S.Maxwell, the first time he has been mentioned in his diary since that first flight on 12th June. Capt Maxwell's combat report says at 3.5 p.m., on patrol at 13,000 feet they met a enemy aircraft, 'Believed to be late type L.V.G., speed at 13,000 ft about the same as F.E.. Machine gun firing backwards'. The narrative continued as follows: 'Whilst on patrol the F.E. crossed the lines to prevent the hostile aircraft approaching the line & pursued it back to just S. of Lille before getting to close range. The F.E. fired six drums and after 2 or 3 minutes fighting the H.A.[6] dived spirally still firing. The F.E. still firing kept close range till at an altitude of 4,500 ft., the H.A. went down vertically into clouds & was lost from view.' Bert, in his diary, says:- '08 Sep A29 Capt

[6] - *H.A. - Hostile Aircraft*

R.S.Maxwell 1.37-4.33 2h.56m Offensive Patrol. Met an Aviatik over Lille & had a scrap. The Hun dived down at terrific speed to earth & got into a spinning nose dive. We followed to 4,500 ourselves & nearly did the same & the Hun fell clean away from us. Confident he smashed up. The other machine with us on patrol had a scrap & coming back, pilot was hit by an archie & arm was fractured & hit in leg but managed to land 1,000 yds this side firing line. We went up in the evening, dismantled machine & got it away.'

A week later he was again flying with Capt Maxwell. Whilst on Patrol at 10,000 feet they met an Aviatik and another biplane, unknown but firing through the propeller. The narrative of the combat report reads as follows: 'F.E. approaching the lines at 13,000 feet sighted Aviatik on the line coming towards YPRES Salient from the north. F.E. dived to 9,000 feet, and opened fire. Aviatik dived firing and F.E. caught up Aviatik, holding fire on the steep part of the dive. On partially flattening out at 4,000 feet F.E. was hampered by second H.A. following an (on?) F.E.'s tail and firing through propeller. F.E. recommenced firing at Aviatik but one gun jammed through faulty cartridge, and the deflector bag broke loose on the other gun. The range at this point was about 20 yards (!!). F.E. then turned and recrossed, landing at ABEELE owing to cover of reduction gear being shot and allowing oil to leak. Both H.A. when last seen appeared to be under full control. Bert wrote: '15 Sep A29 Capt R.S.Maxwell 12.02-12.57 0h.55m Patrol. Met an Aviatik over other side of YPRES started scrapping. After a bit he went down in a stiff nose dive & we followed. Another Hun came behind us & started putting it in. When we turned on him he went down too. Got about (? - word missing from narrative) shots through planes & on through end of crankcase letting all the oil out. We came down at ABEELE, I repaired it & we flew home. During fight the Captain's gun jammed & my deflector bag came off. Very lucky for Fritz.' That day, on the pock marked ground below, 41 tanks assisted the infantry in their advance. Their deployment wasn't all the surprise it should have been. A German kite balloon observer had spotted and reported their movement twenty four hours before they went into action. The Battle of the Somme still had two months to go before it finally petered out.

Bert Stanley flew on patrol for 2 hours 26 minutes on 16th September. On the 17th Capt Maxwell wrote another combat report at 10.45 a.m. On that day in the area of WERVICQ-BOUSBEQUE, they were flying a long patrol at 13,000 feet. They were to meet an H.A (No.1) 'With a stationary engine[7], fixed tail plane, otherwise like Fokker biplane, but shorter in fuselage.' H.A. No.2 was an Aviatik. The narrative reads as follows: 'F.E.2d going S. from PASSCHENDAELE sighted H.A. No.1 going W at about 9,000 ft. F.E.2d went on going South in order to dive at H.A from the South. F.E.2d dived at H.A. from the direction of the sun, and when at a range of about 100 yds., H.A. turned S.E. under F.E.2d which pursued down to 5,000 ft. (firing 5 drums) to a point S. of BOUSBEQUE, when H.A. went down in spinning nose dive, but could not be seen lower that a few hundred feet owing to clouds. F.E. started to regain height and from 7,000ft the wreckage of the H.A. was distinctly seen through a large space in the clouds at S.E. corner of large wood S. of BOUSBEQUE.'

H.A.2: 'F.E.2d at 10,000 ft at 11.10 a.m. saw H.A. over ARMENTIERES, being shelled at 12,000 ft., F.E. followed H.A. back to LILLE firing 3 drums, but failed to get nearer than about 150 yds. No decisive result was observed.'

Bert Stanley had this to say about it: '17 Sep A29 Capt R.S.Maxwell 9.50-12.08 2h.18m. Chased a Roland Scout (?) engaged him & brought him down he crashed from about 5,000. Verified by 2 pilots at Bailleul & one of our own pilots flew over & saw wreck. We also engaged two other Huns but both managed to eventually get off.' The first aircraft engaged in the narrative was Capt Maxwell's fourth and last victory on F.E.2ds. The next of a further five was on 18th January 1918 whilst flying Sopwith Camels and Commanding No 54 Squadron. Stanley's confirmed score was now three!

Capt Maxwell was to write another combat report on 22nd September with Bert as his gunner, but Bert was getting more laconic with his descriptive notes in his flying diary and says very little about the action:- '22 Sep A29 Capt Maxwell 9.33-12.22 2.50m Patrol. 2 scraps with Fokker Biplane and Aviatik.' He flew another 2 hours 56 minutes that day. Another two sorties the next day, and a further two the day after. Then on 26th September there is one of those poignant little notes that appears in diaries recording an event that must have had a profound effect on the writer. Bert wrote about it in his flying diary as follows:- '26 Sep A8 Lt Livingstone 6.12-8.00 Patrol Obs 1/AM F.Dearing 9882 Died of wounds at 1.30pm. Buried at C.C.S. (Casualty Clearing Station) 27.9.16. A brave big-hearted lad. God Bless him.' Dearing now rests in Ligsenthouk Military Cemetery, Belgium, regrettably I have been unable to trace and details of the action in which he died.

---

[7] - *Stationary engine - An in-line engine.*

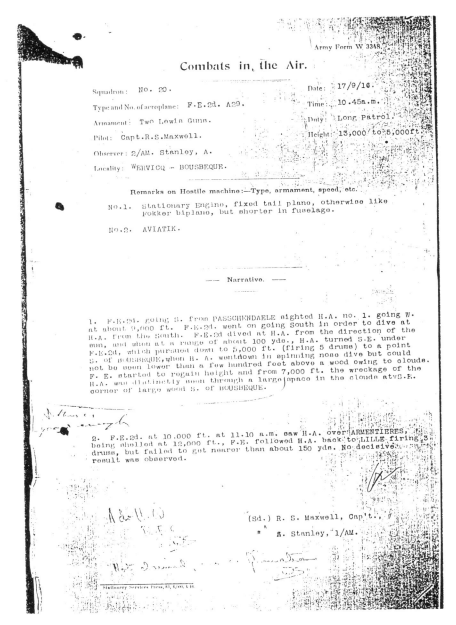

Army Form W 3348.

Combats in the Air.

Squadron: NO. 20.

Type and No. of aeroplane: F.E.2d. A29.

Armament: Two Lewis Guns.

Pilot: Capt.R.S.Maxwell.

Observer: 2/AM. Stanley, A.

Locality: WERVICQ - BOUSBEQUE.

Date: 17/9/16.

Time: 10.45a.m.

Duty: Long Patrol.

Height: 13,000 to 5,000ft.

Remarks on Hostile machine:—Type, armament, speed, etc.

No.1. Stationary Engine, fixed tail plane, otherwise like Fokker biplane, but shorter in fuselage.

No.2. AVIATIK.

—— Narrative. ——

1. F.E.2d. going S. from PASSCHENDAELE sighted H.A. no. 1. going W. at about 9,000 ft. F.E.2d. went on going South in order to dive at H.A. from the South. F.E.2d dived at H.A. from the direction of the sun, and when at a range of about 100 yds., H.A. turned S.E. under F.E.2d, which pursued down to 5,000 ft. (firing 5 drums) to a point S. of BOUSBEQUE, when H. A. went down in spinning nose dive but could not be seen lower than a few hundred feet above a wood owing to clouds. F. E. started to regain height and from 7,000 ft. the wreckage of the H.A. was distinctly seen through a large space in the clouds at S.E. corner of large wood S. of BOUSBEQUE.

2. F.E.2d. at 10,000 ft. at 11.10 a.m. saw H.A. over ARMENTIERES, being shelled at 12,000 ft., F.E. followed H.A. back to LILLE firing 3 drums, but failed to get nearer than about 150 yds. No decisive result was observed.

(Sd.) R. S. Maxwell, Cap't.,

" A. Stanley, 1/AM.

Stationery Services Press, 83, 8/40, 4 16.

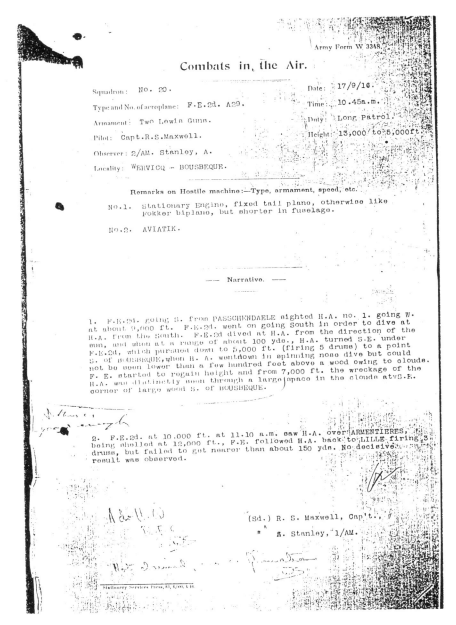

Copy of the Combat Report referred to in the text, dated 17/9/1916.
(Courtesey: Public Records Office ref: AIR 1/1220/204/5/2634/20).

Sergeant Observer A.O. Stanley - promoted to this rank 10th October 1916.

October 1st saw Bert promoted to Air Mechanic First Class and his pay increased to 5 shillings and sixpence a day. Ten days later he was promoted to Sergeant and on that day, during a break in the rain, his diary records:-
'10 Oct 9.15-11.10 1h.55m Patrol. Met a Hun & had a scrap just north of Armentieres. A large machine which proved too fast for us on the dive. Got undercarriage & prop hit. Dropped a drum (magazine) over which stuck on plane (wing) & got home.'

PART TWO

SERGEANT STANLEY - PILOT

'I know I shall meet my fate,
Somewhere high above the clouds;'

W.B.Yeates - An Irish Airman forees his own death[8] (1917)

On 20th November 1916 Bert was posted home for pilot training, having spent 310 days in France and 106 hours 09 minutes in the air. I expect he was pleased it was all over. His flying to date had certainly been rugged to say the least. Stuck out in front of the pilot like the figurehead of one of Nelson's Frigates, acting as his windshield in temperatures well below zero; flying at heights without oxygen where today it is considered mandatory; having to fire, fight, reload and clear stoppages on a temperamental Lewis machine gun with freezing and bleeding fingers; having to observe and seeing everything that was coming at you, both from the enemy in the air and from the earth below and having to hold on for dear life while your pilot attempted to throw you out of the machine by his evasive manoeuvring. Yes! I imagine Bert was greatly relieved when he was posted home for pilot training!

There is a gap of nearly three months from the time Bert Stanley left France and making the first entry in his Army Book 425 (Pilot's Flying Log Book) on the 16th February 1917. Assuming he took 2 weeks leave there is a period of 10 weeks which is unaccountable. Perhaps this period was taken up in some kind of ground school although neither two of the better known WW 1 authors (McCudden, *Five Years In The RFC* and Ira (*Taffy*) Jones, *Tiger Squadron*) two NCO observers who returned from France to learn to fly say what form it took. Denis Winter in his book *The First Of The Few* gives a rough outline of what the officer cadet at Oxford had to endure, but nothing is told of what routine a war veteran NCO had to contend with. Regrettably Dennis Winter seems more concerned with commissioned ranks and the then more glamorous fighter pilots. None-the-less it is a brilliant book. McCudden appeared to start flying training as soon as he completed his two weeks leave, although a crashed machine and bad weather held him up for a few weeks!

---

[8] - *Sgt. Stanley had an Irish mother.*

Maurice Farman S11 Shorthorn. On 1st March 1917 Stanley flew A7001 solo after 60 landings and 5 hours 50 minutes dual (Photo:Chaz Bowyer)

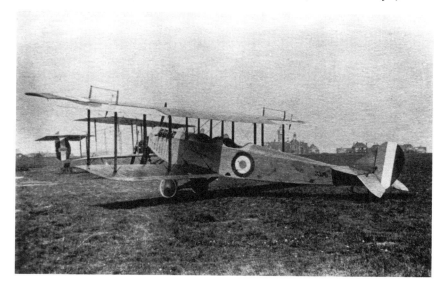

A French Curtiss JN-3/4. Most RFC 'Jennies' in the UK had been transferred from the RNAS (Photo: Phillip Jarrett)

Bert had been posted to No 8 Reserve Squadron at Beaulieu, Hampshire. The airfield in those days was situated close to the village of East Boldre. The new Second World War base was built further to the west on Hatchet Moor. He was in the air for 2 hours 15 minutes during his first week. Fourteen landings under 'Temporary Control' took 5 sorties to complete. He appears to be confused what month it was, February becomes January and then back to February in his log. I know the feeling, I never knew my arse from my elbow during my early days of flying instruction!

A further 8 sorties accounted for another 44 landings and another 3 hours 15 minutes in the air. In one 45 minute sortie Bert shot 13 landings - one every 3 minutes! Then, after a total of 60 landings and 5 hours 50 minutes in the air, on March 1st 1917 at 0810 hours Bert soloed Maurice Farman S.11 Shorthorn No A7001. He took 20 minutes to shoot 2 landings. He flew a further 4 solo sorties that day - 2 hours 50 minutes in all.

Curtis JN-4s (Jennies). RFC pilots learning to fly in formation, Texas, USA, 1917 (Photo Chaz Bowyer)

By the 3rd March he had completed the course at No 8 Reserve Squadron with 10 hours 55 minutes flying time of which 5 hours 5 minutes were solo all completed within 3 days! Bert must have felt quite at home in the 'Shorthorn'. Like the F.E.2b it had the engine to the rear of the pilot and the pupil was stuck out in front of the nacelle like the gunner in the F.E.. The tail was held on by twin booms. However, unlike the F.E. it had twin fin and rudders and, like its 70hp engine, looked and was puny by comparison.

I am sure Bert couldn't help thinking of that robust machine which saw him through so many scrapes a few months before!

Bert was then posted to No 16 Reserve Squadron also at Beaulieu. He was airborne 11 days later in a Curtiss JN-3/4. Nicknamed - 'Jenny' and built in the USA. It took 10 minutes to climb to 3,000 feet! He soloed it for 7 minutes after 1 hour 40 minutes dual. Its serial number was A620 and must have been the oldest 'Jenny' on the unit! (He never flew it again; it must have been saved for first solos only!) On the 'Jenny' he flew 'five mile circuits' (?), a cross country to Upavon-Netheravon-Beaulieu when he recorded, '...clouds very low - very bumpy!'

This photograph clearly shows the observer's position in front of the pilot in a B.E.2c. His gun had to be physically lifted onto another bracket to change the direction of fire. This aircraft, 2650, served with 21 & 27 Squadrons and was built by The Daimler Co Ltd, Coventry (Photo Chaz Bowyer).

After 25 hours 7 minutes (solo time - 17h.37m) Bert started to fly the B.E.2e and 2c, soloing after 15 minutes dual. On 6th April 1917, the day the United States declared war on Germany, he flew a 'Puff Target' sortie, (whatever this means). Another 'Puff Target' sortie and a 'Mirror' (whatever this was), two solo night landings, which took 8 minutes (No dual!), two photographic sorties and one on General Signals. On 9th April 1917 (I was born on the same day six years later!) he was graded '1st class pilot'. He needed to be since it was said more pilots were killed during their flying training than on the Western Front!! His course was completed on 13th

April, he had been home for 144 days.

There was no waste of time! Six days later on 19th April he found himself back in France flying a B.E.2e of No 13 Squadron at Savy (shared with No 35 Squadron flying Armstrong Whitworth FK8's). His total flying time solo was 23 hours 23 minutes. Some 3109 B.E. c,d, and e's were built for the RFC and no less than 1126 found their way to the western front. It first flew in June 1914 and first arrived in France at squadron strength in April 1915 with No 8 Squadron. It performed well in Home Defence being the vehicle for the destruction of no less than 5 enemy airships.

In its khaki brown 'western front' paint it looks a rugged purposeful aeroplane, but the initial error in its design was that the pilot sat in the rear cockpit and the observer sat in the front. From this position the observer, under the centre section and amid wires and wings, was unable to bring his gun to bear without shifting it from one mounting to the other. Thus in combat it was virtually helpless. The B.E.2e was underpowered by an RAF (Royal Aircraft Factory) 1a engine which dragged it to a height of 6,000 feet in 20 minutes where it flew at 82 mph. 9,000 feet was its maximum height and its endurance, so they say, was 4 hours. In short it was probably the most inferior Allied aeroplane flying on the western front. It must have required great courage to fly them in action. I have stood in awe on the balcony of the Imperial War Museum gazing at the one survivor hanging from the roof.

When Albert Stanley arrived in France, the Battle of Arras was ten days into being, a battle intended to be a subsidiary to a French attack further south (which failed). The RFC was to suffer more casualties in that month of April (known in the RFC as 'Bloody April') than any other month during the whole of the war. 316 airmen would be killed or missing - one per every 92 hours flown. Not many you say by comparison with the tens of thousand soldiers who would die in the land battle below. But if you consider the total RAF commissioned aircrew flying on the western front in October 1918 was approximately 3,700, the casualty percentage in 1917 was very high.

Manfred von Richthofen was to gain 30 of his 80 victories over the Arras front during March and April and had begun to lead his big formations out of Douai - right in the centre of the front. His 32nd victory on 2nd April had been a No 13 Squadron aircraft. Commanded by Major E.W.Powell, No 13 Squadron's task in this battle was artillery co-operation, photography up to 4,000 yards behind the German lines (against that prevailing wind!), close reconnaissance and contact patrol work. The weather was awful, it had snowed heavily. There had been heavy gas shelling and there was mud!

On the edge of this holocaust Bert practised his landings, went twice to St.

Omer to collect a new machine and after pottering around for a further 5 hours 16 minutes on the 25th April took Lt Courey over the lines for a shoot[9]. He returned after 54 minutes 'Engine dud'. At 6.40 a.m. they took off again in another machine and for 1 hour 5 minutes at a height of 2,000 feet they reconnoitred Arras, Roeux, Fampaux. They were attacked by a 'Hun Scout' and Stanley's aeroplane needed, '...a new plane, elevator and patch fixed!' After 3 'shoot' sorties in the River Scarpe Monchy area on 29th April, while flying with Lt Bonner for 2 hours 10 minutes at 2,500 feet, the trailing edge of the aircraft was hit by a shell!

By now he was flying a regular 2 hour sortie day, which on several days increased to 2 sorties. In the remark column of his log book appear such comments as 'Patrol', 'Battery silenced', 'Hun', 'Photography OK 36 plates', 'New tail plane Archie' and so this dangerous work went on and on. April saw another 17 hours 50 minutes in his log book consisting of 13 sorties 7 of which were over the lines.

On 7th May, Capt A.Ball VC,DSO (2 bars).MC etc was shot down and killed on the same front (No 13 Squadron had been his first). At that time Bert was 4,000 feet over the line with Lt Rawlins for 3 hours 5 minutes carrying out a shoot and comments 'Huns'. On the 19th he was attacked again while flying with Air Mechanic Wardlow. They were taking 17 photos at 3,000 feet. On the 27th his engine cut out and he was compelled to force land ('A1', he says!). The month of May finished with 49 hour 33 minutes flying, 33 sorties, 27 of which were over the lines. 'Weather dud' appeared in the remarks column 3 times!

June sorties appear to be flown a greater height, probably due to better weather. But the climb to 8,000 feet must have been difficult and dangerous with their eyes peering into the sun and watching for the enemy with every swivel of the head. Most of his flying over the lines consisted photography flights, by necessity flying straight and level for the semi automatic cameras were fickle things in those days. And... always, patrolling high above, the enemy, hiding in the sun, stalking, waiting to pounce, like a cat onto a mouse. And... the black acrid puffs of exploding artillery shells in the sky. It was almost like standing daily on a firing step in the trenches exposing your head and shoulders inviting the enemy to take a pot shot at you. Flying lacked the mud only - until you got back on the ground!

The Battle of Arras was petering out and to the north the great Flanders

[9] - Shoot - Spotting for the artillery which naturally tended to focus the enemy's attention upon you.

offensive had begun. It was to finish in November 1917 with the capture of Passchendaele after a half a million men, British, French, Canadians, Australians, New Zealanders and Germans had become casualties in an unimaginable horror of appalling slaughter in blood and mud. There were 70,000 British and Commonwealth casualties in the first four weeks (enough to fill an arena the size of Wembley Stadium.) Again for little or no territorial gain. I imagine that fighting under these conditions could have led you to think you had nothing to lose if you died. Haig and his General staff threw human lives away as they would a handful of confetti at a wedding. Fifty miles behind the line, they never bothered to go forward to see what the troops were enduring - a negligence that should have been punished - not rewarded. (Wasn't Wellington's example ever mentioned at Sandhurst!?)

On 6th June Capt Cunnell and his gunner, 2nd Lt Woodbridge, flying an F.E.2d from 20 Squadron (Bert's old Squadron) shot down 4 aircraft, one of which was piloted by Richthofen. Wounded in the head Richthofen did not return to the front until 16th August. Cunnell died 6 days later, his observer Lt A.G. Bill taking control of the F.E. and flying it back to base.

At Messines, in the first ten days of June on a front of roughly 10,000 yards, 2,233 guns fired 2,843,163 rounds weighing 64,164 tons, i.e. a gun to every 4 yards and 6 tons of ammunition for every yard of front attacked. On the 7th the ridge at Messines, which had been mined, was blown up with over 400 tons of Ammonal. I find this piece of intelligence nauseating. My father must have seen it all, probably took part in the bombardment; he was in France at the time with his artillery regiment. During the same period Bert plodded along the line 8 times in a B.E.2e. Taking pictures of the battle at a height of between 2,000 and 7,000 feet and once at 500 feet in a storm!

During that June Bert flew 32 hours and 33 minutes. Two sorties were 'Practice scrap with Nieuport', during one of which they 'Lost gun'; obviously caused by the observer in the front seat moving the gun from bracket to bracket, missing one so dropping it over the side. It was just as well it happened on a practice flight. (A Lewis gun weighed 17 lbs and a full magazine, the large one, with 97 rounds weighed 8lbs 11ozs a total weight of 26lbs 1oz!!). Twenty sorties out of 32 were over the line; one at 1,500 feet for three hours with Lt Banks conducting '6 successful shoots'. Lt Banks was with him on two occasions when they were attacked by 'Huns'. They must have been sufficiently scared for him to record 'Gun jammed'.

Sometime during July the squadron moved to the south west of Savy to Etrun. For the first time in his log book Bert records flying an R.E.8. The R.E.8 was another aeroplane that had an evil reputation in the RFC. The early R.E.8's had a tendency to spin in the hands of inexperienced pilots.

If tipped up on its nose on landing the position of the fuel tanks made it certain that it would catch on fire. However substantial modification made it almost a new aeroplane and it eventually outlived its evil reputation, but not in July 1917.

The R.E.8 was designed as a standard corps reconnaissance and artillery aeroplane to supersede the B.E.2c. In appearance not unlike the B.E.2's which was not surprising since it came from the same stable. The wingspan of the R.E.8 (42 ft. 7ins) was 2ft wider than the B.E.2 and the fuselage (27 ft. 10ins) just a few inches longer. The pilot now sat in the front cockpit and had a forward firing Vickers synchronised gun and the observer in the rear with a Lewis gun mounted on Scarff ring. This meant he had a greater field of fire and unlike the F.E. and the B.E. did not have to lift the gun onto another bracket to keep an enemy in range. It was powered by a 150 h.p. RAF engine which pulled it to 6,500 in 16 minutes and sped it along at about 100 mph. However, it took 22 minutes to climb to 10,000 feet and 40 minutes to 13,200 feet.

This is undoubtedly the finest picture I have ever seen of an RE8. Taken in 1918 it is a machine of No 15 Squadron RAF. It shows the pilot and observer seated and possibly all the ground crew that serviced it. C2464 was built by the Daimler Company Ltd at Coventry (Photo Chaz Bowyer)

On 6th July, flying in a B.E.2e with Air Mechanic Wardlaw at 8,000 feet photographing, they were 'Hit by archie'. With the same observer in an

R.E.8 on the 20th they 'Brought down Hun', between them - Bert's 4th. It had taken him 15 minutes flying time to convert onto the R.E.8 before taking it across the lines. However, he had 3 quick sorties during the month to practise landings. Lt Hyde and Lt Vautier were the unfortunate observers! The reliability of the R.E.8 appears to be questionable, two 'dud engine' remarks, and a 'Centre Section blew out' at 7,000 feet which must have caused him a lot of concern. He also recorded, for the first and only time, that the camera had jammed (at 7,500 feet after taking 8 pictures). Otherwise, of the 34 sorties he flew 24 were over the line. He totalled 36 hours 16 minutes in July. The R.E.8 sorties over the line were considerably shorter than those flown in B.E.2e's.

R.E.8's of 15 Squadron (the white band in front of the fin is the squadron marking) lined up beside the road near the town of Albert, 25th March 1918. A typical scene of a R.E.8 airfield in France. No 15 (B836) was rebuilt by No 1 (Southern) Aircraft Repair Depot at Farnborough. No 13 (B2276) was built by D Napier and Son Ltd (Imp. War Museum ref:Q11987).

On 29th July Bert went home on leave, during which he confided in his sister-in-law Violet that he thought it would be unlikely that he would ever come home on leave again. He gave her the tiny brown jug to remember him by. Since April the RFC had suffered 520 casualties, killed and missing.

Returning to France on 18th August 1917, Bert took straight off to take 20 photos over the lines. No practice circuit and landing, straight off at 8.55.

a.m with Air Mechanic Wardlaw as his observer. A 'dud engine' brought an 'ANF patrol'(?) on the 19th to a rapid conclusion. August 20th saw him and his observer, Lt Austin, landing in the fog at '70 Squadron'. They had been in the air 3 hours 15 minutes, having taken off at 5.30 a.m. No 70 Squadron was then based at Liettres, having recently been re-equipped with Sopwith Camels. A month before they had been at Boisinghem equipped with Sopwith 1½ Strutters and commanded by Major A.W.Tedder (later to become Air Chief Marshal in WW II). Liettres was 25 miles north west of Etrun and their course was roughly parallel to the front line. There must have been

Preparing to start an R.E.8 of 69 Squadron (No 3 Australian Flying Corp) for a night bombing raid from Savy. Note forward firing gun and Scarf ring for rear gunner (Imp. War Museum ref:E(AUS)1178).

some very anxious moments on their return flight. Fog obscured the ground and they were not able to see the many airfields on their route. In addition, to add to their discomfort, they were harassed on their way by 'Huns'.

Four days later Lt Dykes was with him when, after 10 minutes, they were compelled to land, no reason is given for this sudden departure from flight. 'A1' says Bert! There were two interesting sorties on the 25th and 26th which sandwiched a propeller test at 10,000 feet. He and Lt Westerby carried out two shoots with 8 inch howitzers; one 52 shots, the other 65 shots, both at a height of 3,000 feet. One can imagine the R.E.8 with its aerial trailing 250 feet below and Lt Westerby giving simple instructions with his morse key on his Marconi radio to the firing battery below. Not unlike a bomb-aimer in the second world war; Bert, meanwhile, searched the sky above.

During the 9 remaining days in August he was in the air 22 hours 37 minutes; of 11 sorties 9 were over the lines. Two were of 3 hours or more, 3 were in excess of 2 hours. There was little time to dwell on his recent leave! September came and apart from cryptic notes in his remarks column, 'Weather dud', 'Very Low mist', 'Archie very hot', 'Photos dud', 'Aerial dud', 'Photos OK, new batteries, jamb' 'Shoot 2 explosions', 'ANF (?) - quiet'. A dull, dangerous routine. Each sortie over the front only identified by initials decipherable, alas, by the person who made the entry in his log book. 'NGL' appears after two and I am wondering if it meant No Good Landing!

I found a Combat Report in No 13 Squadron files dated 3rd September 1917, submitted by a colleague of Bert's, Sgt R.C.Taylor. They must have known each other well. He was flying an R.E.8 with Lt F.D.Steel as his observer photographing at 7,000 feet. (Bert, this day, was flying at the same time on a photographic sortie at 8,000 feet with Air Mechanic Wardlaw. They took off at 8.30 hrs and flew for 55 minutes. The log records 'Overline Photos OK'!) The hostile machines recorded in Taylor's report were Albatross D111's. The narrative gives some idea what they were going through:- 'About 9.10 a.m. when on photography, seven hostile machines attacked us while over O.B.16. (a map sector). Six of these dived on our tail in V formation. The nearest hostile machine commenced firing at a distance of about 35 yards. Observer opened fire on this machine and saw his tracer bullets hit the pilot whose machine immediately rolled over and over, and went down out of control and was wrecked. The observer immediately opened fire on the next nearest machine, and after five bursts of fire the hostile machine commenced to spin and was seen to fall from 5,000 feet, and disappeared into clouds at about 3,000 feet still spinning and was not seen again. Observer then cleared a stoppage in his gun and opened fire on the next machine with the third drum. By this time our machine had descended to a height of 3,000 feet over the British lines, when the remaining hostile machines turned back. Our machine being hit through the right hand rear strut, right hand aileron strut, right hand top plane and tail plane, we returned to landing ground.'

Army Form W. 3348.

Combats in the Air.

Squadron: No. 13

Date: 3rd September, 1917.

Type and No. of Aeroplane: R.E.8 1350.

Time: 9.10 to 9.20 am.

Armament: 1 Lewis gun, 1 Vickers gun.

Duty: Photography.

Pilot: Serjt. R.C. Taylor.

Height: 7000 feet.

Observer: Lieut. F.B. Steel.

Locality: O.I. 16.

Remarks on Hostile machine: Type, armament, speed, etc.

Albatross Scouts biff. Front guns. Speed 110 miles p.h.

—— Narrative. ——

About 9.10 am. when on Photography, seven hostile machines attacked us whilst over O.o. 16. Six of these dived on our tail in V formation. The nearest hostile machine commenced firing at a distance of about 75 yards. Observer opened fire on this machine and saw his tracer bullets hit the pilot. Whose machine immediately rolled over and over, and went down out of control and was wrecked.

The observer immediately opened fire on the next nearest machine, and after five rounds of fire the hostile machine descended to 5000 and was seen to pull round over Pont, but climbed again at about 5000 feet still fighting, and was not seen again. Observer then cleared a stoppage in his gun and opened fire on the next machine with the third drum. By this time our machine had retreated to the height of 7000 feet over the British lines, when the remaining hostile machines turned back. Our machine being hit through the right hand rear strut, right hand aileron strut, right hand top plane and tail plane, we returned to landing ground.

Officer Commanding,

13th Wing, RFC.   R.C. Taylor Sgt. (Pilot)

Forwarded.

A.R. HQ. This Army confirms that the Hun was undoubtedly out of control to the ground about O.16.   A.G.R. Garrod. Major, Commanding No. 13 Squadron, RFC.

Copy of Sergeant R.C. Taylor's Combat report. Major A.G.R Garrod, CO of No 13 Squadron, who signed this report retired Air Chief Marshal Sir Guy Garrod GBE, KCB, MC, DFC. At one time Air Commander South East Asia in WW 2. (Courtesy: Public Records Office ref:AIR 1/1719/204/5/2634/13).

The report was counter-signed by Major A.G.R.Garrod who was then in command of No 13 Squadron. A post script to the report written in Garrod's hand reads, 'AA HQ Third Army confirms that the first machine crashed out of control to the ground about O.16'.

The last four entries in Bert's log book are made in ink, which was unusual, as all previous entries had been made in indelible pencil. The hours flown up to 25th September total 30 hours 45 minutes, all 18 sorties were over the lines. There are five days of flying unaccounted for in his flying log book.

On 30th September 1917 Sergeant Albert Oscar Stanley (6717) and Air Mechanic First Class Arbour Hood Wardlaw (78979), his observer, took off from Etrun at 1050 hours in R.E.8 A3731 to carry out a photo-recce of the British 17 Corps front. At that time *Vizefeldwebel*[10] Hamster of *Jasta 37* flying an Albatross DIII (or DV) was also in the air and had already shot down, east of Tilloy, an R.E.8 at 1055 hours (British time). At 1105 hours he was credited with shooting down his second R.E.8 that morning, the latter flown by Albert Stanley and Arbour Wardlaw. They crashed to their death east of Arras and south west of Fresnes-les-Montauban. I pray that death came swiftly to them and that they were spared the horror of an 'ordeal by fire' or the endless waiting for the ground rise up and pound them to death.

Hamster was known to have scored one more victory, a Sopwith Camel on the 23rd November 1917. Nothing further was heard of him after that.

Uncle Bert, Sergeant Albert Oscar Stanley, flew with No 13 Squadron more than 180.16 hours (107 plus sorties over the lines including 44 plus with his observer AM 1st Class Wardlaw) and 106.09 hours (55 plus operational sorties), with No 20 Squadron. I also found in that cardboard box a weighty, ponderous bronze medallion, four and three quarter inches in diameter. His name is inscribed on it. 'Next of kin plates,' they were called. Some 1,150,000 of them thumped on to the door mats of homes through out Britain and what was then the British Empire, giving cold comfort to those who picked them up, reminding them sadly of better days when they either succoured their young or played with them as brother or sister. With each medallion was a printed letter from Buckingham Palace, which read:-

---

[10] - *Vizefeldwebel - Literally vice-sergeant (lance-sergeant).*

'I join with my grateful people in sending you this memorial of a brave life given for others in the Great War. George R.I. '

6717 Sergeant Pilot Albert Oscar Stanley

HMS Pathfinder - A name which became synonymous with RAF bomber operations in W.W II.

Stoker Second Class Henry Arthur Bartlett.

This is the second medallion we have in our family. The first commemorated the death of my mother's brother, my uncle, Stoker Second Class Henry Arthur Bartlett who on 5th September 1914 was torpedoed by a submarine when serving in HMS Pathfinder. He had joined the Navy just prior to the war and died when he was 20 years old. He was probably one of the first naval casualties. I don't think my mother ever recovered from the shock. Henry and Albert shared one thing in common, having no known grave their names are carved on stone memorials. Henry at Chatham in Kent and Albert, together with Arbour Wardlaw his observer, at Arras in France.

My father joined the 1st Essex (Heavy Battery) Royal Artillery, Territorial Army in 1913.He said he did this because of his love for horses. He was a gentle man and I loved him very much, but he would never talk to me about his war experiences. He just quietly said it was a war to end war and must never ever be allowed to happen again.

Those Allied and German lives given in the belief that their cause would bring peace to the world were betrayed 21 years later by the events of 1939, caused by complacent politicians and a megalomaniac named Hitler.

CHAPTER ONE

IN THE BEGINNING

'For I will walke this wandering pilgrimage,
Throughout the world from one end to the other end.'

From Daphaïa - A Elegy by Edmund Spenser
The Oxford Book of English Verse - Oxford University Press 1930

On my 17th birthday, in April 1940, Germany invaded Denmark and Norway. Later that year Dunkirk came and went. That summer, I watched the Battle of Britain rage above me. Contrails weaved their deadly pattern in the clear blue skies and men, in the springtime of their lives, died during those beautiful cloudless days. I watched London burn and picked up hot shrapnel splinters from the ground.

Nightly I returned to the office in London to 'fire watch' - to extinguish any fire bombs that might land on the office building. I was petrified and in the morning walked streets carpeted with fire hoses and lined with smouldering buildings. The New Year came and I found myself with an ear infection. I went to see my doctor. I proudly told him I was about to join the RAF as a pilot. He laughed in my face and said, 'With your medical history they won't have you in the Pioneer Corps let alone the Air Force.'

This had never occurred to me and I was shattered. I had been a sickly boy and spent much time in hospital where a surgeon whittled away at my mastoid process. (I still remember, with revulsion, the ether pad being placed over my face!) My doctor explained that anyone who suffered 11 mastoid operations, eight on one ear and three on the other, stood no chance of getting into any of the services.

There wasn't much I could do about it now, a recruiting sergeant at Romford had tested my urine and my signature was on an RAF form. I considered myself practically in uniform! A few weeks later I was summoned to the RAF Selection Board and Medical Centre somewhere near Euston Station. Here I filled in a form concerning my medical history. Most of the questions were straight forward until it came to ears. I knew I could not disguise the trenches behind each ear that gave the game away. In the event I told a lie, I said I had one operation on each ear and left it at that.

No 4 (Ilford) Squadron ADCC (Air Defence Cadet Squadron) at weekend camp, Nazing, Essex, April 15th 1939. The food was disgusting. Cadet FB Clark is extreme left, front row. I had reached my 16th birthday one week before.

I performed all the medical co-ordination and eye gymnastics required of me with ease; my feet had yet to get flat and my teeth were OK, but I needed a denture - the pieces remained at the bottom of my kit bag for years. I then found myself sitting before the ENT (Ear Nose & Throat) specialist. 'What's this?' he queried, 'A mastoid operation on both ears? We'll have to have a good look at that.' My heart sank as he probed and then looked again. 'A perforation there, nicely healed,' was his only comment. From a distance he whispered words. I told him without difficulty what they were. It was nice when he stopped, as his assistant also stopped jabbing his finger in and out of my ears. 'Good,' he pronounced, 'Nothing much wrong there.' The recent visit to my GP had prepared me well!

The selection board then questioned me, the ADCC (Air Defence Cadet Corps) had long before provided me with the answers. Finally they told me I had been selected for pilot training, but in view of my age (I was just under 18) they would send me home on deferred service. In the meantime they suggested that I took a course at evening school to improve my mathematics and to gain some knowledge of navigation. 'See you in three months,' they said.

I duly attended classes at a local technical college. There I met Ron Say,

Fg/Off Ron Say with his daughter Valerie.

a man older than myself who was married and had a small daughter; we became firm friends. His help and encouragement was invaluable and I spent many happy hours with him and his family.[1] Three months later, to my surprise, I was called; many of my friends had waited longer. I reported on 21st July 1941 to No 1 Air Crew Receiving Centre (ACRC), St John's Wood, London, at Lord's Cricket Ground. ACRC, or *'Arsey Tarsy'* as we called it, was a masterpiece of improvisation - an excellent piece of forward planning. The unit was previously based at Cardington where, due to the rapid expansion of the RAF, it had outgrown its boundaries. When I was summoned, it had recently moved to London.

Here large intakes of aircrew recruits were received, housed, fed, kitted, drilled, inoculated, lectured, administered and disposed of. At Lord's they were received, in requisitioned flats they were housed, in Regent's Park Zoo they were fed, in a commandeered garage they were kitted-out, in empty streets they were drilled, in a cinema and drill hall they were lectured, and in a former ministry office block (Abbey Lodge) they were administerd, inoculated and finally posted to ITW's (Initial Training Wings).

Lord's was barely an hour from home and I went there with a neighbour, Eric Spinks, whom I hardly knew. I had never been inside Lord's before. The nearest I ever got was standing outside in the pouring rain with my father watching the 'No Play Today' sign go up. How my father loved his cricket. This time the gates were open when we arrived and we were greeted by a cheerful sergeant who said, 'Now you are in try and get out!' He motioned us to sit in a stand next to the pavilion. We took our seats - our game had begun. I was put into bat in the pavilion long room where, standing in line with others, the first ball was bowled. We were told to drop our trousers and, in front of the portraits of the all time cricket greats, that great service ritual, an FFI (Free From Infection!) was conducted.

---

[1] - *Flying Officer Ron Say was a navigator when he died in a Wellington of No 20 OTU, Lossiemouth. My wife still writes to his widow, now happily re-married and living in New Zealand near her daughter and grandchildren.*

The innings over, we were mustered into a gaggle of 45 and introduced to our flight commander, Corporal Berry, who said he was, 'Doing time in the RAF.' He was young, but not quite as young as most of us. His buttons glowed like small suns, his boots mirrored reflections, his jet black brilliantined hair was sleekly brushed away from his forehead and nary a bristle on his face. His forage cap miraculously sat on the side of his head and it was true to say he walked beside it rather than under it. The pile had worn off his uniform and here and there a small patch of oil or grease remained from labours of a more arduous past. In the morning it hinted at creases in the right places, but as the day drew on, others, like the erosion of soil, took their place beneath the arms, over the breast and in the crotch of his trousers. Obviously the Air Force did not replace their uniforms light-heartedly!

Cpl Berry and his merry men at ACRC July 1941. Clark is 3rd row from the front, 7th from the left. Immediately behind me is Sam Standfast who asked, 'When do we go in leave?' We met three years later in Stalag Luft III.

He spoke with an unidentifiable brogue. To stress a word of command, an out of place aspirate would creep in, but never when talking normally. He coupled commands with fierce expressions on his countenance which at first frighten us to death but in less than a minute his face would burst into a grin. We were billeted on the top floor of Bentinck Close, in Prince Albert Road, a one time block of luxury flats. The lift did not work. We rose at

6 a.m and paraded for breakfast at 7.30. We dined three times daily in Regent's Park Zoo and always waited an hour outside for our turn to eat. Once at the table NCO's harassed us to get out! Fortunately during the twelve days we were there it only rained twice! Our main diet was mackerel which we swore were given to us because the seals wouldn't eat them!

1386200 AC2 (U/T Pilot) FB Clark July 1941
- just 18 years old.

There was little we could do to relieve the boredom of these tedious periods. However, there was a cage of gibbons close to the entrance of the dining hall. For the want of something better to do someone imitated the 'whooping' noise they made. The effect was electric. The gibbons suddenly came to life and 'whooped' around their cage swinging madly from end to end. The unholy row created was intensified by the yells at us to be quiet. All would be silent for a moment until someone would let out another 'whoop' and off they would all go, monkeys, officers and NCOs alike. We nearly died laughing!

Within three days we were kitted out and emerged from the darkness of that former garage with a stuffed kitbag! We were ordered to change immediately and 'Get fell in!' my day finished with painful and blistering feet! We pounded the back streets daily and when proficient in the rudimentary movements of foot drill, Corporal Berry said it was time we went on a route march - the first of many. We always managed to stop at the same cafe where Berry was first to be served and was never asked to pay (presumably because he brought us in regularly!). A good thing, since we couldn't afford to pay for him on 2/6d (13p) a day!

A lecture on personal hygiene was given by a doctor in a cinema. He was greeted with tumultuous applause. He was nonplussed, hung his head and pawed his foot like a horse, but he soon got going and had his audience in fits of laughter. The only thing I remember of his talk was, 'Cupid's arrows were usually shot after the chemist shops were closed!'

Another lecture took place in a drill hall, given by the Commanding Officer, a group captain. He welcomed us into the Force and gave us a real blood and guts talk - a real Nelson touch this! He ended with, 'Any questions?' Well, he asked for it. Someone levered himself to his feet and asked a question, it was a very good question considering we had only been in the RAF ten days. 'When are we going to get some leave?!' This boy had learned fast! I met him four years later, in quite different circumstances. We shared a room in Stalag Luft III!

Inoculations, vaccinations and blood grouping caused enormous casualties, men went down like ninepins, both before and after the jabs, I don't know how many stayed down for good. Afterwards our '24 hours light duty' consisted of scrubbing and polishing floors! There were 'aptitude tests' and I vaguely remember trying to conquer comically conceived gadgets and answering questions, all to determine one's intelligence. At least I was intelligent enough to know I couldn't beat them at that game. After that I went home for a few hours, taking my abandoned civilian clothes. It was great to be fussed over and made me appreciate what I had left behind, Mother's cooking was always good. I got those boots off and relaxed.

Once back at St John's Wood, Eric Spinks and I seldom went out during the evenings, we were both exhausted from the day's exertions. We remained in bed during the frequent air raids, until ordered to shelter on the ground floor. Here the windows were bricked up and the atmosphere soon became foul. After this we never complained about living on the top floor. Those occupying the ground floor not only had to endure this nightly intrusion but had to remain behind in that dreadful fug after we had gone.

My posting to an Initial Training Wing was unexpected. My letters home say 35 of us with surnames beginning with the initial letter B & C were posted to RAF Station Hemswell, Lincolnshire. Station records say 49. The majority of the intake went to Scarborough which we knew was a 'pukka' ITW. We had never heard of Hemswell! We presented a cigarette lighter to our corporal, he had mothered us well! Early on the morning of 2nd August 1941 I took my leave from Eric Spinks[2], buckled on my pack, swung my kit bag over my shoulder and staggered down stairs. Outside it was raining.

[2] - *Eric was subsequently discharged from the RAF. The Wellington he was flying crashed, his hands were mutilated by frost bite. I never heard the full story, his parents moved house and we never met again.*

CHAPTER TWO

ROYAL AIR FORCE STATION HEMSWELL, LINCOLNSHIRE

'Lie in the dark and listen,
It's clear to-night so they're flying high.'

'Lie in the dark and listen.' - Noel Coward
War Poems from the Sunday Times - 1945

We left St John's Wood for Kings Cross by truck, it was a Saturday, 2nd August 1941. Letters say we sang loudly all the way and passers-by threw cigarettes at us - shades of Tipperary! What we sang is not recorded, which is a pity, there wasn't much to sing about in those days. We left Kings Cross at 11.10 hrs, changed at Retford for Gainsborough where we finally left the train. We were mortified to find our kit had gone somewhere else! The sun was shining in Lincolnshire. A dilapidated single decker bus met us at the station. A feeble attempt had been made to camouflage it, but succeeded only in making it look even more decrepit. Hemswell was 9 miles from Gainsborough and 12 from Lincoln - in the middle of nowhere, so we thought!

On the bus Sergeant Bryant introduced himself, a regular airman who, but for the war, would have retired. He was in charge of us, he said, and was returning from an officers' training course. (He was commissioned later). Now we were all together perhaps there was something we would like to know about Hemswell. He patiently answered our questions. There was a sigh of relief when he told us that there was an ITW at Hemswell. We were its second intake, the first hadn't been very successful. Also based at Hemswell, he went on to say, were two bomber squadrons, No 61 and No 144. They had been there since the airfield had opened in 1937, although he had heard they were under orders to move. They were equipped with a mixture of Hampdens and Manchesters. The Manchester, he said, had an engine problem and there had been a number of fatal crashes on and around the airfield. We gathered they were unpopular both with the air and ground crews.

A road sign heralded the approach of an aerodrome and a hush of expectancy came over us. The bus laboured up the 200 foot climb to the summit of the Lincoln Cliff. At the top of the hill we passed a magnificent windmill. The tension built up, a hedge obscured our view, we were grinding to a halt, a noisy change of gears jerked us forward in our seats. A tall black fin came into view and then, slowly, the Wellington aircraft to which it was attached. Yet another and there in the distance, across a wide expanse of airfield, seven or eight more were dispersed. Black, dirty black, Mark 1c Wellingtons, their fat, pugnacious bellies almost dragging in the dust, their cockpit and turret covers idly flapping in the wind. Beyond, four huge 'C' type hangers cast their saw-toothed shadows onto the surrounding buildings.

Empty hangars on a derelict airfield. Hemswell 1986.

'It looks as if 61 and 144 have gone,' said Bryant regretfully, 'I wonder who this crowd is?' We passed a Wellington at a dispersal close to the roadside and saw painted below the pilot's cockpit a small red and white chequered emblem - the national emblem of Poland. 'What a turn up for the book!' said someone. We stopped briefly at the guard room, then dismounted at station headquarters then marched off to barrack block 'D'. Later drawing blankets from stores and had our first meal in the nearby dining hall. Of the now ten ghosts in Room 1, I can only remember six, then only five by the names they were known to me. They were John Burnup, 'Blackie' Blackman, 'Jock' Connell, 'Charlie' Chaplin, 'Butch' Butcher, and someone called Bob. It was inevitable in such company I too would lose the name I was christened with and being a Clark became 'Nobbie'!

John was rotund and hearty, a former police inspector, a graduate from Hendon Police College (I met him for a brief moment after the war, he said he had been a flying instructor). He and Butch were the only married men on the course. Butch was the eldest and from the West Country, never ruffled, and appeared to weigh up every spoken word. Jock, tough, lovable Jock, was from Glasgow. A heavy beer drinker, as young as he was. Charlie, the youngest, unassuming, non-smoking, non-drinking, non-swearing type. Took everything in and at first said nothing[1]. Blackie, from the Midlands, dark features, young and like myself overjoyed that he was now old enough to join the RAF. Bob, a tall erect young man just from school, who had a lot to say - I wonder if he survived?

That night we removed the blackout curtains from the windows and opened them wide. The last Wellington had taken off, probably on a training flight, we were soon asleep. A barely audible sound of a far off air raid siren woke me. In the night sky above I could hear the sound of unsynchronized aircraft engines. Otherwise it was peaceful. From my bed I saw the red obstruction lights on top of the hangars suddenly flick out. A truck engine started and hurriedly crashed into gear - presumably taking men out to douse the paraffin lit flare path. The unmistakable whine of a falling bomb filled the air not unlike a mosquito diving towards an unprotected ear. There was a flash and a crump, yet another and still another, like giant footsteps coming nearer and nearer. The next shook the barrack block. A pane of glass shattered to the ground. There was a murmur of protesting voices and bodies flung themselves to the floor. I waited for what seemed an age for the next blow; it never fell. A voice in the darkness roared out, 'Missed! You bastards!!' Amid laughter we clambered back into our beds, only to fling ourselves out again as an aircraft swept low, strafing the airfield. Some wag said the enemy had soon got to know where we were!. My research into the Station ORB (Operational Record book) confirmed that the damage was four holes on the airfield, one broken pane of glass and a bullet hole through the flare path truck.

Hemswell was built during the panic expansion programme just before the war and opened in 1937. It was still very new and I suppose the last word in Bomber Stations. A crescent of four huge 'C' type hangars dominated the scene. In the shadow of which were grouped the engineering shops, barracks and other buildings. The barrack blocks were two storeyed, 'H' shaped buildings, built of yellow brick and flat roofed, situated on three sides of the parade ground. On the fourth side was the airmen's mess and the NAAFI canteen. 'D' block was nearest to the airmen's mess. It had eight rooms; a sitting room, a cleaning room, a drying room and underneath an air raid

---

[1] - *Later a Double DFC!*

shelter. In the centre was the washroom; I can still remember the early morning frenzy of activity and the shortage of basin plugs, a famine throughout the RAF!. The married quarters were at the rear of 'D' block, then occupied by the WAAF. The officers' mess was outside the gate of the camp.

'D' Block with broken windows - Hemswell 1986.

The next day was Sunday. Blackie and I set out to explore. Like iron filings drawn to a magnet we made our way to the hangars. It was a glorious afternoon and at a distant dispersal, in a crescendo of noise, an engine was running up. Nearer a Wellington started up; the propeller first revolving slowly, then with a puff of black smoke, the engine burst into life, spinning the propeller like a berserk windmill. In the wake of the slipstream a small cloud of scurrying dust bent the grass as if in prayer to Mecca. 'Are you ze boys to fly?' asked a smiling Polish squadron leader from behind us. Blackie and I looked at each other and answered together 'Yes, sir.' 'You will get parachute and be back here in five minute.' 'Very good, sir,' we chorused.

We had no idea where the parachute section was, but we soon found it! We were back in five minutes, clad in a bulky green jacket (a parachute harness-cum-immersion suit which later went out of fashion) and holding a parachute pack in our hand. The prompt and sympathetic attention the parachute section gave us was staggering. A standard utility van took us to the Wellington we had watched starting up. On arrival our squadron leader motioned us out. He was dressed as we were, but carried a helmet. I looked at the helmet and back at Blackie who shrugged his shoulders. A hole appeared in the nose of the aeroplane and a ladder felt its way onto the ground. The Pole put his thumb up, I moved towards the ladder, eager hands helped me up.

Our squadron leader opened up the engines, tested the magnetos, throttled back and signalled 'chocks away.' Moments later we moved from our hard standing onto the grass airfield. He wasted no time, turning into wind he took off. (Hemswell's runways were laid late 1943). The air was smooth and at sometime during the flight the rear gunner eased me into the rear turret. He indicated by signs how the controls worked. I scared myself windless! With agonizing difficulty I gingerly centralised the turret and timidly peeped behind me. With immense relief I saw the gunner - God bless him - through the perspex window in the door and thought salvation was at hand; time to escape this horrific, claustrophobic, mechanical bubble. He grinned and stuck his thumb up, spread his fingers and indicated he would be back in ten minutes, during which time I learnt just how the tail feels on a donkey. I was pleased to get out. Two memories of that first flight remain with me, the sight of Lincoln Cathedral below, and a railway train, the white smoke pouring from the funnel of its locomotive and drifting across the countryside, how could one ever forget that?

We landed smoothly on the grass airfield, stopped and taxyed quickly back to dispersal. Blackie and I scrambled out of the nose. In the sunlight I saw his face, 'You look terrible, Blackie,' I said. 'For God's sake don't remind me, Nobbie - I feel it! Excuse me.' He dashed off and was back in a few minutes, feeling a lot better, he said, but looking as if he had been buried for a week! We thanked our pilot and the same van returned us to the hangar. We were cock-a-hoop having got ourselves airborne within 24 hours of arriving on the unit. We were greeted by a loud and unfriendly voice, 'AIRMEN! YOU! AIRMEN! COME HERE!!' it shouted. 'You know what, "Blackie," I said, 'I think he means us.' It is true to say I have never seen a man look so angry, (unless you count schooldays when 'Shonk' Findlay, starting with me, flogged the whole form. He was hopping mad too).

He did not bother to return our salute. 'Were you in that aircraft?' he demanded, waving his arms in the direction of about twenty. 'Yes, sir,' we said. 'Do you know what you have done?' he shouted, almost weeping with rage. 'No, sir,' we replied sheepishly. 'You stole the march on these boys,' he roared, dramatically stepping aside, disclosing four small boys dressed in ill-fitting ATC uniforms and looking sorry for themselves. 'I take the trouble to bring these ATC boys down here,' he went on, 'to fly and what do I find?

I find the aircraft has left the ground taking you with it. What're your names? Where're your 1250s? (Identification Card). You'll hear more about this. Now get away from me!'

We saluted and turned on our heel. A few paces later Blackie spat out of the corner of his mouth, 'Bastard!' The venom with which he said it shook me - so out of character. 'I say, Blackie,' I said, 'he was a two and a half ringer - a squadron leader you know.' Blackie turned on me and hissed, 'What do you want me to say - two and half bastards?!' I now knew why the parachute section had been so co-operative! 301 Squadron ORB (Operational Record Book) records: 'On the 3rd August 1941 ATC cadets were conducted over the Squadron and 12 of them were given flights.' There was no mention of two intruders! Our flight caused a sensation, not only among our course members, but also among the airmen of the camp where word circulated that, 'Those bloody cadets in Block 'D' have put one over on that bastard ....' It would be churlish of me to disclose his name. Apparently he was as unpopular with the airmen as we cadets were! The last word was said a few days later when our officer in charge suggested, before any of us flew, perhaps we would make sure there were no ATC cadets about! He looked up from his notes, rubbed his nose with his finger and winked! I was to fly another four hours at Hemswell, still as a passenger, before we moved on.

That evening a corporal suddenly appeared at the entrance to our room. Gently swaying like a stalk of corn in a zephyr, he announced in a broad Scottish accent, 'I'm Fotheringham, Corporal Fotheringham. I am in charge of this room.' We looked up with interest at this wiry, blond haired, tough little man. 'He's pissed,' I thought. 'As I said,' he repeated, 'I'm in charge of this room. All I want you to do is to keep your bed spaces polished and the room clean and tidy. If there's anything wrong with this room when the SWO (Station Warrant Officer) comes 'round in the morning, I get kicked, if I get kicked believe me, by Christ, you'll all get kicked.'

He moved from the door, took off his cap, threw it onto Jock Connell's bed and continued, 'Well, let's get to know each other, you know who I am, now who're you?' He stabbed his finger, first at John Burnup and then went aggressively around the room asking our names. He then turned to Jock Connell who had is hands clasped behind his neck, his back leaning against the head of his bed, his legs stretched and crossed before him. 'And who are you?' demanded Fotheringham. Jock answered in an even broader Scottish accent, 'I'm AC2 Connell,' paused and then said deliberately, 'Jock!' 'JOCK!?, JOCK!?' Fotheringham repeated incredulously, 'Wadya think this is?' jabbing his finger angrily at his corporal stripes, 'Scotch Mist?! And which part of Scotland do you come from?!!' he demanded loudly.

Jock told him and, to our amazement, they embraced each other like long lost brothers. Fotheringham thought Jock was having him on with a phoney Scotch accent and later confessed that he was only trying to scare us. He had just returned early from a 48 hour pass, was 'cheesed off,' and more to the point - broke. Nobody thought Jock Connell would complete the course. On fortnightly pay nights he would get roaring drunk. 'DON'T MAKE A NOISE!' Jock would roar, 'You'll wake Corporal FOTHERINGHAM - HAM - HAM, HE,HE,HE, FOTHERINGHAM - HAM - HAM. Nobbie, do ya wanna buy a battleship?!' Much later I was there when they pinned wings on him, gave him three stripes and sent him to North Africa. I never knew what happened to him after that.

That first working morning reveille was announced over the Tannoy at 06.30, followed by a yelling Fotheringham making a whirlwind circuit of the room. (As he subsequently continued to do.) 'WAKEY! WAKEY! SHOW A LEG! RISE AND SHINE! GET UP YOU LAZY BASTARDS!'. Breakfast over, we marched off to a wooden hut, filed inside and sat down. A middle aged Flight Lieutenant came in, quietly countermanding Sgt Bryant's loud call to attention. 'Sit down men,' he said. He removed his hat and gloves placing them on the table before him. His hair was thinning and he looked the school master he was. Still standing he announced. 'My name is Craggs. I am the officer in charge of you and I am responsible for your course of instruction. Sgt Bryant, whom you have already met, is responsible for your welfare and your discipline. If you have any problems inform Sgt Bryant who, in turn, will inform me.' He then turned and pointed to a broad, smiling, athletic man with corporal stripes and a gleaming brass PTI (physical training instructor) badge above them. He continued, 'This is Corporal Hart, whom you haven't met before. He is responsible for your physical fitness and will assist Sgt Bryant in the administration of your discipline.' The knowing look he gave him did not fail to register on us.

He explained that Hemswell was a Selected Station. A new experiment (we groaned!) its two-fold purpose was to relieve the congestion at the larger ITW's and to bring aircrew cadets into direct contact with the daily routine of an operational air station. The normal practice kept cadets undergoing initial training away from aircraft, thus allowing them to concentrate on the shortened course without distraction. However, he continued, we would have to work harder at Hemswell, since many of the facilities available at the larger ITWs would be denied us. Not the least of our problems was his lack of knowledge of navigation. We couldn't believe our ears, it must have shown on our faces. He smiled and continued saying that he could learn just as well as we could and in any case he was looking forward to the experiment. He was true to his word.

The course would last two months. The first two weeks would be entirely devoted to mathematics at the end of which there would be an examination. Failure would mean removal from the course without any further consideration as aircrew. I winced - maths was not my strong subject. After the mathematics examination, the course proper would start, he said. The subjects to be taught would be the Effects of Poison Gas, Air Force Law, Hygiene, Armaments, Aircraft Recognition, Signals (Morse and Aldis up to eight words a minute) Meteorology and last, but not least, Air Navigation. At the end of the course there would be an examination, failure would again mean the end of training for aircrew. In addition there would be an hours drill or physical training (PT) a day - half an hour before breakfast and another session in the afternoon before tea. The rest of the time would be our own (sic) to do with as we pleased. He would hold evening classes for anyone who wished to attend.

A Wellington Mk Ic HF598 of No 300 Squadron 'Mazowiecki' loading parachute retarded mines. Note the Polish chequered insignia on the nose of the aircraft (Photo: Polish Aircraft Archive via Chaz Bowyer)

The arrival of No 300 Squadron 'Mazowiecki' and No 301 Squadron 'Pomorski' at Hemswell from Swinderby in July 1941 must have had a profound effect on those left behind by the exodus of those two popular RAF Squadrons, No 61 and No 144. Their departing airfield 'beat up' was still talked about! The Poles made a magnificent contribution to the then depleted ranks of Bomber Command. With the *Wehrmacht* then only twenty one miles from our shores morale at Hemswell could not have been higher. The few parades the Poles held on the parade ground emphasized their national pride with their strange rifle and goose stepping drills. Otherwise their uniform differed only in their cap badge, and their rank which they wore on their lapels. If aircrew they wore a metal flying badge - and all airmen wore bell bottom trousers!

A mutual comradeship seemed to be achieved by the booming announcements over the Tannoy system, first in English and then in Polish; one message in particular. It always came after a day of hard work and an afternoon of increasing tension, during which English and Polish ground crews had prepared the aircraft for the night's operations. Winding the main spring, so to speak. The Tannoy would boom out: 'ATTENTION! ATTENTION! Operations for tonight have been cancelled. I repeat, Operations for tonight have been cancelled.' An ironic cheer would go up from the British barracks. Then the message would be repeated in Polish: *'UWAGA! UWAGA! Dzisiaj w nocy operacje sa wstrzymane. Dzisiaj w nocy operacje sa wstrzymane.'* An ironic cheer would then go up from the Polish barracks. The armourers cursing their luck would then go out with their tractors and trailers to retrieve their munitions and unwind the mainspring. Such an event occurred on 3rd August 1941, the same Sunday Blackie and I went exploring. Operations were cancelled at take-off time, at 22.25 hours to be precise.

On 4th August, 301 Squadron started to re-equip with Wellington MkIV's (a MkIc re-engined with a Pratt & Whitney Twin Wasp). They had so much trouble with them that for a short time they reverted to flying Ic's on Operations. On the night 6/7th August 1941, 14 aircraft from Hemswell went to Frankfurt, 300 Squadron lost one, another landed away with casualties, There was severe icing. That evening we started to dig our aerodrome defence positions. It was an arduous, blistering task and took four men three evenings to dig a trench 8 ft long 4 ft deep and 3 ft wide. Corporal Hart and Sergeant Bryant helped us.

Twenty of us visited Kirton-in-Lindsey, a modern fighter base (opened in 1940) 5 miles North of Hemswell. No 121 Eagle Squadron were there and the 'Stars and Stripes' fluttered from a flag pole at dispersal. They had Hurricane IIb's. and we watched a pilot practising landings. He took off into wind, climbed, stall turned, landed down wind, took off, stall turned and landed into wind repeating this manoeuvre several times. It seemed unusual at the time, but a year later I found myself doing precisely the same! It was rumoured that during a recent fighter affiliation sortie one of their pilots had cut a Manchester in half!

Back at Hemswell our youthful enthusiasm found us watching an operational take off. We had chosen a beautiful evening, very little wind and a cloudless sky. A Polish officer took us out to the duty pilot's caravan, a black and white chequered vehicle with a perspex dome in the roof. From there we could look down the flare-path, a line of goose neck flares, each small flame flickering as unseen breezes rushed swiftly across the field.

The night's silence had long been shattered by the starting of unsilenced engines. Twin blue exhaust flames danced in the darkness as the engines were run up. Above the engine noise the sharp staccato of machine gun fire could be heard. A short burst from each rear turret, tracers flashing into the sand butts like a lightning strike from the sky. Slowly each aircraft moved forward, like black monsters leaving their lair to hunt nocturnal prey, navigation lights gleaming like cats' eyes in the darkness. Gently bouncing, brakes squealing and protesting as they moved toward the point of take-off.

In the interior gloom of the caravan we could make out a man holding a telephone in his hand. He barked out an order in Polish and a green light stabbed the darkness from the glass dome. The first of the queuing aircraft cleared its engines, turned and lined up with the goose necks. The brakes squealed and hissed as it manoeuvred into position. Again the green light stabbed the darkness, the rear turret rotated onto the beam. The engines were opened up against the brakes, the noise was deafening. The tall fin of the 'Wimpey' wagged like a disapproving finger, the whole aircraft vibrated madly. The brakes released it, moved slowly forward under full power. With quickening pace it passed where we were standing, the slipstream flattening the grass about our feet. A green circle of light shone onto the passing fuselage, briefly illuminating the letter 'N' in its beam.

She gathered speed, sluggishly the tail came up, the rudder moved from side to side as if waving farewell. The flame from each goose neck beat wildly in the passing turbulence. The noise and the small white tail light disappeared into the darkness. We all instinctively moved forward, crouching, watching in the gloom for space to appear between the wheels and the ground. 'She's off,' we said.

The performance was repeated again and again. They were taking a lot of the airfield to get off, thereby creating an unbearable tension among us. We stayed until five had gone when Jock, in his broad Scottish accent, spoke for all of us saying, 'Let's go home. It's too bloody nerve wracking here.

It's giving me the creeps just watching!' By that time 'N' droned overhead, on course for Germany.

On that night, 8/9th August, 12 Wellingtons from Hemswell went to Hamburg - one of 5 from 300 Sqdn returned early, inter-comm failure. 301 Sqdn lost one, four crew died, two were POW. That same night an enemy aircraft attempted to land on the airfield. He fired a Verey cartridge and on the R/T (Radio Transmitter) asked permission to land. The ORB said, 'Permission was not granted and the enemy aircraft departed!' The following day was a memorable one for us - our kit turned up having being adrift for 8 days.

The night of 14/15th August, 11 Hemswell aircraft went to Hannover, of the 6 from 301 Sqdn, technical trouble grounded one, one was attacked three times over Bremen, and one, severely damaged by Me.110 cannon and machine gun fire, landed at Bircham Newton. The next day I went out to the airfield to look at a damaged Wellington, she was on her belly and looked a complete write off. Much of the tail fin was missing and there were enormous holes in the fuselage and wings. She had been 'coned' by searchlights over Bremen, then attacked by night fighters. It said much for its Geodetic construction that had held it together! One airscrew blade on the port engine had a hole through it the size of a tennis ball. The rear gunner was also there looking at the damage. Much of his turret was missing and he said not a round of ammunition remained. He had a minor flesh wound, lost the heel of a boot, and there were a number of holes in his flying clothing. Miraculously no one else in the crew was hurt. He claimed two fighters destroyed. I can still see him standing beside his turret telling his animated tale with his hands and his broken English, smiling and laughing as if it were a huge joke. God knows what the one that landed at Bircham Newton looked like!

Two nights later 9 aircraft from Hemswell went to Cologne. One 301 Squadron aircraft was hit by flak and without flaps overshot the landing field, colliding with a lighting system 'Totem Pole'. Enemy aircraft attacked landing aircraft - there was no damage. The next night, 18/19th August, 10 Hemswell aircraft went to Duisberg - 300 Sqdn sent 7 aircraft. 'Z' crashed on take-off. I recall laying in my bed looking at the ceiling, smoking a cigarette. The noise of aircraft taking off kept me awake. They roared off at regular intervals, the sound of their engines echoing across the countryside, changing note as they became airborne and fading in the distance. My mind unconsciously followed each aircraft down the flare path and into the air. One... Two... Three... Four... and so on. There was something unusual about that engine note, not the same as the others. A distant fire bell rang.

There could be no doubt this aeroplane was in trouble. A bright yellow light illuminated the darkness, its source so far away that the crash onto the ground could not be heard. The yellow light faded and then burst brilliantly into red, filling the night sky. Then with the explosion of the first of the bombs, came the shock wave. A coloured flare arced its way into the night. The noise of exploding bullets, triggered off by the heat of the dying fire, continued long after to break the night's silence. Aircraft began to take off again, what could have been in the thoughts of the crews as they passed over that smouldering wreck? It was a moving cacophony. Sleep after that did not come easy.

There was no laughter in the camp the following day. In the evening Jock Fotheringham came into our room, he was drunk and still severely shocked from his experience on the fire tender the previous night. He sat on a bed and poured forth his story. An engine of the aircraft caught fire on take-off, the fire tender was well on its way before the aircraft hit the ground. Before they could reach the burning wreckage a figure sprang from the rear turret and went back into the blazing furnace and dragged two men clear. The fire crew reached him in time to prevent him from going back a second time and to certain death. The heat, the exploding bombs and ammunition prevented them from getting any closer. Jock Fotheringham, having told his story, then held his head in his hands and sobbed, 'God! the stench of burning flesh, Why? Why? Why?'

A few days later the wreckage with its practically unharmed tail fin, from which pieces of burnt fabric gently fluttered in the wind, was removed. The rear gunner was awarded the *Virtuti Militari*, Poland's highest award for bravery. The captain and 2nd pilot were killed and the observer injured, the remainder of crew saved.

On 21st August, Air Vice Marshal Ujejski came to Hemswell, there was an impressive parade ground turnout by the Poles. In the afternoon sun the AVM presented decorations to the personnel of 300 and 301 Squadrons. The following night No 300 squadron sent 6 aircraft to Mannheim. The next day we took our maths examination. Our confidence was such we all went straight into the next part of the course! It was remarkably well organised by the specialist sections of the unit, while Craggs concentrated on navigation. The other instructors worked us hard, there was no slacking.

We eventually persuaded the armament section to allow us to visit their precious bomb dump. We were threatened to secrecy! Inside the maze of earth protected shelters we were shown the latest 2000 pound bomb[2], and case upon case of mustard gas bombs. No wonder they were touchy about their bomb dump! We were pleased to leave the place. Each day's end was punctuated by the lowering of the RAF flag to the notes of a bugle sounding the last post. Everyone near the parade ground stood to attention as the flag was gently hauled down reaching the ground as the last bugle note sounded into the autumn evenings. It signalled the time to black out the barrack windows and start revision of the day's instruction.

On such an evening the Tannoy belched forth an urgent call. 'Attention! attention! in a few moments the Station Commander will make an important announcement.' We stirred on our beds and looked up from our books with interest. 'This is the Station Commander speaking,' said the box on the wall, 'From intelligence reports just received, the embarkation of troops and tanks onto barges is taking place in the coastal areas of France, Belgium and Holland. Coupled with large concentrations of troops and gliders assembled on the airfields it is evident that the enemy intend to make an assault on our shores tonight. Accordingly, at 0400 hours tomorrow, defences will be manned to repel any attack that may be forthcoming on this airfield.' 'Christ,' said a voice within the room, 'this really is it!' The voice from the box continued, 'This is the sort of message you must now be prepared to receive as it is evident that preparations for the invasion of this country are now being made. However, in order to test the airfield defences, at first light a mock attack will be carried out by a regiment of locally based troops. Thus the order to man the airfield defences at 0400 hours will stand. That is all!' With a 'click' the box went silent.

'Christ! He had me really worried,' said Bob. 'Me too', said Blackie. The door of our barrack room burst open and in came Sgt Bryant. 'What're you looking so bloody cheerful about, Sarge?' asked John. Bryant grinned, 'Didn't you hear the news?' he said, 'you fall in outside at 0400 hours tomorrow morning, now you babes get some shut eye, you are going to need it. Good Night!'

Jock started to blaspheme, flinging the exercise book he had been reading on the floor he then jumped on it! '"Fly with the bloody Air Force," they said to me when I joined up and what have I bloody well done?' He kicked the book unceremoniously across the floor. 'I've bloody near ruptured myself with P.T. for an hour every day, I've crushed beetles on that bloody square, I've dug a fucking trench and all I have to show for it are blisters on my

<hr />

[2] - *Much later hydrogen bombs weighed 42,000 lbs!!*

hands and feet. For God's sake, when I get into that trench in the morning fill the bloody lot in on top of me!' With that he jumped into bed and pulled the clothes over his head!

It was a cold damp dark morning when we fumbled our way to our trenches. As the grey light of dawn emerged, a thick clinging mist hung everywhere, reducing forward visibility to the end of one's nose. Away to our left a series of loud explosions shattered the morning silence, the battle had begun. In our trench we heard much, but saw nothing. A Tiger Moth fussed about overhead like an angry wasp; the Station Commander was obviously enjoying every minute of it. We four in our trench slowly froze. Five hours later Sgt Bryant put in an appearance and said, 'OK lads, it's all over, report for classes in half an hour.' He then walked off; it was just as well he did otherwise the four of us could have finished the rest of the war in the guardroom!

The 'battle' was an unqualified success, for the 'brown jobs' that is. They had infiltrated behind our lines, having spent the night in the married quarters. It would be ungallant of me to suggest they shared the beds with our WAAF! At first light they came running out from their lair under a smoke screen flinging tear gas bombs and thunder flashes right, left and centre. We didn't have a pick axe handle between the lot of us, which was just as well; Jock would have killed all of them with it. We had one casualty from a thunder flash thrown into a trench. Someone named Bunker got hold of it and threw it out. Unfortunately it landed back into the trench where he crouched with his hands over his ears. It went off under his backside, splitting his trousers and surely making him the unofficial world record holder for the high jump! The Station ORB for the 24th August reports: 'Anti Invasion exercise for all personnel.' The 'enemy' were the 7th Battalion of The Royal Norfolks. Two nights later, the 26/27th August, Hemswell sent 9 aircraft to Cologne, 'business as usual.'

I was astounded to find that my pass mark for the Maths exam was 88%. Seven had failed. We went off to celebrate at the 'Moncks Arms,' Caenby Corner and got drunk.

Wednesday afternoons were devoted to sport, all the camp taking part. Sometimes we played net ball against the WAAF. Our team was the first to beat them. Anyone who tells you that net ball is a dull sport has never played it, at least not the way we did. Once I got my face slapped, even though my intentions were strictly honourable - no one believed me! Afterwards we took tea together.

On the night 31st August/1st September, 6 Hemswell aircraft went to Essen, 4 from 301 Sqdn, one suffered flak damage. Letters home say I had difficulty existing on 17/6d a fortnight (88p!) because bills for laundry, soaps and polishes came to 3/6d (18p)!! On 7th September, main force attacked Berlin and Kiel involving 248 aircraft - 18 were lost, the highest so far! On 13/14th September, Hemswell sent 14 aircraft (part of 147) to Brest to bomb three warships hidden by a smoke screen. Meanwhile we took our final examinations. I wondered where success would lead us and if anyone on our course had been deterred by what they had seen. There had been few undisturbed nights. In two months 89 operational sorties had been flown with the loss of 4 aircraft, two over Germany and two on the airfield.

The Moncks Arms, Caenby Corner, Lincoln -
an oasis in the middle of a desert.

On the night 29/30th September, 10 Hemswell aircraft went to Hamburg. We had already gone on 7 days leave. It was a great to be home again after two months absence. A week later my parents saw me off at Kings Cross. I arrived back at Hemswell on a Saturday evening.

On the night 12/13th October, 21 Hemswell aircraft went to Bremem, - 300 Sqdn lost an aircraft after it radioed, 'target attacked.'

The examination results took a day or two to come through. I was pleased to see that my name, with an average of 85%, was in the middle of the 13 who passed, Jock Connell was the only other pass in our room. That evening we all went to a dance in the NAAFI to drown our sorrows or to celebrate our success. Our quiet, shy, retiring, Charlie decided it was time he came out of his shell and knocked back the four whiskies I was passing back from the bar. We waited for him to collapse on the floor but he didn't! Later he was seen cuddling a pretty little WAAF in a corner. At the end of the evening guiding her towards the door to leave she was heard to say, 'I must get my hat.' Charlie replied, 'You don't need a hat where you are going!'

He was posted to another ITW for a second try and eventually flew Stirlings on operations long before I went on ops. How lucky could I be? I met him 2 years later wearing his double DFC.

On 26/27th October, 14 aircraft from Hemswell went to Hamburg, 300 Squadron sent 9 and recorded that they had now dropped a total weight of 1,000,000 pounds of bombs!

I entered a decompression chamber believing this would be the 'moment of truth' for my ears! I was relieved to find no problems at 24,000 feet! Outside it began to get cold and wisps of snow chased us as we marched and counter marched on that damned drill square. Bryant never let up! Rifles dropped from freezing hands brought him down on us like a ton of bricks! On the night 29/30th October, 301 Sqdn sent 7 Aircraft to Brest. 2 aircraft would not start due to severe cold!

Another month went by and the weather worsened. Flying schools were way behind with their training schedules. We went over old navigation exam papers again and again and with a slight variation recommenced the ITW course. We spent our evenings either in the NAAFI drinking beer or in the Church Army hut eating sausages, beans and chips! Night 1st/2nd November 16 Hemswell aircraft went to Kiel.

We heard that the 13 who passed the course would be promoted to Leading Aircraftman (LAC) backdated to September. We start counting the pennies, 5 weeks back pay, doubled to 5/-d a day (25p) a further 2 shillings (10p.) a day flying pay when we commenced flying. Crikey! we would be millionaires! When at last the 13 names appeared on Promotion Routine Orders (PROs) we busied ourselves sewing propellers on our sleeves. Jock Fotheringham spoilt the magic moment by waltzing round the room singing, 'LAC One! Two! Three! Get some service in!'

The Station ORB said farewell to the station commander, Group Captain Pendred, on 6th November. I never saw him apart from his helmeted head in a Tiger Moth when he flew over his bloody defence exercise! In 1986 Air Marshal Sir Lawrence Pendred died at the age of 87. His obituary said he was distinguished for his roles in RAF Intelligence and Flying Training over many years' service. The Air Council recorded its appreciation for his 'very valuable contribution in raising the standards in RAF Intelligence.' I do hope he had the sense of humour to chuckle with me at that one!

On the night of 7th/8th November, taking off at 1816 hours, No 300 Squadron sent 6 aircraft to Berlin - 4 crews failed to reach the target due to bad icing, the starboard engine of one failed. On another the port airscrew and intercom failed. They also sent 4 aircraft to Mannheim, losing two. Shortage of fuel caused one of the remainder to crash-land and another to land at Manston. 301 Sqdn sent 6 to Berlin, one returned due to icing, one bombed Minden after radioing, 'engine on fire abandoning aircraft,' but returned safely! They also sent 3 to Mannheim, losing one. One landed at West Malling and one landed at Wattisham! An unsuccessful night's work for Bomber Command, little or no damage being done to any of the targets and at loss of 9.4% (double previous losses). The next major raid on Berlin did not take place until January 1943.

There were rumours that we were to leave Hemswell and we were not unduly worried when the Ground Defence Unit (later the RAF Regiment) asked us to stand guard over the camp while they gave a party. That particular night, we drew five rounds of ammunition and a drill rifle (which, if fired, would surely have done more damage to us, than the enemy!). We drew lots for duties and luckily I drew only two periods. My beat, lasting two hours, went from the defence hut to the bomb dump, where I reported in, from bomb dump to dispersal, report, from dispersal through the hangars to the Guard Room and report. From the Guard Room down the road outside the camp to married quarters and back to the defence hut.

My first spell started at 2200hrs and finished at midnight. As I set out the last aircraft had just taken off and was climbing for height over the airfield. It was a lovely clear cold night and in the near distance I could hear the sound of a band thumping out popular melodies. I took my rifle and slung it over my shoulder and walked off into the darkness in unison with the music. It was an uneventful tour of duty.

Back at the hut a card game was still in progress. I flung myself down onto a mattress, drew blankets over my head and went to sleep. It seemed only minutes later when a hand shook my shoulder and a voice told me it was 4 o'clock. I got up and a dirty mug of steaming hot muddy cocoa was thrust into my hand which I hastily drank. I left the hut, the chill of the night air shocked me awake. A crescent moon hung in the clear sky. The darkness and the silence, both blinding and deafening, clung to me like a garment. I pulled the collar of my greatcoat up, slung the rifle over my shoulder thrust my hands deep into my pockets and made my way to the bomb dump.

On my way from dispersals the flare path came into view. The flames of the goose necks rippling as the early morning breezes rustled across them. A far off pundit pulsated its red coded message into the sky like a friendly beckoning finger. I walked into a hangar, its huge doors open wide in case of emergency. The pungent smell of dope filled my nostrils. It was silent, a striking contrast from the every day activities of men, whining drills, the ringing note of steel upon steel and the slap of compressor belts. An aircraft with an engine removed loomed before me, the fire proof bulkhead gaping like a fatal wound. It looked dead. High in the roof a breeze clutched at the huge blackout curtains slapping them noisily. I swung round, quaking, and hurried on my way.

Outside the sound of distant aero engines brought me back to reality. I could see navigation lights drifting among the stars. A green light flashed from the caravan. Aircraft were now joining the circuit. The landing lights of the first pierced the darkness and it gently touched the earth. They were now coming home and with them for company my fears left me and I continued on my way. During that night, 9/10th November, Hemswell sent 11 aircraft to Hamburg, 300 Sqdn sent 6. The ORB says they left their new Wellington MkIV's behind and reverted to their clapped out Mk1c's! The next day we left for ACRC London, leaving behind many friends and many brave men.

I found an old RAF exercise book from Hemswell and in it I had written:

'The bombers are still roaring off into the beautiful Autumn twilight. Into a setting sun that silhouetted an old windmill in a background of golden glory. A windmill that for a hundred years had with its arms gently caressed the Autumn breezes long before threshing propellers had thrust these machines of destruction into the air. The last of the swallows were swooping low gathering their final harvest before they too would fly their annual migration South.' (I really was carried away!)

In 1986 I visited a derelict Hemswell airfield; 'D' Block had broken windows and to my sorrow the windmill had gone.

CHAPTER THREE

AN AIRMAN WANDERS

'These are the days that, to their upmost hour,
The upper and the nether millstones grind.'

'The Heirloom,' by Lord Dunsany

War Poems from the Sunday Times 1945.

The change at ACRC was a great shock to us. The relationship between cadets and NCOs since we were last here had hardened. Gone was the laughter and joking of light hearted recruits. In its stead was a rigid and petty discipline. Articles of kit regularly disappeared and an NCO openly boasted he was selling RAF blankets by the dozen. There were rumours that a tyrannical NCO had been flung into the Regents Park Canal at night. It was an unhappy lot after Hemswell.

We were billeted in a block of flats in Hall Road. A cookhouse beneath the building spared us the indignity of having to queue at the zoo for meals and we were constantly harassed by NCOs who invented petty tasks for us. Most of us from Hemswell stuck together. Those who lived in London took every opportunity to get home, travelling by bus to avoid Military Police patrols at the railway and underground stations!

The 13 graduating Hemswell geniuses were posted to an EFTS at Perth. The failures went to ITW at Scarborough for another shot. We drew our flying kit from stores, filling another heavy kit bag. The posting was on the notice board for no more than an hour when, par for the course, it was rescinded. The geniuses were to go to ACDW (Aircrew Disposal Wing) at Brighton, the dunces still went to Scarborough!

Four of us went out on a binge and got drunk. The following morning, dressed in full marching order, a pack on my back, a kit bag on each shoulder and a small steel helmet stuck on my large sore head, we marched to the transport which was conveniently drawn up half a mile away! The pain in my head was a fitting addition to the pain in the arse this place had given me! We were accompanied on the journey to Brighton by a party bound for AONS (Air Observers' Navigation School) at Shoreham. They were straight from ITW and had been in the RAF just 3 months! While their morale was soaring into dizzy heights ours was at an all time low. In retrospect, we were very lucky for the extra living time being given to us.

At Brighton Station we were met by a howling gale and freezing rain. Still more depressed, we fell in and marched off down the hill towards the promenade below. In these conditions we spent more time on our backsides than on our feet, steel studded boots and icy streets not being renowned for their frictional qualities. Our blasphemy shocked passers-by, we had at last lost our sense of humour! Finally, we dragged our wet and miserable selves through the magnificent portals of the Metropole Hotel, our home for the next two weeks.

The following day, 7th December 1941, the Japanese attacked Pearl Harbour!

Our fourth floor room in the Metropole overlooked the sea and we slept in a bed for the first time since Hemswell. Discipline was tough but there was none of the pettiness we'd experienced in London and, of crucial importance, we fed well! Our days were occupied with lectures and drilling on the promenade. There was little doubt we would take our place alongside the infantry should an invasion come. Hopefully it would only be a contest in foot drill! At 22.30hrs there was a curfew on the seafront and no one was allowed on the promenade.

On 11th December 1941 HMS 'Prince of Wales' and HMS 'Repulse' were sunk by Japanese torpedo-bombers off the coast of Malaya. One of the survivors of the 'Repulse', Chief Petty Officer Cyril Haskey, was the father of a boy named Paul who was born in his father's absence; it would be two years before they met. Many years later Paul was to marry my daughter and become the father of my grandchildren.

There was plenty with which to amuse ourselves in Brighton. The Old Hemswellonians decided one evening, after a few pints, to take in a show at 'The Hippodrome'. We were in fine fettle when we reached the theatre. Max Miller and Hershal Henlere were on the bill. The banter between us in the third row and the stage was unbelievable. Fortunately both the audience and the artists took it in good part.

Eventually a roller skating act came on. Two girls gave us a hair-raising demonstration at the end of which they asked for a volunteer to assist them. We got 'Chappie' Chapman to his feet, a big boned, swarthy complexioned individual from the Midlands. He literally teetered drunkenly towards the stage. Once there Chappie clasped his hands above his head like a boxer entering a ring and acknowledged the thunderous applause. There was a whispered conversation after which Chappie, with thumbs tucked under his braces, took a step forward and bowed to the audience. The girls, each taking a firm grip of one of his wrists, proceeded to skate in a circle. Slowly at first, they circled Chappie and began to spin him like a top. Then, after a matter of a few seconds, and to our horror, Chappie was flung out horizontally and whirled through the air with the girls leaning back to counterbalance his weight. The rolling drum accompanying them made a loud thump, the girls stopped and Chappie was deposited between them. The girls then curtsied, Chappie gave a sickly grin, went green and, as if pole-axed, collapsed flat on his back. Pandemonium broke loose throughout the theatre. Two of our chaps leaped to their feet, rushed on to the stage, picked up Chappie and carried him off feet first. It stopped the show. Fully twenty minutes after, giggles were still coming from the audience.

Many years later as I was telling this tale when one of my listeners started to laugh until tears rolled down his face. I was perplexed and asked why, since my tale wasn't as funny as all that. He said we didn't know how funny it was. He went on to say he had been based at Reading at the time and had gone with some others to see a show at the Reading Hippodrome. It was the same bill. They had in their mess a regular army sergeant who was built like a barrel; five foot tall, five foot round the waist and wore size twelve boots. He was a prodigious drinker and when they departed for the theatre it was estimated that he had polished off 14 pints of beer.

They were in the front row and when the time came they pushed their tubby sergeant up on to the stage. He too was whirled round like a top and when the drum stopped rolling he too was dumped on his feet between the girls who curtsied. He, however, rocked gently backwards and forwards on his size twelve boots and with a tremendous 'Whoosh' deposited his 14 pints of beer into the orchestra pit. It had been terribly difficult to restart the show following the uproar from the audience!

There was a call for a 120 volunteers for a posting to South Africa. Only 100 would go, but all would get Christmas embarkation leave. Jock and I talked it over and decided that if we waited until last we could get the leave without going on the draft (all Christmas leave had been cancelled!). So we waited until the mad rush of volunteers had subsided and then went to the table to register our names. The officer said it was unlikely we would go being number 116 and 117 on the list. However, if there was a vacancy we might be lucky enough to get on the draft!

Jock and I pumped each other's hand and congratulated each other. 'The easiest bit of leave I've ever wangled,' I smirked, 'Not a hope of going on that draft and who knows, we may get another spell of embarkation leave when our next posting comes along!' I enjoyed my Christmas leave, and so claimed Jock when we met again at Brighton. We unpacked and went to look at the notice board, primarily to gloat over that posting to South Africa. With usual orderly room efficiency the list was in alphabetical order and as both our surnames began with 'C' we were in the top half of it! Like it or not we were on our way to South Africa. Jock's language was superb. He swore for fully five minutes without repeating himself! (We both wanted to go to Canada or the USA.)

On the last day of 1941 we moved to a town of wooden huts called RAF Padgate outside Warrington in Lancashire. The camp was surrounded with barbed wire and rested under a perpetual cloud burst. The two-tiered bunks were damp and one step off the concrete paths brought mud up to your eyes. Padgate was also an initial intake camp. We saw raw recruits being put through their paces, poor buggers! We had certainly had it easy up to now! Two days later we collected tropical kit, another ruddy kit bag! It was a comical outfit, shorts hanging down below the knee and a sun helmet the size of a bell tent!

The January weather was bitterly cold and there was little or no fuel on the camp. In spite of terrifying threats to anyone caught doing so, the lavatory doors had long been broken up and burnt. I thought it would not be long before nothing remained of the loos but the concrete floor and the china fittings!

In one week our orders came to move. A band wheezed onto the parade ground and then wheezed off with us marching behind it to Padgate Station where we boarded a train. Within an hour we were in Liverpool Docks. For two hours we stood at the quay side, 'two deep facing the boat,' as that old RAF saying goes. Eventually we walked up a gang plank and into the bowels of the 'Otranto', a P & O ship of 20,000 tons, built in 1925 for the Australia run; with an enormous top side, she was totally unsuitable for the Atlantic gales with which she now had to contend. At the water line we stopped and entered a mess deck, a quarter of which was taken up by long tables each seating 18; our claustrophobic home for the next six weeks. We spent the rest of the day watching the army come aboard.

That night a khaki figure appeared at the head of the stairway and with a bellow like a mad bull turned the lights out. I abandoned my hammock, now hanging from one hook, and in the dim blue light of the emergency system flung my blankets onto the metal deck in disgust and spent a sleepless night on cold steel. The next day smoke belched from the huge funnels and tugs fussed us into the open waters of the Mersey. On water as smooth as glass we passed a ship sailing towards Liverpool, her rigging and decks one mass of waving khaki figures. A derisive cheer went up and floating across the intervening water a lone voice called, 'You silly buggers you're going the wrong way!'

HMT Otranto at the dockside (Photo: National Maritime Museum ref:P23715).

That night, suspended from the deck above, a sea of prostrate, hammocked, sleeping bodies rocked in unison with every movement of the ship. Morning found us anchored in Belfast Lough. Around us were assembled ships that were to form our convoy. Next day we steamed out of the Lough. One of the ship's crew said it was the largest convoy he had ever seen. A mist obscured our last view of British green hills, 18 months for me, for many who were watching - forever.

In the murk of heavy rain and dark low clouds driven by gale force winds, we steamed through mountainous seas, seemingly down the middle of nowhere. The food was nauseating. Keeping station with us among a motley collection of cargo ships were two other troopers; 'Orantes', our sister ship and the 'Louis Pasteur', a French boat with one funnel that bucked about like a bronco. In the van was a small armed merchant cruiser which flew the Commodore's flag. On our flanks, scattered on the horizon of foam flecked water, was a destroyer escort and a battlewagon, 'HMS Resolution'.

At first I seldom slept at night, the stench from vomiting bodies and the thought of being trapped below if a torpedo struck us kept me wide awake! Daylight hours did nothing to allay my fears. A Focke-Wulf Condor shadowed us through gaps in the cloud, doubtless informing U-boats of our position. A wily bird this, just keeping out of range of our spasmodic anti-aircraft fire. When at last free from the rain, the windlashed sea and out of range of shadowing Condors, porpoises played beside our bow. Flying fish stretched their wings and glided silently before us. At night a phosphorescent sea lit the bow wave, a bow which turned the water over like a plough turning over the sod, leaving turned green sea to briefly mark our passing.

HMS Resolution - so close we could have spat on her deck
(National Maritime Museum ref:N6198).

Three weeks later the black smudge of land appeared on the horizon. We were amused by our small escort of destroyers cleaving their way up and down, like a litter of puppies on their first day out, signal lamps flashing mutual back-slapping messages which we could clearly read. Impromptu exhibitions of exuberance seemed to be part of Navy tradition. A few days earlier the 'Resolution' had made a high speed run through the convoy, signal lamps flashing and coming so close to us you could have spat on her deck. For one awful moment we thought that she was going to run us down.

We steamed down a horrific avenue of twelve or so sunken ships, only the funnels and masts showing above water. Some U-boat commander must have had a field day! With a clatter and a splash, we dropped anchor opposite the distant white buildings of Freetown which shimmered in the haze. We were soon surrounded with bum boats. Black faces grinned up at us offering wares we were forbidden to buy. After five days we upped anchor and went. A few days later, in a heavy swell and without ceremony we crossed the Equator. A case of meningitis sent shivers through the ship and amid prayer the canvas-wrapped body of its lonely victim slid into a watery grave.

The unrelentless monotony of it all was punctuated by blasts from the siren of the Commodore's ship indicating a change in the course we were steering. The skipper of a small merchant ship conversed with our ship's doctor through an Aldis Lamp and carried out a minor operation. '...A-CRUSHED-HAND-I-DO-NOT-LIKE-THE-LOOK-OF-IT....'. The lamp winked the whole gory story and we, although infants in the art of Aldis Lamp reading, read on! Instructions from us, a pause.
'OK-HAVE-DONE-THAT-THE-PUS...'
Ugh! One could almost feel the pain, but our morbid curiosity kept our eyes glued on that flickering lamp.

The convoy finally broke up and in the grey light of morning we sailed through the harbour entrance and drew alongside the quay at Durban. I must have been the

Bum boats at Freetown

only serviceman passing this way who never saw the lady dressed in white singing to the troopships at the entrance to the harbour! We went on shore for six hours. I was pleased to be out of that stinking, U-boat fear ridden troop ship. We had journeyed from a blacked out, austere land, into an exotic life style; we ate fine food at low cost and feasted on the blaze of electricity that lit the city at night. This was the holiday city of Durban in February 1942.

The following day we disembarked and boarded a train standing in the dockyard. The army watched us disembark with envy. They had a long way to go before their disembarkation into some of the bloodiest battles of the North African Desert. There can be few train journeys more beautiful than the one we were taking, winding through green hills, multi-coloured wild flowers growing beside the track adding great beauty to the natural scene. It was during lunch on the train that I first met Bill Flanagan. He sat facing an open window, the wind tugging at his unruly mop of blond hair. A tall man with a magnificent body rippling with muscles and a snake tattooed on one of his arms. He spoke loudly in a voice that boomed throughout the dining car. He told me that before the war he had been in the Royal Marines but had been invalided out when a shell dropped on his foot!.

Our escorts were two South African Air Force (SAAF) sergeants - a mean looking pair. They wore the slim, smart SAAF standard issue sun helmet, a khaki bush jacket and their slacks were tucked into small canvas leggings over brown boots. Each carried a small riding whip which they slashed against the side of the carriage as they strode up and down the corridor yelling their heads off. They created an ugly mood and fortunately they struck no one. Bill said he would kill anyone who struck him with a riding whip!

The train stopped from time to time and a few of us got down to pick wild peaches that grew at the line side. This infuriated those sergeants so much that we decided the next time we stopped we would all get down, which we did. The engine driver was most co-operative! He would pull up where the peaches grew and blew his whistle when he wanted us to get back on board again! In retrospect, I am not so sure the driver was on our side, so many of us were soon holding our bellies in pain!

Leaving Pietermaritzburg we found ourselves in a horrendous storm. Rain bucketed down and lightning crackled, striking the ground around us. The thunder was deafening, like sitting inside a base drum with someone pounding it. The storm still flickered behind us as in the gathering dusk we saw the twinkling lights of Ladysmith. We climbed into our bunks and later awoke to find ourselves in the suburbs of Johannesburg. A further 30 miles on we were shunted into the siding of a small station called Lyttleton, 5 miles from Pretoria. We left the train, put a pack on our back and began the one and a half mile march to 75 Air School, a bungalow encampment in a valley shimmering in the heat.

We could see the hangars of two large airfields, Waterkloof and Zwartkop and beside the camp was a smaller airfield from which Tiger Moths were flying. We assumed we would be airborne in no time. It was a miserable disillusion that helped only to make light work of a hot march in the burning sun over rough red earth. We were the second RAF intake, the first had been here one month. SAAF pupil pilots resented our intrusion; it delayed their flying training. They called us 'The Blue Plague!' They said a signal was sent to London requesting '500 Hart Airscrew' and they got 500 'Hart Aircrews' (Hawker Hart) If they had only asked for 50 maybe Jock and I would have got the two embarkation leaves we had planned!

We were unhappy to learn we had to go through ITW again followed by ATW (Advanced Training Wing), taking three months in all. There was the usual threat if one failed! However our quarters were superb and we ate well. I wrote home saying with each meal a whole month's butter ration appeared on the table! Soon after arrival, the OB's (the Ossewa Brandwag, an Afrikaans, Anti-British organisation) beat up one of our number with a bicycle chain in Pretoria. After that we never travelled alone when we went there or just avoided it altogether. Pity, it was a beautiful city with streets lined with flowering jacaranda. We had no such problems with Johannesburg, it was easy to get to and we never waited long for a lift outside the camp.

One week after our arrival at Lyttleton, Air Marshal Arther Harris was appointed Air Officer Commander-in-Chief (AOC) Bomber Command. It is an understatement to say he was to have a great influence on the lives of many of the aircrew cadets who were then under training!

The two NCOs who accompanied us from Durban played a great part in our daily lives making it very difficult for us. In short, they were a couple of mean bastards! One was a South African amateur boxing champion and we put an RAF chap into the ring with him. I think his name was Percy Northrop, a public school boxing champion at the same weight! To look at him you wouldn't think he could punch his way out of a paper bag! However our champion won and we considered we'd had the last laugh!

In Johannesburg there were numerous servicemen's clubs who among other things made introductions to families with whom one could stay. It was such an organisation that introduced me to a family who lived in Lower Houghton. Their name was Drury-Shaw, he was a gynaecologist. They had a beautiful home opposite the Automobile Club into which we used to dash for a swim before breakfast! I have long since lost touch with them and I am told a motorway now runs through Lower Houghton where they lived. They were very kind to me during my stay in South Africa and always welcomed me as one of the family whenever I went to visit them - as they did many of their other RAF guests.

At Swartkop were a number of stubby nosed Curtiss P-36's Hawks. Their 1200 horse power Wright Cyclone radial engines laboured as they clawed their way like a swarm of angry bees into the rarefied air (we were 6,000 feet above sea level). We were horrified to see one streaming black oily smoke from its engine as it swung down to earth. A geyser of dust and smoke shot into the air then, in silence, the smoke drifted away and the dust fell slowly back to the ground.

The 'Old Hemswellians' at 75 Air School, February 1942. Front row - left to right: 'Jock' Ian Craig, Norman Brockhouse, 'Jock' Bill Connell, Jack Churcher. Back row: Ken Carter, 'Chappie' Chapman (of roller skating fame), Gordon Cornish, John Cleames, self. We were ten in all but Ted Cederval is missing (probably taking the picture).

From Waterkloof, Hawker Harts and Hinds of 23 Air School, an SFTS, (Service Flying Training School) flew over the camp during their landing circuit. How I had admired Harts at Hendon when I was a boy! The small landing field next to the camp was occupied by No 4 AD (Aircraft Disposal). Here they assembled and test flew Tiger Moths. The pilots made a habit of fish tailing or side slipping over our huts when coming into land, the engine barely ticking over. You could almost touch them as they flew over.

Lyttleton, with all its local air activity was just about the most frustrating place for any embryo pilot to be!

March found us through ITW and into the Advanced Training Wing (ATW) where we were integrated with the SAAF. Needless to say we got on extremely well together, spending most of our spare time in our new swimming pool or on the tennis court. The tuition differed little from that we had already received in the UK. It was a great bore but perhaps I needed it all pumped into me a second time. The final results showed me bottom of the class in Theory of Flight. Clearly I had forgotten why I had come to South Africa. At last I was posted to an EFTS (Elementary Flying Training School).

Of the original 10 that came from Hemswell four were posted with me, Jock Connell, Ken Carter, Ian Craig and Ted (Seedy) Cedervall, Bill Flanagan came too. It was two days after my 19th birthday and ten months after I had first reported to Lord's Cricket Ground.

CHAPTER FOUR

AIRBORNE AT LAST!!

*'I've chased the shouting wind along, and flung
My eager craft through footless halls of air.'*

'High Flight' by Plt/Off G Magee, Jnr. RCAF. Killed 11th December 1941

It took six hours by rail to cover 135 miles from Pretoria to Kroonstad[1] in the Orange Free State. The countryside was flat and uninteresting. Metalled roads finished a few miles south of Johannesburg. Long distance road travel in South Africa 1942 was a primitive, bone shaking, dusty affair on tracks where graders smoothed the ruts and ridges. Red dust flung up by vehicles could be seen for miles. Mind you, 6 hours for a 135 mile train journey wasn't exactly pushing it!

In the troop carrier enroute for the station. L to R, 'Jock' Cambell, Hargreaves, Shropshall, self, Ken Carter

A Chevrolet troop carrier took us from the station to No 7 Air School, which was situated about two miles to the north of the town. In March 1942 it had only been established 5 months and still needed much work on it. Unlike Hemswell there were no massive buildings. The three small steel Bellman-type hangars, the single storey working and living quarters strung out behind them were all within the apex of an 'L' shaped flying field.

---

[1] - *Kroonstad - Vir Plesier, Gesondheid en Vooruitgang (For pleasure, health and progress - town slogan 1947!*

We were two in a frugal room lit by a paraffin hurricane lamp, our furniture two beds and a chest of drawers. A native boy kept us clean and tidy. My room-mate was Ken Carter, from Hemswell, a handsome, photogenic fellow of medium build and a shock of black hair which he was continually combing. The Pupil Pilots' Mess was a large corrugated iron clad building which had the name 'Baldwin Steel' stencilled in red paint on every sheet. Mr Baldwin, with his iron sheets, must have clad every military installation in the Union. We fed like kings and paid 1/6d (8p) per day messing for five course meals and our own table napkin! I was now complaining in letters home that income tax now removed 6/-d

On the train to Kroonstad

(30p) a week from my pay and mess bills were 10/6d (53p) making me 4/-d (20p) a week worse off than before!

The camp had a mascot, a shaggy black and white coated dog of doubtful parentage called 'Jankers'. He was a friendly little beast. Everyone made a great fuss of him and he of us.

The day after we

A truly frugal room

arrived we were allocated flights. I went to 'D' Flight commanded by Capt Hellet. He told us as this was a new school and we were No 3 Course, a course that would take three months to complete - a high standard would be expected of us. Alternate mornings would be devoted to either lectures or flying. There would be two examinations, one half way and one at the end of the course, failure meant dismissal!

In contrast, the 'palatial' mess at No.7 Air School

Lieutenant Dennis Compton SAAF, my
ab initio instructor at Kroonstad

Our day would begin at 05.45hrs and at 06.30 we would parade outside the Chief Ground Instructor's (CGI) office for roll call[2]. He then paired us off and introduced us to our flying instructors, nearly all of whom were SAAF. Most spoke with the distinctive Afrikaans accent, rolling their 'r's, virtually dispensing with 'h's and doubling the length of most of their 'a's. My partner was Ken Wood, a small, fair haired RAF chap. When we were called a tall gangling figure came forward. He wore a peaked cap and was dressed in khaki, his shoulder straps bore the two gold pips of a lieutenant and a red stripe indicating that he was prepared to serve outside the Union. His pilot's badge was whiter than that of the RAF and in its centre was the picturesque arms of the Union of South Africa.

He introduced himself as Dennis Compton - a wizard with the 'joy stick' not the cricket bat! I estimated his age to be about 22. He shook us by the hand and suggested we went and looked at a Tiger Moth. We walked out in the early morning autumn sun to the neat rows of yellow Tiger Moths standing in front of the hangars. Amid great activity, members of the senior course were making ready to take to the air. Propellers were being swung and engines were bursting into life. Ground crews fussed around the aircraft like fathers around small children. Compton went to the nearest aircraft and stepped onto the cat walk of the lower wing. He let down the side flap of the rear cockpit and motioned Wood into the bucket seat. From the ground I looked over his shoulder into the green interior. There really wasn't much to explain, he said, pointing in front of the windscreen to the ignition switches.

His long arm reached inside the cockpit and he started with the flying instruments on the instrument panel. He said they were the airspeed indicator (ASI), the altimeter, the pitch indicator (which we were to ignore - it was useless!), the compass and the turn and bank indicator. There were only two engine instruments, he said, the revolution counter and the oil pressure gauge. He waggled the 'stick' and pointed into the green depths to the rudder bar, the petrol cock, the throttle and the mixture control (which was wired in position). Pointing to the Gosport tube mouthpiece he then waggled the tube to which the earphones were connected, 'Our inter-comm,' he said. He lent over and moved a lever backwards and forwards, the springs activated by his movements groaned and slapped the side of the fuselage. The tail trim was worked by altering a tension spring attached to the control column.

Stretching up he pointed to the forward starboard interplane strut, saying

---

[2] - The CGI was a bulky, smiling Flt/Lt and one of the few RAF officers on the camp (the Station Commander, Wg/Cmdr A.R.L.Duke and the Chief Flying Instructor (CFI) Flt/Lt Pope were two others).

that the red sleeve seen there should always be removed before take-off since it covered the pitot head which operated the ASI and the altimeter! The fuel gauge (a glass column shrouded by a metal tube) was on top of the fuel tank in the centre section. A simple instrument he said - the engine was gravity fed. The rear-view mirror was to keep an eye on us and below it was the venturi tube through which air passed and spun the gyros working the turn and bank indicator. The spring loaded plate on the forward port interplane strut was calibrated in miles per hour, an emergency ASI. The Handley Page slots on the leading edge of the upper wing were wired in the closed position and were inoperative.

He then took us through the starting procedure with the air mechanic. He finished his lecture in his heavily accented English saying, 'The air mechanic (which sounded more like "ear mechanic") will then swing the airscrew and the engine should start, if it doesn't you have to go through the whole damn procedure again. If it doesn't start then, there's no telling what the air mechanic will shout at you!' He said that was enough for one day and made his way back to the flight office. Ken and I went to the parachute section to collect our parachutes, the ear pieces for our helmet and a SAAF flying log book.

The next morning we pushed the CGI's ancient car off the small space that served as a parade ground and had the roll call. Afterwards those who were flying would report to the flights to push out the aircraft. Flying commenced at 07.30hrs and Ken and I reported to the flights[3]. One by one we trotted the small biplanes out of the hangars, the tyres gently humming on the tarmac. Propellers horizontal, we placed them facing into wind in four long rows, 'A','B', 'C' and 'D' Flights, their orange, white and blue roundels on yellow wings and fuselages gleaming in the early morning sunshine. A coin was tossed for the privilege of the first ride; Ken called correctly, I watched them go. It was not long before I was standing beside the aeroplane, its propeller slipstream gently tugging at my unbuckled helmet strap. Bending double, I passed the lower parachute harness straps through the loop and clipped them into the quick-release box. Ken jumped down from the wing, grinned and put his thumb up.

I was trembling with fear when I put my fleece-lined boot on the wing and hauled myself into the bucket seat. Ken passed the Sutton Harness straps over my shoulders and I checked the sequence numbers on them before buckling

---

[3] - *This was to become the established routine: 07.30hrs start and by 17.00 the last aircraft would usually be hangared - a long day for all concerned.*

myself in. I clipped home the ear tubes. Ken patted my helmet. I fished under the rubber padded fuselage for the Gosport tube mouthpiece and said into it, 'Ready, sir'. 'Are you sure that your straps are as tight as you can get them, Clark?' he asked. 'Yes, sir,' I replied. 'OK, we'll taxy out.'

He waved his hand at the mechanic standing at the wing tip and returned his salute. The throttle lever at my left hand side moved gently forward, a needle moved across a dial, the engine responded, increasing in power. We moved forward, bouncing over uneven ground, zig-zagging our way to the take-off point. We stopped across wind and a voice in my ear enquired, 'All clear, Clark?' I twisted my head round and scanned the sky - it was empty. On the ground behind us a crocodile of aircraft, the next detail, pranced and weaved their way to where we were waiting. 'All clear, sir,' I replied, trying to suppress my excitement. 'OK, now pull your goggles down over your eyes. I don't ever want to see you flying with your goggles pushed up on your forehead. Have you got that, man? OK! Here we go, man.' Everything was 'man' and pronounced in clipped Afrikaans English more like 'men'.

The throttle lever began its ghostly movements again as we turned into wind. The engine roared into full power. A slight pressure on my buttocks told me that the tail had come up and with it came a clearer view ahead. The airspeed indicator began recording our forward speed and the propeller's slip-stream, faintly smelling of petrol, whipped back with an upsurge of fury. We bounced a little then, quite suddenly, the ground fell away below us and we were climbing into the still morning air. 'That's Kroonstad down there,' said a voice seemingly from the bottom of a pit. 'You can see the railway running from Jo-berg in the north to Bloemfontein in the south and from Bethlehem in the east. The river skirting the town is the Valsch which meets up with the Vaal somewhere or other. That steel structure down there with the sun glinting on it is a grain elevator. Remember it, it's quite a land mark around here. More often than not you will see that before you will see the town. Have you got that, man?' I nodded to the face in the mirror and looked over the side. There, straggling below, was the small dorp of Kroonstad covering no more than 4 square miles. I could make out Cross Street, the one main thoroughfare, where the few shops and hotels were. To the east the slow moving waters of the Valsch meandered through willow lined banks, spanned by a white concrete bridge to the south[4]. To the north west and close to the flying school was the shanty town of the native compound. Rising

---

[4] - *Some of us flew under it until Bill Flanagan was extremely embarrassed to find ropes hanging from it to prevent us from doing so! I must admit I never did - fly under it that is!*

above all was the grain elevator.

Cross Street Kroonstad - not unlike a scene from an American Western

'Clark!' the voice startled me, 'I want you to take over for a bit. I don't see why I should do all the work. In future when I want you to take over I'll say, "You've got her!" and you'll reply, "I've got her, sir!". You got that, man?' 'Yes, sir', I replied. 'OK, you've got her, man.' 'I've got her, sir.' 'The aerodrome is just over there to starboard, steer in that general direction and keep a very good look out for aircraft already in the circuit and those like us, about to join it. Do your best to hold this height.' I felt a slight knock on the stick. 'And, man, don't hold that stick as if your very life depends upon it - relax!'

Two arms appeared from the front cockpit and the body to which they were attached stretched itself. The aircraft, so beautifully suspended in the air before, wallowed and danced its way back to the airfield. The arms went back into the cockpit. 'I've got her, man,' said the voice from the pit and I, thankfully, removed my hands from the stick, my feet from the rudder bar and replied, 'You've got her, sir.' The throttle eased back gently and slowly we lost height. The wind hummed in the wires as we crossed the line of white oil drums that marked the boundary of the field. Skimming the grass the nose of the aircraft slowly came up. The gentle undulating undercarriage and the scraping of the metal tail skid told me that we were down. Dennis Compton filled the flight in my log book with his own hand:-

Date: April 14, Aircraft Type: Tiger, No: 2273, Pilot: Lt Compton, Pupil: Self, Duty: 1. Air Experience, 1A Familiarity with cockpit layout. Hour: 07.30, Day Dual: .30 (Minutes).

Slowly a new confidence was born. Daily I filled in my log book. I recorded those horrifying first spins (2 left, 2 right). A week after the first entry and 7 hours 10 minutes flying. Dennis said, 'I think you are ready to go solo. I'm going to fetch Captain Hellet to give you a check. Don't worry, just do as well as you have been doing and you'll be off. Good luck, man!' My confidence left me when the white overalled figure of the Flight Commander got into the aeroplane. I swung on take off, over corrected and swung in the opposite direction. I over-shot the field on the first landing approach and felt his hand on the throttle as I moved it open to go round again. 'Christ, Clark! You left that late,' exploded in my ears, confirming my own thoughts. I thought the second landing was

The Grand Hotel Kroonstad - 1942

quite good, he must have seen the smirk on my face in his mirror. His voice in my headphones left no doubt what he thought. 'Very nice, Clark,' he whined sarcastically, 'very nice, and WHO THE BLOODY HELL TAUGHT YOU TO LAND ON TWO WHEELS? EH, MAN?' His white clad back doubled forward and he beat his fist on the side of the aircraft. 'Now snap out of it and show me what you can really do.'

I did, and when we kangarooed to a halt at the end of the third landing he yelled, 'I'VE GOT HER!' and taxyed back to the flights with the tail up. The propeller convulsed its last revolutions as he scrambled out of the front cockpit. He gripped my shoulder, smiled and said. 'Don't worry, Clark, you'll be OK. Seven and a half hours flying is too soon, that's all.' At 10 hours 5 minutes there came a repeat performance. No matter how he cajoled, bullied or pleaded with me I just could not pull off that third good landing which would get him out of that aircraft and leave me to go off on my own. In the meantime 'solo' parties were going on in the mess and instructors were gorging themselves on 'solo cakes' bought for them by the more fortunate pupils. I added up my flying time on the second page of my log book and carried forward the total to page three.

Then one morning I was sitting in the aircraft with the engine ticking

They had all gone solo before me - left to right: Higgs Shropshall, Allen, Waldron, Richter (SAAF), Paul Jones (SAAF - who was to survive a terrible crash at Vereeniging), Farrer, Killingbeck (SAAF - ex Shanghai Policeman).

over, waiting for Dennis to take his seat. Without a word a white clad figure clambered into the front cockpit and strapped himself in, it was Hellet. His voice came over the gosport, 'Morning, Clark, three good landings is all I want. OK? You've got her.' I crossed my hands in front of my face and uncrossed them again signalling the waiting airman to remove the chocks from the wheels. We were away. After the third landing he said nothing. As I re-positioned the aircraft for the fourth take off two shoulder straps were flung back and struck the windshield in front of me. 'Thank God for that,' I thought. 'OK, Clark', he said, 'Just one circuit and bump, that's all. Don't forget if you are in any doubt use your engine and go round again. She'll tend to float a bit more without my weight, so watch it when you land. Oh, by the way we are fed up with cake in the Flight Office. I want a tin of biscuits from you for all the trouble you've caused me.' 'So that's it,' I thought, 'You've run out of cake for your coffee!' 'I'm going to sit on one of those drums (white oil drums marking the edge of the field) and have a quick smoke, give me a lift on the way back. Good luck.'

I went through my cockpit drill: trim well forward, fuel, cock 'on', contents OK. 'Anything coming?' I asked myself, a quick look round - all was clear. 'God, I'm hot,' I thought. I turned into wind, 'You can't delay it any longer - this is it.' A clammy hand inside my glove pushed the throttle forward, 'We're moving - check the swing you fool. Christ! The tail came up quickly,' I muttered. 'Must say the forward view has improved without someone sitting on top of your nose. Are we unstuck already?' I started to sing, 'Oooooh an AVI-ATOR LAY DY-YING.' 'What a bloody silly song to sing - WATCH the airspeed. You are over the wood turn port across wind - there's the small dam coming up, turn down wind. I'm really going to get pissed tonight.' I burst into song again, 'AT THE END OF A BRIGHT SUMMER'S DAY-YA.' The town's native compound moved slowly below me, it was time to turn across wind. 'Cut the engine, trim back and turn in,' I mumbled to myself, 'Christ! You're UNDER-SHOOTING, you're way back, open up a bit, relax, relax stupid. What the hell's that silly bastard running for? Stick back, back - JEEZ! - what a bounce! Engine! ENGINE!! open up the engine, Nobbie! OPEN UP!'

I slammed the throttle wide open, the engine yelled loudly in protest. In the panic I told myself, 'Steady yourself, move the trim slightly forward. Throttle back a wee bit don't overtax the engine. Now once more and this time pull your finger out! OUT!! OUT!!!' The second attempt was a little better, but she floated like hell so I took the motor and went round again for a third shot. Over the wood, turn cross wind, over the dam, turn down wind, over the compound, turn across wind (I would have been lost but for those ground-marks!) Throttle back, and turn in for the final approach. 'What's all that smoke?' I asked myself as a white vapour curled its way across my path. We flew low over the oil drums, the engine barely ticking over. 'Hold it, now back, back, back.' There was a rumble as wheels and tailskid met the grass, we were down.

'Better go back for Hellet,' I told myself. With a burst of engine I turned the aircraft and taxyed back toward the oil drums, my hands trembled, I was more than glad it was over. I stopped and Captain Hellet swung on to the wing and threw his parachute into the front seat and climbed in after it. The hair on his uncovered head rippled in the slipstream as I zig-zagged back to the flights. The engine coughed to a standstill, he climbed out and gave me a wink, 'Well done, Clark,' he said, 'There was no need to try and knock me off those oil drums you know! That second attempt would have been OK if you'd have left it. By the way the wind direction changed - that's why they lit the smoke candle!' Ken and Dennis, coming out for the next detail, waved their arms in congratulations. Dennis said, 'Now we can get down to some real work, man.'

My log book says it took 3 checks and 13 hours 20 minutes flying time to go solo. In the mess that evening I was welcomed back to the fold where for the past week they had written me off as the course's first failure. I got drunk among friends.

Tiger Moth 2273 - Paddy Seddon at the controls

The month of May came, so beautiful in England, the embers of autumn in South Africa. With the schooling we had already had we found g r o u n d s c h o o l reasonably easy and consequently had more time to ourselves. At first we spent some of it in Kroonstad, but we were never well received there. Our infrequent trips into Kroonstad took us past the so called 'Native Compound', a wire enclosed area of tumbledown shacks, filth and poverty. We all thought that something, perhaps a pestilence, from areas like this would eventually engulf this otherwise beautiful country. Perhaps, in the light of today's events in South Africa, we weren't far wrong. One cannot help feeling there has been plenty of time to put such matters right.

I had 3 hours 35 minutes solo time when the time came to execute my first solo spins in sight of the airfield. I was not happy when I found myself flying an Australian-built Tiger with plywood leading edges which restricted its climbing performance. The airfield was already 4,500 feet above MSL[5] and it took a long time for that Aussie Tiger and I to claw our way to safety height. I got there eventually, above a corner of the airfield. I turned steeply in either direction looking for any aircraft below. With my heart in my mouth I closed the throttle and eased the stick back into my stomach. The nose came slowly up above the horizon and the needle of the air speed indicator moved swiftly across the dial as the airspeed fell off. The aircraft paused and hung silently, motionless in mid-air as though waiting for its next command. Gingerly I pushed my right foot on the rudder bar and the starboard wing dropped. It began slowly gyrating towards the earth. Curiously the aircraft appeared to remain static while the earth below spun madly. I counted two complete turns and hastily recovered. Sweating, I coaxed the aeroplane back up to safety height, no laughter, no song, and

[5] - *MSL - Mean Sea Level.*

repeated the performance this time to the left. I hurried back to the airfield landed and climbed out. Back in the crew room, my legs still shaking, Bill Flanagan called over 'How'd it go, Nobbie?' I smiled and lied, 'Swell, Bill, no problem!'

Later, in the crew room, Bill Flanagan was discussing spinning. He laughed at my puny four turns performed solo that morning and said tomorrow he would show us a real spin. We all watched him take off and climb into the morning sun. The glinting speck turned steeply first one way and then the other. A wing dropped and slowly the spin began. We began loudly counting the number of turns, 'One!...Two!...Three!...,' silently the aeroplane spun its way to earth like a matchstick caught in a vortex of draining water. Rooted to our feet, we no longer counted but watched him get lower and lower, every one of us going through the motions of recovery in our minds. Still spinning he disappeared behind a row of tall trees that obscured our view. We waited for the inevitable plume of rising dust and smoke which would tell us that machine and earth had met.

It never came. A drunken biplane appeared over the trees, crabbing its way back to the field it landed, bouncing to a halt. It taxyed in, Bill climbed out, his face green and with one hand clutching the side of the cockpit puked in front of us! We dubbed him 'King Spin' on the spot. Later Bill explained what happened. After the fifth turn he decided it was time to pull out but for some reason or other he couldn't. He then panicked and even altered the pressure setting (which retarded the needle) on the altimeter to give himself more height!! He was much too close to the ground when he decided to bail out. Then it happened, she came out of the spin herself, so low, he said, he thought the wheels were going to touch the ground!

We started aerobatics. Loops and stall turns didn't bother me, but during the first slow roll my feet left the cockpit floor and waved aimlessly about. Dust sprinkled my face like a gentle shower of rain and I hung grimly to the sides of the aircraft. I could see Dennis smiling at me in the mirror. His last pupil, he said, could not roll to the left so he started me going that way. When I finished the course I was unable to roll to the right!

At the end of May the weather began to change. Dark clouds sped their way across the sky and upper winds of 90 mph were recorded. We watched a wall of dust march across the *'Bundu*[6]*'* towards us. In the evening sky the sun displayed its dying embers in a last defiant gesture to pierce the murkiness that was bearing down upon us. There is seldom a sunset in South

---

6 - *'Bundu' - Afrikaans for the deep countryside.*

Self in flying kit worn for the camera!

Africa without beauty, but this one was awe inspiring both in its beauty and brilliance. It looked as if it was to be a final display of glory before the end of the world! With the sunset came the dust, blotting out every detail not only of sight but of mind. The storm went with the same suddenness as it came, leaving a thick mantle of red dust over everything. The night was unusually quiet, there wasn't a cricket to be heard, the dust must have covered them too.

May 30th/31st 1942 saw the first 1000 bomber raid on Cologne. At Kroonstad I bent my first wingtip! Course 2 left for FTS and we were given a weekend pass, so I hurried off to the Shaw's in Jo-berg. When I left to return, Anne, their daughter, offered me a box of good luck charms. I took an owl, to see in the dark, and a black cat for luck! I tied them to a strap on my helmet, they stayed there a long time and they served me well! Back at Kroonstad Course 4 had arrived. When Dennis returned from leave we started instrument flying in preparation for night flying. Cocooned under a small canvas cover over the rear cockpit in oven-like heat I chased illusive instrument needles, sweat pouring down my face and down my back. My first dual cross-country was in a Hornet Moth. Nosing our way across the Veldt with a finger on a map and pencil on a Navigational Computor MKIII (RAF spelling), we worked out navigational problems. They sent me off solo on the same trip a few days later. On the home leg I simply climbed and headed for the silver grain elevator on the horizon!

Formation flying was only flown with an instructor. At first I bounced around like a rubber ball, never daring to get too close, sweating profusely and pumping the throttle backwards and forwards like a piston rod. I enjoyed it enormously until I flew with an instructor named Becke who screamed abuse at me. His pupils said he behaved like that all the time, we all thought he was sick! Eventually, we started night flying. Aircraft purred overhead with their red and green navigation lights cutting through the darkness. In the cockpit green luminous dials and needles bobbed in front of you. At first I never knew where the ground was and confused the flare path with the lights of Cross Street!

I was standing beside the first flare with an Aldis lamp in my hand and Capt Hellet at my side. An aircraft was making an approach, its engine throttled back, feeling its way onto the ground. He was far too high and Hellet exploded with rage, grabbed the Verey pistol and fired it. The shot, nearly removing my head as it left the barrel, curled away into the darkness and exploded into two red stars. The engine burst into life and then cut out. Continuing its downward path

DH Hornet Moth 1545 at Kroonstad

the aircraft struck the ground with an almighty thud, bounced and slewed to a stop. We rushed over, fearing what we might see. A voice in the darkness bellowed, '...AND DON'T FORGET TO SWITCH THE BLOODY SWITCHES OFF!' and we knew, in-so-far as the bodies were concerned, everything was under control.

I flew to Potchefstroom first with Dennis and then afterwards solo. On my day there was a very high wind and I had a mechanic at each wing tip right to the point of take off. I wondered what folly this was to turn me loose in the eye of a gale, however I went! Once airborne I turned north and pointed the aeroplane at the black slag dump of the worked-out Lace diamond mine. Over it I looked down into its black hole and climbed to get a glimpse of 'Potch' in the far distance. I landed among friends and wasn't allowed back that day. That night there was one heluva party in their mess and I was suffering when I flew home the following morning. Later we saw a film of Lt Nash-Webber and Colin Clarence (A SAAF pupil) flying in and out of that hole at Lace mine. Hellet roaring with laughter with the rest of us and saying 'That's damning evidence, Nash!'

I sweated and cursed in the Link Trainer and saw a spectacular prang into the aircraft lines by a member of the junior course. Debris floating about every where, couldn't have done better myself! Then came the final flying test with the CFI, Flt/Lt Pope, an elderly first world war pilot. In the mirror

I watched his eyes disappear into the top of his head as I blacked him out in a steep turn! I remember how perfect that turn was, the aircraft gently bumped as I flew it through her own slip stream! Then suddenly it was all over, exams were finished. The last flight entered in the log book and the summary completed:-

Day: Dual 35.50 hours, Solo 34.55 hours.
Night: Dual 3 hours Total 73.45 hours.
5 hours on Instruments and 8.15 hours in the Link.

The aeroplanes were on parade as usual,
their engines strangely silent

I wandered up to the flights for the last time. The aeroplanes were on parade as usual, their engines strangely silent. I opened my locker door and dragged out my parachute prior to returning it to the parachute section when the Flight Commander's door opened and Nash-Webber walked into the room. His parachute was flung over his shoulder and his helmet balanced on top of his head. He looked at me and smiled, 'Hello, Nobbie, off tomorrow?' 'Yes, sir,' I replied. He put his foot on a bench and asked, 'Glad it's all over?' I looked at him and said, 'Well I wouldn't say that, I've had a wonderful time here, but naturally I'll be pleased to move on to the next stage.' 'I guess you're right. You'll enjoy flying the Hart, Nobbie, it's a fine aeroplane.' He turned to go away, but stopped and took another look at me. 'How about one last trip? I'm just off to Zwartkop, it should be quite a ride.' He was true to his word. We flew low all the way to Jo-berg where we climbed only high enough to pass over. We landed at Zwartkop and while

Nash went about his business I watched someone struggling to land a Westland Wapiti!

The flight back was as exhilarating as the one out. We were hugging the contour of a small hillock and in the valley before us was a lake covered with birds. I sent up a silent prayer and fearfully curled myself up, waiting for the bird strikes to come. I was amazed when there weren't any. I looked behind - there wasn't a bird to be seen! Seconds later they came bobbing up to the surface completely unconcerned! We arrived over the field, the sun sinking, the sky a brilliant red and the first dorp lights beginning to twinkle below in the dusk. Alas, this flight was never recorded in my log book.

A week later I had a letter from Ted Cedervall, who was flying another 15 hours with the junior course. It said that Dennis had crashed while doing some unauthorised low flying near Parys and had put himself into hospital, he had also put two black eyes on Ken Wood. Nash-Webber had been with him in another aeroplane, both were now grounded. In a PS at the bottom of the letter he wrote, 'A Hart did a slow roll over the hangars here a day or two ago. Flan ?' (Bill Flanagan)

Dennis Compton's bent Tiger - the aircraft
I had so carefully soloed!

Six months later a letter from Dennis Compton said he was still grounded and waiting for the verdict of his courtmartial. Nash-Webber had lost a pip but was flying again six months after the incident. Dennis went on to say he was now engaged to the girl he had courted in 2273 (the aeroplane in which I first soloed and he pranged!). He congratulated me on getting my wings and regretted he could not make the ceremony as he was going to Durban on leave.

Many years later I was in Malta looking at the RAF Memorial to those airmen who died in the Middle East and did not have a known grave. On panel 17 I saw the name Lieutenant Dennis James William Compton, SAAF. I found it difficult to suppress a tear. I recalled walking at his side at Kroonstad, his tall figure clad in a white flying suit, bent double by the straps of his parachute harness tight about his groin. The thumb of his left hand, as was his habit, tucked under the quick release box, his right hand gesticulating as he talked on our way to the aeroplane. I remembered his smiling face in the rear vision mirror as he sat and watched me from the front cockpit. He was a fine instructor, with the patience of Job.

He was 'missing presumed dead' on 16th August 1944, flying a Marauder of No 12 SAAF Squadron. In September 1944 the SAAF comprised one third of all the RAF command in the Mediterranean Theatre.

The RAF monument in Malta for missing airmen who have no known grave.
Panel 17 showing Lt. D.J.W Compton

CHAPTER FIVE

VEREENIGING - HOME OF 22 AIR SCHOOL

'From somewhere in Africa,
This Christmas and New Year,
To all at home I'm wishing,
Victory, Peace and Good Cheer!'

A printed message on a Forces Christmas Aerogramme
sent home from Vereeniging in 1942.

On the 4th July 1942, the 15th Bomb Squadron flying RAF Bostons recorded the USAAF's first offensive mission over Europe. At that moment we were bumping across the threshold of 22 Air School Vereeniging in a another Chevrolet troop carrier after a dusty ride from the railway station.

Vereeniging, in the Transvaal, is 40-50 miles South of Johannesburg and situated on the north bank of the Vaal River. It was here, in 1902, peace terms were discussed by the British and Boer Generals. The square shaped airfield was to the west of the town. It was bordered on the north by a railway, the east by the domestic site, the west by a row of tall poplar trees and to the south by a dusty road to town. It had an incredibly large number of hangars (13 in all). Most camp structures were corrugated iron clad or roofed by Mr Baldwin! The giant cooling towers of a nearby electricity generating station made a magnificent land mark. The largest in the Southern Hemisphere when opened in 1936.

We were Course 19 and in a camp so well established the pupil pilots' quarters were well appointed. We were five to a comfortably furnished room, Ken Carter, Bill Flanagan, Brian Leuty, myself and another, whom I cannot recall, who later had rheumatic fever and was grounded. A cheerful Bantu boy called Daniel looked after us. Included in our numbers from Potchefstroom were Gordon Cornish from Hemswell days and Nigel Pleasance whom we knew on the 'Otranto'. He and I became great friends. The course was divided approximately 50/50 RAF/SAAF.

The pupils' mess was at the end of the lines - a large building. We from Kroonstad complained having to pay 2/-d (10p) a day more for messing, moreover we considered the fare not as good! The next day the routine was outlined to us. It was a six months course flying Hawker Hart, Hind and Audax aircraft. Our training could be summarized simply as follows: the first 3 months in ITS (Initial Training Squadron) learning to fly the aeroplane, take 'wings' exam, the second 3 months in ATS

The Pupils' Mess at No. 22 Air School

Daniel who cheerfully looked after us

(Advanced Training Squadron) learning to fight it. God help us if we were ever sent to war in it! SAAF regulations required us to replace our white flashes in our forage caps with a blue one with a white edge. SAAF pupils now wore a similar band around their caps. We drew our parachutes and I reported to 'A' Flight 'A' Squadron Commanded by Capt C.W.Wulfsohn SAAF. I remember little of him except like most SAAF instructors he was continually binding that it was about time he was sent to that Valhalla of all SAAF pilots, 'Up North' (to fly operationally in the Desert.) This was an obsession with all the SAAF and the cause of much of the animosity between the SAAF and RAF. Our intrusion into their flying schools meant a delay before they could go 'Up North'. They were like a bunch of bloody lemmings - in July 1942 there was still far too much war left to fight.

The Hawker Hart (first flew 1928!) was a beautiful aeroplane and my first impression was that I would never be able to fly it - it was so much bigger than a Tiger! I had already forgotten we had been told, 'If you can fly a

Tiger you can fly anything!!' I was thrilled to think that I would fly it, (and find it easy) - a boyhood ambition coming true! The instrumentation was simple. The flying instruments on the panel were the same as a Tiger, an ASI, an altimeter and a turn and bank indicator. Two additional engine instruments to the Tigers' rev counter and oil pressure gauge were an oil temperature gauge and a boost gauge. Also on the panel were twin magneto switches, a starting magneto switch, an engine primer pump (for starting) and a faulty fuel gauge! The tailplane trim was actuated by a wheel on the left of the cockpit, above it were the throttle and fuel mixture control levers with a friction nut to tighten them. A wheel on the right of the cockpit wound the radiator in and out, its position shown by an indicator in front of you, immediately below it was the compass and to its left, the fuel cock. Aerobatics were performed with the radiator retracted and locked up. Failure to lock it resulted in it crashing inboard with a mighty bang when you were inverted, showering you with oily dust and cigarette ends jolted from the cockpit floor.

Hart cockpit

The control column broke in the middle. It had a spade grip, in its centre was the wheel brake lever, the brake pressure gauge being on the floor. The Audax had a gun firing button at the top of the spade grip. This fired the forward firing Vickers machine gun situated on the left hand side of the fuselage. This gun was a bastard to cock, almost impossible to clear a stoppage and delighted in tearing skin off knuckles. Somewhere there was a hand pump to operate the gun's interrupter gear. There was an added luxury of a lever which adjusted the seat height and the joy, as a pupil, of flying from the front cockpit! This beautiful package was bathed in an aroma of 77 octane fuel and yellow doped fabric!

Starting required two men, standing on the landing wheels, each frantically turning a handle to overcome the engine's stubbornness to fire. Once the 525 horse power Rolls Royce Kestrel Engine had started it uttered a noise in the reduction gears, a murmur, not unlike the purring of a cat. It was an unforgettable experience on the senses of sight, smell and hearing. A great joy to fly - in all an everlasting memory. My instructor was an SAAF Lieutenant, A.D. Maxwell, built like a front row forward, who wore a large moustache below which he lodged a pipe with a silver storm cover over the bowl. He puffed at it continuously in the air and on the ground. On an early sortie together I saw a cloud of smoke whipping out of the rear cockpit. I could see Maxwell's head bobbing up and down and his arms flailing. I yelled down the Gosport, 'Are we on fire, sir?' 'FIRE?' he screamed back at me 'FIRE???! No, you damn fool yong[1], I'm lighting my bloody pipe!' A minute or two later his head reappeared, complete with pipe and storm cap, puffing away contentedly. There was no doubt in my mind if we hadn't been on fire he had.

I shall always remember him dressed in white overalls; one hand thrust deep into his pocket; his flying helmet askew on his head, exposing an ear; his parachute flung over his shoulder; puffing at his pipe as we walked on the tarmac discussing our last flight. He had already seen war service with No 41 Army Co-operation Sqdn SAAF in Ethiopia flying Hartebeests (a Hart Variant built in South Africa). In April 1941 he nearly lost his balls at an airfield near Addis Abbaba. Clad only in a towel and armed with a revolver, he held off a pack of looters who had broken into his room! 22 Air School was full of instructors who were ex-No 41 Squadron SAAF!

The first time we were airborne he flung the aircraft into a steep turn, thrust the nose down and at full throttle flew low between the trees to the emergency landing ground. Here, seeing the wind sock hanging limp from its mast, he pulled up into a stall turn, straightened out, throttled back and landed. The tail had barely touched and my breath barely recovered when he banged the throttle wide and climbed away. A few hundred feet up he stall turned, straightened up and yelled into my ear, 'You've got her, Clark. Land straight ahead!' We repeated this performance several times. I could not help thinking of that Yank at Kirton-in-Lindsey in his Hurricane! He suddenly climbed to 4,500 feet, put the aeroplane into a spin and yelled. 'You've got her! Get her out, yong!' which I did! It was a highly unconventional first flight in a Hart!

Maxwell's idea of an emergency landing usually occurred after lunch when he would land at the ELG in haste; hopping out smartly from the rear

---

[1] - 'yong' - Afrikaans the translation of which I don't know, but it was always 'yong' - what're you doing, yong? Come here, yong!

Hawker Hart over the Bundu

cockpit, leaving me to keep the engine running while he relieved himself at the wingtip!

Bill Flanagan soloed first. There was no doubt it was him aerobating that Hart over Kroonstad mentioned in Cedervall's letter. When I mentioned it to Bill he just winked and said Kroonstad was a long way outside our local flying area! It took me two shots and 3 hours 25 minutes to solo. It was an uneventful flight just up and down with no fuss except from Maxwell who was hopping mad and said I should have soloed earlier! Maxwell was particularly edgy during those first three weeks. He kept on bawling me out for swinging on take-off, which I was sure I wasn't. He irritated me with his continual, and in my view, uncompromising, nagging. I vowed in some small way I would get even with him.

My opportunity came sooner than I expected. He gave me a height test, climbing to 10,000 feet which, on the High Veldt, was 15,000 feet ASL. Here we stayed for about 30 minutes. Lack of oxygen made flying hard work and I was pleased to get down again. A few days later I was surprised to see the altimeter winding up to 10,000 feet again. I said nothing but chuckled to myself. Maxwell was wheezing away in the back cockpit, his voice sounding like an out of tune violin with a string or two missing! It had been his third height test sortie that morning. We had been up there about 15 minutes when there was a rumble and an explosion down the inter-comm. 'Clark, you bloody fool, *yong*!' My helmet momentarily swelled about the ears as the blast filled them and then filtered away. 'Didn't I give you a height test a few days ago?' he croaked, his first shouting effort had been too much. 'Yes, sir,' I replied sweetly, 'I thought you wanted to give me another.' 'This is my third today,' he whispered hoarsely, whereupon he pushed the stick forward and down, down, down we went like a hawk pouncing on its prey. Maxwell went mad and threw the aeroplane into a series of wild aerobatics, one following the next. He was hopping mad, and presumably endeavouring trying his best to make me airsick. And I? I just sat back and enjoyed every second of it! (Smug bastard, wasn't I!)

The first anniversary of my joining the RAF slipped by uncelebrated. A few days later a third 'Pip' appeared on Maxwell's shoulder and with it much of the bite in his bark disappeared. After six weeks we, as the Junior Course, attended our first wings parade, a simple ceremony held within a half circle of aircraft. We would be attending this ceremony twice more before we would lead the parade and receive our brevet.

Jock Connell arrived with the new Junior Course and I logged my first 100 flying hours. We were now four from Hemswell days. With the first half of ITS behind us we began cross-country, formation and night flying. Or rather, the course began them while I smartly retired into hospital with tonsillitis. I surfaced nine days later only to be grounded for a further six. By which time I was well behind the others and it was touch and go whether or not I would be relegated to the Junior Course.

My first day back in the air I flew a dual cross-country. I went solo the following day. I was to proceed to Nigel, report in, then fly to Standerton, land and refuel, returning to base via Frankfort. A total of 2 hours 45 minutes flying time. The trip to Nigel was uneventful although an Oxford taking off nearly decapitated me as I was completing my landing run. The airfield was on a hill and I was obscured from view. The leg from Nigel to Standerton was simple, I followed the railway line! Standerton was an SFTS, flying Miles Master II's powered by a 870hp Bristol Mercury Radial engine. The School suffered from bad serviceability and accidents, which, it was rumoured, were due to the subversive activities of the Ossewa Brandwag! They were way behind with their training schedule. Those who started SFTS here at the same time as us at Vereeniging had flown few hours by comparison.

Bill Flanagan landed at Standerton shortly after I did and together we endured the good natured banter from old friends concerning the age of our aeroplanes. My aircraft was refuelled first and I climbed into the cockpit with all the airs and graces of an intrepid birdman. My friends clustered round while the mechanics removed the starting handles from the stowage clips in the rear cockpit. Amid a ripple of laughter I heard a voice shout, 'What the hell are those for, Nobbie? To wind up the elastic?!' I replied with two fingers on my right hand! The handles were put into position by two mechanics balanced on the wheels. They were ready to start up. I gave the Ki-gas pump a few strokes to prime the engine, flicked up the switches and yelled 'Contact'. The mechanics turned the handles furiously and the airscrew turned slowly. The engine caught, misfired and caught again this time bursting into life with a puff of smoke pouring from the exhaust. I throttled back letting the airman get away from the slipstream and then slowly but deliberately strapped myself in.

I was fastening the straps of my helmet when I noticed that the airscrew was slowing down so I opened up the throttle a little wider and was pleased to see the needle of the rev counter swing up the dial again. I continued to adjust my helmet - 'Damn!' the airscrew was slowing down again. I opened the throttle a little more and to my horror found that it was now fully opened and the engine sounded suspiciously as if it was about to stop. I hastily looked around the cockpit and my heart missed a beat when I saw the petrol cock was still in the 'Off' position. Frantically I turned it 'On' but it was too late, the engine gave its last dying gasp and I was facing a dead prop and an irate ground crew! Alas my red face and my frantic actions had given the game away. My so-called friends rolled on the ground, helpless with laughter. On my left another engine burst into life, Bill had started up. Quickly running up his engine and testing his magnetos he throttled back and waved the chocks away. With a nod and a grin in my direction he taxyed out to take off leaving me alone to my shame.

The banter continued, intermingled with the profanity of the two air mechanics laboriously attempting to restart my engine. I noticed that the attention of those around me was focused elsewhere and I looked over my shoulder in the direction of their stares. A fire engine started up and rang its bell urgently. There in the air about a hundred feet up was Bill's aircraft, the engine stopped, the prop lifeless. For the want of something better to say I muttered to myself, 'Christ, Bill, you've had it!' The aircraft went into a violent sideslip, straightened up, touched down superbly on three points and came to rest with the dead airscrew almost touching the boundary fence. A figure climbed down from the cockpit and calmly lit a cigarette. Not a bad effort for a pilot with only 100 hours flying experience!

I was shaking when my engine finally restarted. I ran it up and tested the magnetos, all appeared to be OK. I waved the chocks away and looked out to the airman standing at the wing tip for the signal that it was OK to taxy out. With a huge grin on his face, he signalled 'OK' with his hand - his fingers were crossed! I took off and circled the field. Below a small cluster of people and vehicles stood around Bill's aircraft. Their faces shone white as they looked up in my direction. It was a superb day and soon my misgivings went and my confidence returned.

Bill arrived back late that evening; as ever, a bundle of energy, laughing loudly and recounting the day's experiences. He said tests on the fuel syphoned from his tank showed there to be more water in it than could have possibly got there by accident. I was lucky they didn't refuel me from that bowser. A few days later a note was delivered to me by a pupil who had visited Standerton. It read:-

> 'He who says he flies THE kite,
> Should never have the fright,
> Of growing red behind the gills,
> When finding he hasn't done his cockpit drills!'

It wasn't a good poem, but I got the point!

A day later I started night flying. Maxwell and I shot four landings and he handed me over for a check flight. The OK for solo was given at 2 am, by then everyone had had enough so we packed up.

The weather changed and dust storms stopped night flying for another five nights. Most of the course had soloed by the time my next session came round. It was a beautiful night, cloudless and lit by a large moon. Maxwell and I roared down the paraffin lit flare path into the beauty and stillness of the night.

Vereeniging lay below, looking like an illuminated spiders web filled with dew. There was nothing but gentle encouragement from the back seat. As I throttled back for the last landing a thin line of sparks showered from the exhaust, like a crowd of lively children just released from school. The glide path indicator flashing way ahead told me my height was right. I moved the throttle forward to warm up the engine should I need the power in a hurry and then moved it slowly back again. The first flare whipped past and disappeared in a flurry as the slipstream caught it. I instinctively checked on the control column and gently eased it back. There was a rumble as all three points touched. A touch on the brakes and we slowly came to a halt. It was the third good landing that night. A voice in my ears asked, 'What time is it, Clark?' I raised my left arm and read the hands of the watch on my wrist with ease in the moonlight. '11.30, sir,' I replied. 'Bright enough to read your watch with ease. Eh! Clark?' he said. 'Yes, sir.' 'OK man, I'm sending you solo now. Just give me one good circuit and landing like we've had tonight and we'll get ourselves off to bed. Don't forget, if you have any doubt use the engine and go round again.'

We taxyed over to the flight office, stopped the engine and got down. He made an entry in the Authorization Book, which I signed before going into the darkness again to wait for the Audax being prepared for me. An hour later, when I took off, the moon had gone. I completed a circuit and came into land, checked at the first flare and pulled the stick back. A small voice within me instinctively said, 'Too high! Too high!' Before I could heed its warning we were down and above the noise of the engine there was a report like a gun shot. We bounced crazily into the air again, a broken bracing wire dangled before my eyes. Another bounce, not so bad as the first, yet another until we came to rest, my feet pounding at the rudder bar to keep the aircraft straight and my heart pounding within my breast.

Maxwell was the first at my side when I climbed out of the aeroplane. He seemed completely unruffled and said, 'Hard luck!, get into another aeroplane before you lose your nerve!' That idea didn't attract me one little bit, as far as I was concerned my nerve had gone anyway. I apprehensively strapped myself into another aeroplane and got the signal to go. I taxyed out, took off, and came in on the approach again. Everything was fine, I checked at the first flare and pulled the pole back. Instinctively the same small voice said again, 'Too High! Too High!' This time I thought I was ready for it and I slammed the throttle wide. Too late, we continued to sink and, as we hit the ground, above the roar of the engine came that same gun shot noise. A broken bracing wire danced crazily before my eyes. I was seized with panic. I struggled for control not only of the aeroplane, but also of myself. We were again in the air and I still had to repeat the whole bloody performance to get back on the ground.

The first flare came, I checked, moved the stick back. 'Christ! There's a fire engine at the second flare!' I observed. 'Gently back, gently does it' I told myself. There was a rumble, the landing was perfect. I taxyed back to the flights, the wings of the aeroplane sagging distinctly more than the last one! I miserably climbed out of the cockpit and on to the ground. Maxwell was waiting for me. 'You bloody fool!' he raged, 'YOU BLOODY FOOL!' he wept.

Next day I flew solo to Standerton again! This time via Witbank (an EFTS) where my landing left much to be desired!

The instrument flying of the Course was above average and was causing the instructors concern. However, unbeknown to anyone, a small plastic window was put in the rear of the hood and the next three tested were confined to barracks for 5 days. They had been seen putting a match box between the hood and the cockpit. The small gap gave them a clear vision ahead. Someone must have been crazy to think of a trick like that! After that exposure we all made normal progress, which was from bad to worse.

An original Hawker Hart, designated Hart II by the SAAF, probably built in the 1930's. It had a tail skid and caused no end of trouble if you landed the slightest bit out of wind!

Regrettably, my reputation reached its lowest level when I ground looped a couple of Hart II's, leaving the starboard wing tip in need of repair. Fortunately for me I wasn't the only pupil who had grounded a Hart II wing tip. Unlike the Hart Trainer, which had a tail wheel, the Hart II had a tail skid and was notoriously unstable on the landing run if you were a few degrees out of wind. They were the very first Harts to be built and retained the gun ring in the rear cockpit. The were designated Hart II by the SAAF.

Maxwell was instructed to improve my landings. As we taxyed out he took a starting handle from its clip in the rear cockpit and thumped me over the head with it! 'Do you feel that, Clark?' he roared. 'Yes, sir,' I replied. 'Frankly I'm bloody well surprised,' he shouted, 'I'll tell you something, you'll feel it a damn sight harder if you balls up any more landings!' I did. Out came the handle and he was good as his word!

We were coming towards the end of ITS. I was greatly enjoying my flying, aerobatics and formation flying in particular. We had one more session of night flying to complete. It was a dark, pitch-black night and occasionally an invisible gust of wind would swirl dust up into one's face. It had been a hot, dry, arid day, one of many recently. Lightning danced a fantastic ballet in the hills so far away that the thunder could not be heard.

Maxwell and I shot five quick landings in this Wagnerian setting. 'Shoot as many landings as you can within the hour - and watch the weather,' was his instruction before he sent me off solo.

On my sixth approach it was obvious I wasn't going to get down. A severe cross wind caused me to drift rapidly across the flare path, so I opened up and went round again. There was panic on the ground, I was the last aircraft in the air. Maxwell was reputed to have said, 'Clark's alright, leave the flare path where it is and see how he gets on his next approach.' It was again obvious that I wasn't going to get down on my next approach. My gloved hand had long forced the throttle wide as a red Verey light followed by another curled into the air. A red Aldis Lamp flashed at me through the darkness followed by a white one winking slowly in morse, 'W-I-L-L C-H-A-N-G-E F-L-A-R-E-P-A-T-H'. I circled the field. One by one the flares were extinguished leaving a black emptiness below. I noticed that as far as the eye could see small bush fires burning red on the ground. Gusts of wind rocked the aircraft roughly from its forward course. The storm was coming nearer, I could now see the lightning attacking the ground.

After what seemed a lifetime a light flickered on the ground, then another until the flare path was reborn out of the darkness. A green Aldis light stabbed in my direction followed by a green Verey light curling into the air. At last I was free to land, I had been in the air one hour forty minutes when I gently touched down. The rain came, the storm beat into the remainder of the night and all the following day. Lightning struck the airfield passing from one hangar to another. It cleared up as suddenly as it had started. We were now haunted nightly by the cacophony of croaking frogs. Hundreds of the green bloated creatures that had appeared from nowhere! A day or two later they disappeared to whence they had come!

ITS was now ending, the CFI gave us passenger tests and we took our 'wings' examinations. We had no failures, although a few had to take a swine of an engines examination paper again. It improved my ego to find my name fifth from the top of the 'passed' list. At my interview with the CGI I was told that he was pleased with my progress, but my landings must improve!

My last flight with Maxwell was as spectacular as my first. Taking place soon after lunch, we landed in some remote field for him to tumble out to relieve himself! We flew very low throughout the whole detail of 1 hour 50 minutes and at one time we flew alongside some overhead high tension wires. I was glad when he turned the aircraft violently away and left them behind!

We landed and strolled away from the aircraft together, he puffing on his pipe and me fumbling for suitable words to say. There was no need to say anything. He took his pipe from out of his mouth and knocked the ash out on the heel of his shoe. 'Well, Clark,' he said with a grin, 'That's it!' I was lucky to have had another patient instructor, I felt many would have washed me out long before, unless of course, he had a wager with someone that I would pass! We attended our second 'wings' parade and moved further up the social scale as the junior course of ATS.

We joined the Advanced Training Squadron in October with roughly 150 flying hours each plus 25 hours in the Link Trainer. I was paired off with an RAF chap called Dick Charlier. Dick was a tall, slim faced individual with a nervous laugh that expressed appreciation of any kind of humour in conversation! We were to enjoy enormously the three months ahead of us sharing, in an Audax, some 60 hours crew flying in the rear seat, or 'dog box' as we called it. The curriculum, in addition to our normal flying activities, included bombing, front and rear gunning, and photography. As an added complication there was a TR9 radio installed in the aircraft. Many gleefully unpacked that obnoxious piece of equipment, the oxygen mask into which they inserted the microphone, little realising that from then on every time they went into the air they would have its clammy touch about their face. Fortunately I managed to stave off that evil day; having to share a head set, I let the mike hang loosely on my breast.

Hawker Audax

We were joined about this time by a SAAF pupil who had been hospitalised for months. He had written off a Hart when he shot up a mine. His court marshal ordered him to pay £900 for the aircraft out of his service pay! It was rumoured that the SAAF only paid £100 each for them!

We had just started ATS when our course had its first serious accident. Paul Jones, a SAAF pupil, taking off in formation was caught in the leader's slipstream and struck the railway embankment on the edge of the field. The aircraft cartwheeled onto its back and caught fire. Paul was a tubby fellow and many of us turned our eyes for we were certain we were watching a funereal pyre. Smoke and flames rose high into the air and out from the middle of it all, like a Phoenix, staggered Paul, badly burnt, but still alive. In the wreckage we found Paul's watch which had been burnt off his wrist! We were to see Paul again just before we left Vereeniging. He was more or less patched up but he never flew again.

The remains of Paul Jones's aeroplane. You can see
why we were so amazed to see him crawl out alive

At about the same time Paul Kruger (A SAAF Pupil) was acting as safety pilot (sic!) for an instructor practising instrument flying. The aircraft went into a spiral dive from which Paul should have taken control and recovered. Unhappily he failed to do so and they crashed cutting a groove in the earth some 50 yards long. The instructor was badly injured but Paul, incredibly, had only superficial injuries. There was also a self inflicted incident worthy of mention. An instructor and his pupil came across a large bird (they thought a vulture), flying at the same height as they were so they decided to attack it! They hit it with the leading edge of the upper mainplane and the impact must have been enormous. When the aircraft landed at Vereeniging it was in a pretty sorry state. What remained of the bird measured just under six foot from wing tip to body. The other half of it, on its earthward plunge, ripped out one of the side panels. The accident report did not mention they were trying to get the bird!

Audax 1875 with its black lines drawn over it.

Dick flew the first sortie and, with me firmly anchored to the floor of the 'dog box' with a 'monkey chain[2]', we carried out an air to air camera gunning exercise. We landed with me standing, looking over Dick's shoulder. For that I got a raspberry from the flight commander and was told in future I would be in the sitting position when we touched down! It was a good start!

Summer working was now upon us. It was usually dark when we started engines - a regular dawn patrol! We would take off at 06.30, drone into the smooth early morning air and finish at 14.00hrs. It was said that an unidentified aircraft had been seen flying high over Durban. It was also rumoured that a Japanese carrier had been spotted off the coast. Consequently a number of our beautiful yellow aeroplanes became camouflaged over night. Others had black lines drawn over them showing the dividing line for the dark earth and the dark green paint. Instructions were issued that in a state of emergency instructors would fly the aeroplanes and the pupils would be the gunners! The casualties among the pupils would have been horrific since they were already squabbling among themselves who would occupy the few crew seats available! I wonder what we would have fought with, we only had 20 pound smoke bombs and worn out machine guns! Perhaps we would have been the first SAAF/RAF Kamikaze outfit!

In the meantime Dick and I completed exercises in aerial photography,

---

[2] - *Monkey Chain - safety strap that was attached to the base of the parachute harness and clipped to the floor.*

using an F24 Camera. With the camera held by hand we took oblique shots, and with it fixed to the fuselage floor we took 'line and feature overlaps' and 'stereo pairs'. For the latter we took two photographs, the first when we approached the target and the second when we had passed over it. When the shots were viewed through a stereoscope the image appeared to be three dimensional. The cooling towers of the power station, for example, looked like small volcanos!

Dick and I found ourselves refuelling at Kroonstad during a cross country. Dennis Compton and Nash-Webber, now 2nd Lieutenants, were still grounded and working in the control tower. Dennis told me what had happened in detail: his fiance had left her coat behind after a mess party and the following day he decided to return it to her by air. He took off with Ken Wood in the back seat and Nash-Webber went along in another Tiger to see the fun. They arrived over the farm where she lived and they decided to beat the place up. During a low level run Dennis remembered the coat and took it out of the cockpit, in doing so it snagged the throttle and closed it. In the confusion that followed the aircraft flew into the ground and bent. Both Ken and Dennis were lucky to survive. I am not sure why Nash lost his pip. I believe he landed to help and broke his aeroplane. They were still very upset about the incident. Dick and I toddled back to Vereeniging via Milldraai.

We progressed to bombing, having learnt to find the strength and direction of the wind with a bomb sight. We then attacked the Camera Obscura with imaginary bombs radioing, 'Bomb gone,' at the point of release. The expected point of impact was plotted in the Camera Obscura below. We soon became proficient at that game and the day came when Dick and I took off in an Audax with eight small white practice smoke bombs attached to the lower mainplanes. You laid flat on your stomach beneath the pilot's seat, your head a few inches from the radiator wafting hot oil fumes into your face. In discomfort you directed the pilot onto the target, pressing the 'bomb tit' to release the bomb. You could see those small white bombs falling until they struck the ground with a burst of white smoke. You then plotted the accuracy of your aim on a chart.

Dick and I had been orbiting the bombing range for some time with one eye on the aircraft at present bombing and the other on a storm which had suddenly blown up from the east. We got the ground signal that the range was clear, but as we approached the target we found it was obscured by cloud. Dick and I decided we would abort the exercise and high-tail it in the direction where we last saw the airfield. It started to rain heavily and in a matter of seconds we were soaked. Dick was flying lower and lower and we were getting more and more anxious as forward visibility was down to almost nil. It was on the tip of my tongue to suggest that we turn south and try to run out of the storm when I recognised the cemetery below us. We were heading straight for the field. I called Dick over the intercom to throttle back and get the speed down as at any minute now he would see the airfield straight ahead. Trusting character was Dick - he did as I suggested and, with the coolness of the master he was, landed the aircraft straight ahead.

We bounced a little and there was an enormous bang. The cockpit filled with white acrid smoke. 'Christ!' blasphemed Dick, 'What the hell was that?' 'I haven't a clue,' I lied. We both knew that one of the bombs had dropped off! We taxyed back to the flights in silence, both horrified at the sight of the windsock flapping wildly in a horizontal position. Dick had landed 90 degrees across wind - in a gale! We waited a while for the usual cheery faced airmen to guide us in. The storm had now reached the peak of its fury and the rain had long since penetrated our Sidcot flying suits, soaking us to the skin and still no airmen! I told Dick to keep the engine running and I climbed out, running over to the ground crew room and putting my head round the door. 'Where do you want this bloody aeroplane put?' I asked. A head looked up from a card game, 'What bloody aeroplane?' it queried. 'The one we've just landed,' I replied as blasé as I could. 'Blimey, Nobbie!' the head said, 'You haven't been flying in this muck, have you?' 'Come to think of it,' commented another unsympathetic voice as they rose to their feet, 'I thought we were a kite short when we put the other lot away!' Dick and I helped the armourer to defuse the remaining bombs and remove them from the lower wing. There were only seven. Dick and I knew roughly where the other one was, but we hadn't recorded it on any chart! We never heard another word, no one saw us land and what was more humiliating, no one had missed us!

We had our first course fatality over the bombing range when Gordon Cornish fell to the ground from his aeroplane. They had a bomb 'hang up' and the pilot tried to shake it loose. Gordon wasn't attached to the aeroplane by his 'monkey chain' and was flung out on to the rear fuselage where, unconscious, he slipped off without a parachute. We had been together, except for a short period, since Hemswell. He was an England Rugby trialist and played for W.R.Hammond's RAF cricket eleven in South Africa. He was a great sportsman, a natural with a ball, and a fine friend. We were all shocked by the manner of his death. We laid him to rest with full Military Honours in the cemetery Dick and I had recently been so pleased to see. A few weeks earlier, Gordon's brother had been killed flying a Spitfire over Malta. We mourned for both and for their family.

Gordon Cornish, killed at No.22
Air School, 17th September 1942.

Night flying now wasn't quite the trial it had been. There were no broken undercarts or busted landing wires, probably due to the brilliance of the moon and the fact we were landing by floodlight! I completed my first solo night cross country.

One night Bill Flanagan, now engaged to be married, came in crying with rage. Both of his hands were swollen and bruised. As he was leaving his fiance's flat one of the Ossewa Brandwag hooligans had gone for him with a coal hammer. It was almost the last thing the poor wretch ever did, Bill put him in hospital! The police, much to our surprise, said, 'Serve him right!' and turned a blind eye to the incident.

I met Maxwell who asked me how I was getting on. We were Senior Course now, and knew it! He took the wind out of my sails by telling me that I held the SAAF record for prangs. In a letter home I said I had six: four undercarts, one tail wheel and a wing tip. I don't believe it - I must have been boasting! I can only remember two wing tips, two landing wires and a burst tail wheel, that was enough!

I was flying a Hind with Lt Marthinusen, a huge man, reputed to be very wealthy. He owned a Stinson Reliant aeroplane and a Cord motor car so he must have been! (There is a Cord at Beaulieu which came from South Africa and I often wonder if it is the same one). Our aeroplane had just come out of the workshop which started the germ of an idea in his mind. 'Clark!', he boomed over the Gosport, 'did you notice any serial numbers on this aircraft?' 'As a matter of fact I did, sir', I replied. 'Oh well', he said, 'Not to worry, and mums the word, man.' He then proceeded to beat up a large house on the banks of the Vaal River. It even surpassed those low level sorties I had previously had with Maxwell and Nash-Webber. When it was thankfully over, and he was climbing the aircraft away, he said dryly, 'The neighbours are rather touchy about this, took my number last time, but I think we fooled them this time.' 'Fooled them?' I said, 'You mean scared them!'

Another example of the South African attitude was manifest when Bill Flanagan was leading a formation of three, with me flying number three. He put the nose down and I watched the slipstream tugging the straps of his helmet. Tucked in close, I waited for the signal for us to break formation. His head swept the sky for a last look around, it was clear. His hand went up and the signal was given and I pushed the stick hard over to the left at the same time pulling back. Number two had done the same to the right. We were less than a thousand feet above the airfield and to my astonishment I just caught sight of Bill finishing off an excellently executed slow roll! Bill had hardly stopped his landing run before he was hauled in front of the OC Flying Wing, Lt Col E A Pope. Bill came out grinning; all the Colonel had said to him was, 'Confine your fancy breaks to the Bundu and not over my airfield. Now get out!'

The last major exercise had arrived and we all looked forward to the break. Our ground crews packed up their kit and moved out to a small airstrip on the banks of the Valldam called Dennysville. Here they lived under canvass, we slept at base. It was miles from anywhere and we were to conduct air firing exercises. We were surprised when we landed to find it occupied by a unit of British Airways with four or five Lockheed Lodestars!

British Airways Lodestar at Dennysville.

Vaaldam was a large dam holding back the waters of a huge man-made lake on which, twice weekly, a BOAC Empire flying boat would land and disembark passengers for Johannesburg, some 70 miles away. During the course of the year we had seen the waters of the lake pouring over the top of it - an incredible sight.

I started well! I was late for the first detail. The officers, without notice, had locked their gate behind them. It was a petty restriction. With the fence too high to climb we had to go back and take the long way round. The OC 'B' Squadron, Sqdn/Ldr Chater, was waiting for me with the engine running. As soon as I put my foot on the step he banged the throttle wide, and pushed the tail up. I clambered in with difficulty and muttered my apologies. I received a curt reply and 5 days confined to camp when we landed.

A few hours later I was up with Dick again enjoying the fun and thrill of firing a Vickers K gun mounted on the scarf ring. The wind tugging at helmet and clothing, the noise and the smell of exploding cordite, the sight of the rounds splashing into the sand around the target (I never hit a thing!). Flying, bombing and firing was still great fun. I certainly was naive, but I don't think it occurred to any of us what a deadly occupation it would become.

A day later I found myself flying with the OC 'B' Sqdn again, this time on a front gun sortie. He ordered me to stand up and look over his shoulder. At the end of each run he pulled on enough 'G' to make me think my legs were going to go through the floor - the bastard!

Hours later I was solo on the same exercise. It was hard work keeping that damn Vickers gun firing; diving down onto the target, struggling to get it into the centre of the ring and bead sight, press the trigger within the spade grip, get off a few rounds and then the bloody gun would stop! You then had to pull up, hold the stick between your legs and attack the cocking lever with both hands in an attempt to clear the stoppage. By the time you were making your next run in you were usually out of breath, temper and minus all skin on your knuckles only to find during the next burst the belt had broken! Thank God no one was firing back at us!

After my third and last sortie of the day, I returned to Dennysville after a similar performance, frustrated, tired and angry. I swung over the strip and looked down at the wind sock. I remember to this day what I said to myself, 'The wind goes in the small end and comes out of the large end so I must land in the direction it is pointing!!!' During my landing run it occurred to my tired, dim-witted mind that the tents at the end of the strip were coming towards me a great deal faster than they should be! I squeezed hard on the brake lever, nearly welding my hot sticky hand to the spade grip. The aircraft and I finally came to rest right in the middle of those tents and a lot of bug-eyed airmen gaped at me from out of the canvas. It was only when Dick wandered over to me as I climbed down and whispered out of the corner of his mouth, 'One of your down-wind specials, Nobbie?', that I realised what I had done! Not a guide rope was out of place when I came to rest, but they had to take a tent down to get that aeroplane out!

The course was almost over and I considered myself fortunate to have flown the Hart Variants. It was a peek into the past and the fulfilment of a schoolboy's dream. What farewell parties we had at the end of it all! First one in town at the Royal Hotel for the Airmen, what a wonderful bunch they had been. I finished the night unconscious, clouted by brandy and a swinging toilet door! Then a party in the Pupils' Mess for all the friends we had made in town. I found myself with a fight on my hands with a room-mate during that one! An unpleasant episode best forgotten.

Then came the party for our instructors where my Flight Commander, Flt/Lt G Kennedy DFM, told me I had been recommended for a commission, but not to expect it yet because of my youth. I could not believe my ears! I didn't dare tell him that in my wardrobe was tunic with both my wings and sergeant's stripes already sewn on it! Maxwell congratulated me on receiving my wings and obtaining my commission. This was what he wanted of me, he said, and I was glad I had not let him down. He certainly had not let me down, I was fortunate to have such a sincere man as an instructor. We were surprised by the appearance of the Station Commander, Group Captain (later Air Commodore), P.R.T.J.M.I.C. Chamberlayne CB, AFC. He was a large man, well loved and affectionately known as 'Tank', always tapping his leg with a fly whisk as he strode around the camp. 'Parades?', he was reputed to have said. 'Parades? There are my parades, up there!' pointing to a formation of aircraft flying overhead. He joined in the drinking, quaffing our loving cup full of beer in one gulp while we chanted, 'He's a bastard, through and through!!'

Our former ITS instructors were night flying and had left the party early, much the worse for wear! They took to the air in formation and, in the gathering dusk, beat hell out of the mess and the town! In the morning we flew a formation with ten or so aircraft. Clark was well out on the beam trying to keep his eyes in focus and his damnedest to keep up. I felt like Dopey of the Seven Dwarfes! What a landing that was!

Suddenly, within an amphitheatre of Harts and Audaxes we marched up and down a few times and saluted this way and that. Our names were called and we stood stiffly to attention before an Air Commodore who pinned a flying badge to our left breast. The authorization to wear it, dated 19.12.42. is stuck in my log book.

There was a telegram of congratulations from Dennis Compton waiting for me on my return to the mess. With our pay, passes and warrants in our pockets we lost no time getting to Johannesburg.

Wings parade 18th December 1942 - receiving my flying badge.

After the parade - left to right: 'Curly' Simpson, Brian Leuty, 'Micky' Muncaster, Self, Esme, Colin Clarence (SAAF), 'Keppie' Keppler (SAAF) and Ken Carter

CHAPTER SIX

CONVERTED, FRUSTRATED, CONVEYED AND CONVERTED AGAIN!

'My Sarie Marais is enshrined in my heart,
Like a flower that will never fade,
and sad was the day when my ship sailed away.'

An old South African ballad.

With the assistance of a servicemen's club in Johannesburg a small party of us decided to take our leave at Knysna. A small town in the Wilderness, Cape Province, well known to Pupil Observers who, for many years, had been training at George and Oudtshoorn, but was virgin territory as far as we were concerned. Before leaving Johannesburg I ordered my new kit. I was cutting it fine, but I managed to get everything with the exception of some pilot officers' ranking braid. One tailor I went to said he had yards of the stuff, and produced an enormous roll of Air Commodores' braid - he must still have some!

We caught our train and for the next two days journeyed through Kroonstad, Bloemfontein, Graaf-Reinet, Oudtshoorn and to George. The journey took us through the Outeniqua Mountains, incredible in its scenic beauty and some of the loveliest country I had yet seen. For nearly an hour we threaded ourselves through George Pass, a blaze of sub-tropical beauty. Eventually below us we saw the small town of George and beyond it, the blue waters of the Indian Ocean. Here we changed trains and arrived at Knysna at dusk; an old bus took us a further five miles to Knoetze. That night we slept in small comfortable beds as one only can after two days on a train. The air was ozone fresh and the surf pounded on the beach just a few yards away. We were there as the guest of an unknown Rhodesian, who put this house at the disposal of the RAF on leave.

We were well looked after by a housekeeper and two native servant girls. The food was fantastic and we were each allowed one quart of beer a day! We swam, surf-bathed, fished, sailed a tin tub on a small lagoon and on Christmas day, my first away from home, we had a lunch of roast duck, chased by oysters we had collected from the sea.

Three days before our leave was to end a telegram came ordering five of us back to Vereeniging. Alas, we finally found ourselves on a train for Johannesburg, leaving behind us a paradise of simplicity and a wonderful memory! We never knew who our benefactor was but silently thanked him for his generosity. We had been recalled to Vereeniging to return our airman's kit to stores, which took two hours! We also found that Bill Flanagan had now married and was honeymooning in the Parys area.

Kysna Station

Royal Hotel

On our way to the Stinkwood Forest, Kysna. This is the only photo I have of Dick Charlier. Left to right: Self, Dick, 'Micky' Muncaster and Mary.

I went to Johannesburg and collected my new uniform from the tailor. Greatcoats were terribly expensive and raincoats were almost impossible to get, so I decided to wait. From RAF stores I bought a roll of barathea for my second uniform to be made up later ('later' was, in the fullness of time, to become five years, when it was made into costume for my wife!). My pay was now 22/-d a day (£1.10) an exorbitant amount in those days. Within three days we were posted to 26 Air School Pietersburg, which is in the Northern Transvaal, about 175 miles to the north of Johannesburg. We were to convert onto Oxfords and it was going to take two months.

About this time in Europe the US 8th Air Force had just made its first bombing raid over Germany and H2S radar was first used by a Pathfinder force. In Russia the battle of Stalingrad was about to end in disaster for the *Wehrmacht*.

After Vereeniging, where I undoubtedly spent the happiest six months of my war service, Pietersburg had little to commend itself. It had none of the recreational amenities that Vereeniging boasted and certainly not the handy convenience of a nearby city. The town itself was small, the population unfriendly if not anti-British, and the surrounding countryside red and arid. The air school was new and, strangely enough, one of two airfields in the area. The other had been used by Imperial Airways in the days of the Cape to Cairo run. From the station, the now familiar Chevrolet troop carrier bore us through red dust to the north. Soon, through a wire fence, we saw the squat black iron clad hangars and the rest of the camp buildings shimmering in the blistering mid-summer heat. Beyond was the flat red brown earth of the airfield.

I shared a room with 'Taffy' Tyler and we sweated as we lugged our kit down to the hut that had been pointed out to us. Our room, not unlike Kroonstad, looked like a cell; the furniture was sparse and there was a mosquito net hanging over each of the twin iron beds. There were insects everywhere, termites, ants and other indescribable flying, crawling objects, filling the air and the earth with movement. Outside the sun beat down remorselessly and the earth baked in front of your eyes. There were much worse places on earth for airmen to be sent (I found one or two later!) but at the time we did not think so!

No. 26 Air School Pietersburg. It was the first time I had worn my new uniform.
I was just 19 years old. Left to right: 2nd/Lt 'Keppie' Keppler (SAAF),
Plt/Off 'Taffy' Tyler, 2nd/Lt Paul Kruger (SAAF), self.

Our day commenced at 04.30hrs and our batman, a tall Zulu, marched to our room on the concrete path outside; his steel-tipped boots delivering something resembling a naval broadside as he came to a halt outside the door, followed by his right turn pounding the ground with a crash. Marching into the room he would come to a noisy halt beside my bed, left turn with stamping feet, salute and then gently shake my shoulder under the mosquito net saying, 'Good morning, sah, it is 4.30, sah! Tea or coffee, sah?!' 'Tea please, Joshua.' 'No tea, sah!' Although he always gave you a choice there was never both to be had, it was just his ritual for starting the day! At the very least, if you chose correctly you got what you asked for! In the pitch black of those early mornings he was darkness personified!

One hour later, after breakfast, we paraded on a small quadrangle, surrounded by ground school classrooms. It was always dark and bitterly cold, a complete contrast to the dawning day. We stood shivering while the roll was called under the supervision of a bullying SAAF major. We started early to utilise the best of the day and ceased flying at noon.

We had come to Pietersburg to convert onto Airspeed Oxfords - a relatively modern twin engined trainer. It was incredible that in January 1943, with 230 logged flying hours and wearing a pilot's brevet we had yet to raise an undercart or move a flap! I found the Airspeed Oxford cockpit confusing. The duplication of engine instruments didn't help. I was familiar with the standard blind flying panel I had 'flown' for 49 hours sweated labour in the Link Trainer. It was a neat panel which sat in front of the pilot and was standard instrumentation in every modern British built aeroplane (except the Tiger!) right into the jet age. It consisted of six instruments: the air speed indicator; the vertical speed indicator (which indicated a rate of climb or dive); the altimeter, (these were operated by changes in pressure and were known as the *pressure instruments*); the artificial horizon; the direction indicator; and the turn and slip indicator (these were operated by gyros and were known as the *gyroscopic instruments*). To the left of the panel was a fuel gauge and below it a gauge selector switch which, when activated, indicated the contents of each 49 gallon main tank, moreover it worked!

The centre panel looked like a totem pole and had a variety of switches, not the least of which were the master electrical switch and indicators showing the position of the undercarriage and the flaps; it was an orderly confusion. Mounted on a central control box were the throttles, mixture control lever, elevator trim wheel (tail trim), main tank fuel cocks, flap and undercarriage levers. At the base of it were two auxiliary tank fuel cocks; when pushed to the floor each drained 29 gallons of fuel into the main tanks. The brake lever was in the centre of the control wheel and was operated by pushing it with your left thumb; the brake pressure gauge was on the starboard fuselage wall.

It required two men, one on each wing, to wind up the two 370-h.p. Armstrong Siddeley Cheetah X engines. Compared with what was to come it was simplicity itself!

In keeping with the rest of the course it took me 2 hours 30 minutes to solo! The course was dull and I remember little of it. Bill Flanagan, as would be expected, broke all regulations by barrel rolling an Oxford, I certainly did not have the courage to do so. We flew 15 minutes out to a landing strip called Papkuil for night flying and only two events out there were worth recalling. Firstly, Jock Rowan, a Scottish expatriate from the Palestine Police and now a 2nd/Lt. in the SAAF, took off in the dark and flew into an ant hill! The impact knocked one of his props off, but without any fuss he did a circuit and landed the aeroplane, reporting there had been a little vibration! He swore the hill wasn't there when he started his take off run, 'Fast workers these termites!' he said.

Secondly, I flew an aircraft back to base taking off in the dark and saw the sun rise. I landed at Pietersburg at dawn and saw the sun rise again. A good line that - to see the sun rise twice in one day! Later, Paul Kruger, who had crashed with an instructor weeks earlier at Vereeniging, invited me to a party. I found myself in a car bumping north on the dusty gravel road towards Lois Trichardt, on the border of Rhodesia. After an hour we turned off down a track to an isolated farm house. After parking the car in the yard we crossed a wide stoop (veranda) and went through a door which opened into a large room. Inside a small band were hacking out a Afrikaans tune. Paul went to a dias at the end of the room where sat an old lady who greeted Paul like a long-lost son. We were both in uniform, he in SAAF khaki and myself in RAF blue. When she saw me she froze, and the room went ominously silent - the atmosphere changing in a moment, making me fear the worst. She said something to Paul in Afrikaans and smiled, saying, 'Oomah says you are the first Englishman ever to cross the threshold of her house, but you are welcome.' With that the music and dancing recommenced and Paul introduced me to some tough-looking characters who led me outside to a row of barrels set up on the stoop. One of them placed a glass beneath a tap and filled it with a golden liquid saying in a strongly accented voice, 'Hev a drink man! Leave the women alone and we'll leave you alone!' I got the message and stuck to the home-brewed peach brandy. They looked after me well and in these unusual circumstances had a delightful evening. Suitably imbibed, or was it embalmed, we made the return trip to Pietersburg which I have to be honest and say I don't remember.

Six weeks and 29 flying hours later we finished the course. The five commissioned at Vereeniging, Johnnie Morgan, Jimmie Muir, Nigel St George Pleasance, Taffy Tyler and myself, plus two sergeant pilots, Brian Leuty and Norman Brockhouse, were given two weeks leave and then posted to CFS (Central Flying School) at Bloemfontein. We were not very happy. The last thing we wanted to become was flying instructors! The remainder of the course went to RAF Gilgil in Kenya where they hung about for a long, long time for a posting to an OTU (Operational Training Unit). Sergeant

Bill Flanagan went with them. I heard that he died as a passenger in a Dakota which crashed when bringing him back to South Africa after the war.

'Taffy' and I in Durban.

'Taffy' and I took ourselves off to Durban. It had changed a lot since I first came the year before. There was now a blackout, since the glow of the town at night had been seen miles out to sea. Everything, including the bars, now closed at 8 pm. We stayed at a small hotel called 'The Waverley' on West Street. 'Keppie' Keppler, a South African with us at Pietersburg, introduced us to two attractive girls. That was how I met Marie, an art student at Durban University, a blonde who styled her hair in the fashion of

Veronica Lake. I don't know whether or not it was the fact that she looked like my favourite film star, but I really fell for her. Like the kids we were, we used to frolic and fumble on the beach on those warm summer nights under an enormous moon. It was all very romantic and frustrating too!

Norman Brockhouse at Lyttleton. Later killed flying a Beaufighter in the UK - 1944

The time came to leave and we caught a train to Johannesburg where I sought the hospitality of the Shaws, playing tennis and dwelling in the luxury of a family home. When I left Johannesburg that Sunday evening for Bloemfontein I was unaware that this was to be the last time I was ever to see them. On Monday morning I reported to CFS. I saw little of the *'Centre City'* as it was known - the *'Fountain of Flowers'* as its name translates. I knew that the RAF were not very welcome there. We were an unhappy lot assembled in the mess that night, although we started to play physically boisterous games as the effects of cheap brandy took command of us! That afternoon we had protested that we hadn't come all the way to South Africa just to become flying instructors. I don't know if this had influenced any decision made, but the following day we were posted to Clairwood Camp, Durban for transit. We were delighted. Regrettably these orders were, in time, responsible for the death of at least four of that party of seven.[1]

In a few hours I was back on the beach in the arms of Marie! My paradise lasted just two weeks when I found myself taking my leave of her, swearing to write to her and never to forget her. For awhile I wrote, but I never have forgotten her! We were ordered off to Capetown and it was rumoured that we were being sent home, it was obvious that no one in Africa wanted us! It was a long journey by train from Durban to Cape Town, two days, it was said. An RAF Hurricane pilot wounded in the Middle East, hospitalized in Pietermaritzburg and now on his way home, suggested it might be a dry one too. Duly warned, we prepared for our journey and filled our railway compartment with crates of beer. We arrived at the Retreat Transit Camp, Cape Town much the worse for wear. The party continued for another three days.

At Retreat I was re-united with Archie (Pip) Hagues, who was to become a life long friend. He came out on the Otranto with me, was held back for some reason or other at Lyttleton, then joined the junior course at Kroonstad. After that he went to SFTS at Waterkloof on Harts, followed me up to Pietersburg and there he was on the same draft home having been six weeks behind me!

I shared a room with Nigel Pleasance who had been a sergeant in the army and seconded to the RAF for flying duties. He was a well built man with a round face which always seemed to be smiling. His wife was serving in the WAAF. We had an arrangement whereby we alternately put one another to bed after the heavy drinking sessions that followed in that god-forsaken camp. Nigel had an extraordinary habit of saying, 'Of drinking old ale there is no end!' Whereupon, out to the world, he would fall flat on his back!

We celebrated the 25th anniversary of The Royal Air Force with one helluva binge in the mess. Being a Transit Camp the mess was occupied with personnel from all three services. Nigel upset the navy by deliberately calling a Commander dressed in whites a steward! 'Steward!' he roared, 'Steward! Bring us another four beers! They also serve who only stand and wait!' - another favourite war-cry of his! I went as white as the Commander's coat. He was not amused and suggested it was time Nigel went to bed. Nigel was in no mood to be told where to go and continued drinking. He eventually left the room and was away for such a long time I went to look for him. I

---

[1] - *Jimmie Muir (later awarded a DFC) and Brian Leuty died flying Lancasters, Nigel Pleasance died flying a Halifax and Norman Brockhouse was killed in a Beaufighter.*

couldn't find him anywhere until a flash of inspiration caused me to open the door of his wardrobe. There, sitting on the wardrobe floor, was Nigel, stark naked and out to the world. It took two of us to get him to bed. That incident ended our five day binge!

We went to Cape Town, to drink at the 'Delmonica', a bar and restaurant with Spanish decor. We took the cable car to the top of Table Mountain and looked down into the docks below at the 'Queen Mary', hoping we would be on the next draft for that - we weren't. The day after my 20th birthday, and two weeks after we arrived at Cape Town, we embarked on the 'Aquitania'. Once on board I was unlucky enough to be put in charge of Italian POW's who were in cages in the bowels of the ship. In all there must have been about 3,000 of them. Although I must have counted them many times, I don't remember how many I had under my control! None of us knew it at the time but they were bound for the USA. The last I saw of South Africa was Table Mountain through a porthole at the back of the ship. It would have been much nicer to have shed a tear from the deck, but it was not to be.

The 'Aquitania' was a ship of 45,000 tons and 901 feet in length. Built in 1914 by John Brown on the Clydebank, she was probably the only passenger ship with four funnels sailing at that time (1943). Once the pride of the Cunard Line she was now ancient and looked it. There was nothing rakish about her lines compared with the other two Cunarders, the 'Queen Mary' and the 'Queen Elizabeth'. It was said that, with a maximum speed of 23.5

Knots (in 1914!), she was fast enough to sail singly, without the encumbrance of a convoy. We prayed whomsoever said that was correct! In accordance with new regulations she was a dry ship, there wasn't a drop of alcohol on board. At least we didn't find any! She was broken up in 1948.

We set course and zig-zagged across a smooth South Atlantic under a hot sun and a clear sky. Every so often we would have our POW's on deck and give them an airing. It must have been Hell down below in the tropical heat. God knows how we would have got them out if we had been attacked by a U-Boat.

A little more than a week out of Cape Town we slipped through the narrows past the ancient fort of Santa Cruz, and sailed into the breathtaking vista of Rio de Janeiro harbour. Here in the shadow of the Sugar Loaf and the encircling mountains we dropped anchor. Our elderly steward told us there was only one other harbour in the world that compared with Rio's scenic beauty and that was Sydney, Australia. We took his word for it!

Under the ever watchful eye of the huge statue of Christ which stands overlooking the harbour we watched from the decks above as busy barges refuelled and revictualled the ship. We gazed longingly at the shore and hoped for some leave but it was not to be. With an air of romantic and unhurried charm ancient ferries powered by beam engines plied their way to and fro across the bay from Rio to Nicheroy. Long-legged girls reclining on the decks of expensive yachts acknowledged our waves and whistles as their craft slid by. We watched aircraft taking off from the small airport inside the harbour, wishing we were flying them.

We stayed in Rio for the best part of a week. Then, one day, machinery began to throb, the anchor was raised and we started to move and I sent up a silent prayer to the statue of Christ for our safety. We sailed through the narrow harbour entrance, past the ancient fort and with ever increasing speed pounded our bow wave onto the nearby shore as we made for the open sea.

Days later, on the Equator and heading in a northerly direction, the sea turned brown, the 'experts' surmised that we had reached the outflow of the Amazon. We continued chugging our weary, boring way north. In anything more than a swell our old ship protested and came alive with creaks and groans from the rigging to the rivets! A little over three weeks after leaving Cape Town we were told that we would shortly be docking in New York. The weather had now worsened, the wind howled through the rigging, and every part of the ship seemed to be moving independently. We were in a force nine gale and we were told we would have to hang about until it had abated before we steamed into harbour. It was a very heavy sea and the old 'Aquitania' was digging her sharp end into the waves, shuddering and throwing the water back over her decks like a duck taking a bath! To add to the excitement the 'Mauretania' and other ships, were looming out of the murky dusk, orbiting in the opposite direction!

The following morning the storm had blown itself out, the sun re-appeared and we made our way to New York. A U.S. Navy Blimp came out to meet us, flying around, its engines putt-putting away like a two stroke motor bike. It was still gusty up there and the wind made her make one or two manoeuvres that weren't exactly in the flying manual; they were having a rough ride. For once I was glad I was down on the comparative calm of the ship's deck.

IBM HQ New York May 1943. Left to right: IBM Manager of servicemens' welfare, John Morgan (pre-war employee of IBM UK, self, T.J.Watson - President of IBM (and owner), unknown G.I. Photographs behind us show future Presidents of IBM, at the time they were both serving pilots - one in the UK and one in the Pacific.

We steamed past the Statue of Liberty and landed our POW'S on Ellis Island. Then slipping down the Hudson and beneath the towering office blocks of Manhattan we berthed in the pier next to the blackened, burnt out hull of the 'Normandie' lying on its side at Pier 88. She had been berthed there since August 1939. However in February 1942 a workman using an acetylene torch allowed a shower of sparks to fall onto a bale of life jackets. The subsequent fire was uncontrollable and she burnt out.

We were given seven days shore leave, reporting back to the ship every night. I have never jammed so much into such a short time. Johnnie Morgan took me to IBM (International Business Machines) headquarters; he worked for them in the UK before the war. In the corridors and rooms of the IBM building at every pace the word 'THINK' paranoiacally glared down at you. A photograph was taken with T.J. Watson, the President of IBM. He was then reputed to be the highest salaried man in the world, his annual salary being $450,000 (in 1943 £90,000, £1 equalled $5!). This excluded any income from the majority share holding the Watson family had in IBM.

In Jack Dempsey's Bar, New York, May 1943.
Left to right: Unknown, self, John Morgan, Nigel St. George Pleasance

The photograph (see previous page) plus a gift box arrived at the quayside just as the ship was casting off. With it was a box of Havanas which I know my father enjoyed! They were to send me many more gift boxes during my RAF service and one, I recall, contained a pack of playing cards for which H.M. Customs hammered me for duty!

During that seven days we went to the services clubs at the Commodore Hotel and the Stage Door Canteen. We drank at Jack Dempsey's Bar, dined at Charles' A La Pomme Souffle, laughed our way through 'Hellzapoppin' and listened to Harry James play 'The Flight of the Bumble Bee'. We were thrown out of a restaurant for asking two girls if they would care to dance which, in the eyes of New York State law, constituted propositioning! We listened to Jazz being played by negro musicians in smoky bars. At Radio City, during the interval of a great Tracy/Hepburn film called 'A Guy Named Joe'[2] we watched the precision dancing of the long legged 'Rocketts', meeting them afterwards at Childs' Restaurant. We certainly made the most of those seven days!

In the meantime the 'Aquitania' was taking on board American troops for Europe. Three men to a bed with an eight hour sleeping shift, as one got out the other got in. When the ship was full the gang plank came up. We sailed out of New York and I watched that Manhattan skyline disappear brick by brick. There were a lot of American servicemen aboard that ship who were never to see it again.

It was to be over 40 years before I set foot in that exciting city again. I was sitting by the fountains in Rockefeller Plaza waiting for Dorothy to come out of a shop when someone sat beside me. He was a reporter from a publication called 'Newsday' he said and gave me his card. He asked me where I usually met my friends in New York and why. I said all my friends had left New York a long time ago and the last time I met them here we were all terribly young. Thanks to the generous hospitality of the New Yorkers we all had many very happy memories to take back home with us. I couldn't say much more, I was choked. At the moment he had sat beside me I was deep in my memories. He couldn't have asked me a worse question.

During our erratic journey across the Atlantic on the night 16/17th May 1943, No 617 Squadron attacked the Ruhr Dams. Eight Lancasters and 55 men were lost. In a POW camp I was later to meet one of the survivors Flt/Lt Geoff Rice DFC, a most brave and modest man. We were firm friends until his tragic death from cancer in 1982. I missed and mourned him. On the 19th we sailed up the Firth of the Clyde and opposite Greenock we dropped anchor in the tail of the Clyde Bank. A paddle steamer took us and our luggage off the ship and deposited us at the quayside where a train waited. It took us to Harrogate and No 7 PRC (Pilot Receiving Centre) at the Queen's Hotel. The place was fairly oozing with pilots fresh home from overseas. There were rumours that we would be here a long time and our next flying would be done at an AFU (Advanced Flying Unit). Not being

_____

[2] - 'Guy named Joe' - *What ever happened to it? I've never seen it on TV!*

needed we were sent home on leave.

Nigel Pleasance said his wife was based at RAF Hornchurch, not far from my home. I suggested he came with me, stay the night and in the morning we could look for her. This we did but found she had just been posted away. Nigel and I took ourselves off to the Officers' Mess and had a pint. After that we went into Romford and had another pint - or two. I arrived home a little worse for wear! My mother did not approve, she hadn't expected me to grow up so soon! Nigel and I were soon to part and we never saw each other again. He was killed on the 18th July 1944.

The next evening I decided to go to the Old Boys' Tennis Club (a small hut with two clay courts) to see if any old school chums were there. There were none that I knew, most of my contemporaries were now in the forces. However, there was a young lady standing in a corner wearing a WAAF uniform. It was unusual for a girl to be at 'the club'. Although our school was mixed, the classrooms weren't, girls were kept strictly to their own part of the school buildings. To be seen with a girl from the girls' school invited a thrashing from the Head! For that reason I suppose we were chauvinistic about our tennis club! However, times had changed, and there turning the pages of the attendance book was this beautiful WAAF. She was still wearing her peak cap set over dark hair rolled up away from the collar of a blue tunic which did not hide her shapely figure. She smiled at me as I walked through the door.

Dorothy (for that was her name!) told me she had never ever been in that building before. It was her younger sister, another 'Old Girl' who had brought her there. 'Come and look through the visitor's book and see who has been home on leave. You might see someone you know,' her sister had said to her earlier. Dorothy had reluctantly gone along and had arrived a minute or so before I did. She hadn't had time to remove her hat. My entrance made a great impression on her, so she tells me, and her charm and beauty certainly made a great impression on me. We talked for some time and eventually I made my way to the door intending to leave. At the door I stopped, turned and went back to her and asked her if she would care to come with me to see a show in London (for the record it was 'Arsenic and Old Lace').

A few days later we packed a picnic, got on our bikes and went out into the countryside. We were both wearing civvies. Dorothy tells me mine were awful, but I remember she looked really lovely in a dress. It was a fine day and we went into a field, spread a blanket and a table cloth on the grass and set up our picnic. We were clearing away when a tree moved towards us! It was followed by a veritable forest of soldiers who were cleverly camouflaged! We had been totally unaware of their presence. I wonder how many more unsuspecting couples they had observed! We adjourned to a nearby pub where someone asked me why I wasn't in the forces as I seemed to be old enough!

Left, Dorothy and sister Billie in Trafalgar Square.

Dorothy was serving in the WAAF as a Leading Aircraftswoman, a Teleprinter operator at No 11 Group Headquarters, RAF Uxbridge. Although she was conveniently close to home and I managed to see her between watches, she worked throughout the day and night on that blasted teleprinter. We managed to see each other a few more times before my leave expired and, when it did, I asked her if she would write to me. She did, regularly, and I kept every letter. They are light and amusing and as I said in one of my letters to her, 'Like a breath of fresh air on a hot Summer's day.'

Foolishly I agreed to play cricket for the Old Boys' Team, they really must have been hard up! I tried to hook a ball on the leg side for six only to succeed in hooking it into my eye. They stitched it up at the local hospital and sent me home with a bandage covering it. The following evening I was in uniform at the request of my father and drinking with him in a local pub, when someone in the bar said, 'Poor boy, he's been wounded!' Before I could deny it the table top was covered with pints! The headache they gave me next day was far worse than the one given me by that damn cricket ball!

I later found myself back at Harrogate drinking in a small bar in the gardens of the Queens Hotel. I recall little of this disagreeably tedious period except when, with many others, I was apprehended by the Military Police and told to put the stiffening wire back into my hat!

CHAPTER SEVEN

THE SECOND YEAR PASSETH!

'The second hand ticks steady;
You have an itching thumb,
Ten seconds - (meanwhile men have died) -
At Last! brakes off and throttles wide-'

'Operation by Night', Flt Lt George Eades.

On the 9th June 1943 I was posted to No 14 (P) AFU (Advanced Flying Unit) at Banff in Scotland. Opened on the 21st April, it was a new airfield and was first occupied only two or three weeks before I arrived. 'Gee whizz,' wrote Dorothy in her first letter to me, 'What a place to be posted to!' My letters to her complained that the nearest town was five miles away, the mess a mile, lecture rooms 2 miles and we walked! (From where?!). Daylight lasted 21 hours, thus I was closing the blackout curtains on the windows of my room, not to prevent the light from shining out, but to prevent it from shining in! To cap it all, the pubs shut at 9.30 pm and, for the time of the year, it was freezing cold!

We were about 50 strong when we started, one officer said he no longer wished to continue to fly and transferred to Flying Control. We wondered what would have happened if he had been an NCO. Our course commander was a West End actor named Sebastian Shaw, whom I saw occasionally on TV after the War.

I got off on the wrong foot with the station commander, who was reputed to be the most senior Group Captain in the RAF. I remember the incident well. I had gone to the serving hatch for a drink (no bar in this mess, just a hole in the wall) and asked the corporal for a Scotch and soda. He said I couldn't have it as he had only one nip left and he was saving that for the station commander. A voice behind me said, 'You can't do that, Corporal. This young officer was first, you must give it to him.' I turned and there stood the group captain. I protested (I had to!) but he insisted and, moreover, said he would pay for it. The glass was put in front of me, the precious liquid gleaming golden in the bottom. I could almost feel the CO's mouth watering as he cast a longing glance at it. With an air of disapproval, the corporal thumped the soda syphon beside it and immediately turned his attention to the Group Captain. I lifted the glass to the spout of the syphon and pushed down the lever. There was an almighty 'Whoooosh' as the gas released a stream of soda water propelling the contents of the glass onto the floor leaving a small quantity of white sparkling liquid where it had once been golden! As I said, it was a splendid introduction to the Station Commander whom I believe neither forgot nor forgave me from that moment! Two days later I was orderly officer[1]!

My course at 14 (P) AFU Banff, Scotland, June 1943.
Front row, 6th from left, self, 8th Archie ('Pip') Hagues,
11th Peter Boyle. I wonder how many of this course survived?

Life was made bearable with a splendid arrangement made with the landlady of the Commercial Hotel in Banff (her husband, the landlord, was at war). We would telephone her telling her the time we would be in town and she would prepare a magnificent tea for us, fresh herrings, drop scones topped off with lashings of butter and jam. After tea we would go down into her cellar, heave up the heavy crates, and generally prepare the bar for the evening. I was behind the counter pulling pints, waiting for her to take over when in walked the Group Captain. He was not amused! By coincidence two

---

[1] *Orderly Officer - an irksome duty, requiring those designated to remain confined to base and deal with all number of problems, regardless of the time of day.*

days later I was orderly officer again!

I asked the local baker if he would bake a cake and send it down to a pretty WAAF at Uxbridge for her birthday. Apart from being sent a month too soon it was well received and huge because of more relaxed food rationing in northern Scotland. Dorothy wrote saying she had never had such a big cake and that the eyes of her Watch popped when they saw it.

We finished ground school and moved to Fraserburgh, to commence flying Oxfords again. This well dispersed airfield had been established since December 1941, but had only been occupied by 14(P) AFU at the same time as they had occupied Banff. At the door of the Mess I was met by the orderly officer whom I knew. Orderly officer was a good duty, he said; you could eat in the airmen's mess where the food considerably better than that of the officers' mess! We went inside and he bought me a beer and then introduced me to those in the ante-room. We eventually came to a Flt/Lt pilot asleep in an armchair. We stopped in front of him and he said, '...and this silly old bugger has a tin leg,' and gave him a hefty kick on the shin. There was a roar of pain and anger as the chap leapt out of his chair and hopped round the room rubbing his leg. My new-found chum didn't bat an eyelid, 'Must've been the other one!' he said.

After a lapse of four months it took me four hours to solo the 'Oxbox' again. We then started to fly during the day with our eyes covered with the darkest of dark glasses. The flying instruments and the runway were illuminated by sodium lamps. Hardly being able to see a thing, it was terrifying and quite the most dangerous flying I had yet done. With such short nights in the North of Scotland at that time of the year, some idiot had to invent a method of simulating night flying. This was it and very frightening it was too! In my log book I recorded that I took off at dusk and landed at dawn having been 3 hours 30 minutes in the air!

At Fraserburgh the course flew 44 hours in 10 days, then they sent us back to Banff, where we flew another 22 hours in four days. Could it be that someone needed us, we asked? At the same time all of the pilot officers were anxiously waiting for our promotion to flying officer to be gazetted - it was long over due!

I flew the Anson on a low level cross-country. Compared with an Oxford it was like sitting in a lumbering flying glass house and you had to pump the flaps up by hand! I was told to weave as if I had an enemy aircraft on my tail. I thought I was doing well until the instructor asked me if I recognised the land mark below. 'You should do,' he said sarcastically, 'that's the second time we've flown over it!'

Later, in the Mess, I was trying to write a letter. My concentration was interrupted for the umpteenth time by the Inks Spots loudly rendering 'Whispering Grass'. The record was wearing out and so were my nerves. I got up from my chair went over to the gramophone took the record off the turntable and flung it across the room. While it was in the air the door opened and in walked the station commander. It shattered into a thousand pieces at his feet. He looked at me and said, 'We shall need a replacement, Clark.' Surprise! Surprise! Two days later I was orderly officer!

It was at Banff I met Peter Boyle again, we were already great friends. He was a tall, spindly man with hardly any chin, an Old Etonian of great wit and charm and totally unflappable. He loved flying and his ambition was to be a sergeant pilot. This he made in South Africa until one day he appeared in the officer's mess with the commission he had already refused. He was unhappy about it and said so. 'It's my father interfering again,' he said. Peter told me that as an airman he would ride in the back of a staff car beside his father, an officer of Air Rank, but that it would stop before entering a town and he would be shoved up front to sit beside the driver! Once through the town they would stop again and Peter would return to his seat beside his father! He never quite understood or forgave that!

We were to fly an unforgettable cross-country together, Banff - Fettercairn - Falkirk - Grangemouth - Banff. The weather was marginal when we took off and climbed above the patchy cloud to the safety height of 3,000 feet and away we went. Peter was navigating and, in spite of changing winds, managed to keep us on course to Fettercairn. As we set course for Falkirk it started to rain hard, so we climbed to get above it and in so-doing so we lost sight of the ground. On ETA (Estimated Time of Arrival) Falkirk, Peter said we had better let down carefully and see if we could get safely below cloud. As we were letting down I saw a hole in the cloud and water below, so I put the nose down and spiralled through it. We broke cloud about 750 feet above the Firth of the Forth. The rain was belting down and visibility at its best, was extremely poor. I was still flying in a circle, completely disorientated, the compass and directional giro slowly revolving, when Peter said suddenly, 'Turn on to north, Nobbie' (He was trying to orientate his map!). All I could say in reply was, 'Where's north?' and turned the aeroplane through 270 degrees to find it!

I was now aware that the surrounding hills were decidedly higher than us. This knowledge had a remarkable, sobering effect on my flying and I soon settled down! Peter then pointed us like a gun and fired us like a bullet into the east/west runway of Grangemouth. I am pleased to say the landing was good, but through the drenching rain we could see a black flag flying from the signal mast; the airfield was closed, flying was cancelled for the day!

Doubtless our relief at being safely down as well as that damn flag had much to do with our hysterical laughter! Grangemouth refuelled us and telephoned Banff enquiring about their weather. They asked Grangemouth what we were doing there since a general recall signal had been transmitted and they had been worried about us. We said we hadn't heard the recall since the TR9 radio set in the aircraft wasn't very good. As for being worried about us, we bet they hadn't been half as worried about us as we'd been!

An Airspeed Oxford on the approach.
V3792 was built by de Havilland (Photo: Imperial War Museum ref:CH11724)

We waited at Grangemouth another hour and then took off in driving rain. An airman from flying control hauled down the black flag to make it legal! As soon as our wheels left the runway, he hauled it back up again and dashed back inside for shelter.[2]

Two or three days later my log book was rubber stamped 'High Average'. and I was off on leave before taking a BAT Course (Beam Approach Training). I saw Dorothy for just one hour during the whole six days. Those bloody teleprinters came between us again.

The day I reported to No 1514 BAT Flight at Coningsby was the second

---

[2] - *Sqdn/Ldr Peter Boyle survived the war only to meet his death flying a glider. I believe it happened not very far from Grangemouth, now the site of an oil refinery.*

anniversary of my joining the RAF. I began to wonder if I would ever see any action! Those who had 'joined up' with me must have been in the thick of it by now - or worse. Coningsby was started in 1937 and was opened late in 1940 as a 5 Group Bomber Station. When we arrived on the 20th July 1943, as Course No 85, new runways had just been completed, and it was rumoured that the now famous No 617 Squadron was about to occupy it. It was an unforgettable 6 days during which we flew a leisurely 12 hours in Oxfords and 5 hours in the Link Trainer. I shared a room with Pip Hagues in the big 'B' type mess. Our batman had been a 'gentleman's gentleman', and both Pip and I were never so well looked after! As soon as we took anything off it was either washed, pressed or burnished. At that time we were undoubtedly the two smartest pilot officers in the RAF!

Here I attended my first 'Dining-in Night' and all course members were on their best behaviour, not knowing quite what to expect. The dining tables were beautifully laid out with white linen, gleaming silver and sparkling glassware. We stood obediently while the 5 Group Commander, Air Chief Marshal Hon Sir Ralph Cochrane; the Station Commander, Group Captain H.L.'Sam' Patch and other brass hats took their seats at the top table. A brief grace was said and we sat down unfolding our napkins onto our laps. The hubbub ceased, the room went silent, 'Did you see that, Nobbie?' queried Peter at my side, 'Did I see what?' I asked. 'A chap wearing nothing but a 'G string' and a respirator has just served Cochrane his soup!' Pip had seen it too! It seemed a strange way to start such a formal evening!

We left the table after toasting the King and retired to the ante-room. It was bare! Every stick of furniture had been removed and put on the lawn outside. To a leisurely beat of a drum a crocodile of officers marched slowly towards us. Trousers rolled up to the knees, tunics open, ties knotted in bows and hats worn back to front, each held a newspaper full of fish and chips which, after climbing through the open windows, they offered around! They were from No 619 Squadron based at nearby Woodhall Spa and had come to join in the fun. It was a riotous night. We played 'high-cock-o-lorum' and 'mess rugby' with a waste paper basket for a ball; how the beer and blood flowed! Someone who dared leave the party early was brought down in his bed. We sang, and we drank, and six pilot officers tossed the station commander, Sam Patch, in a blanket. A 'Lancaster' was built from mess furniture but it crashed to the floor as the crew tried to board it! A nutcase roared through the mess with his hat on fire! We were paralytic when in the early hours we collapsed exhausted on our beds.[3]

The next operation No 619 Squadron flew was to Hamburg on the 24/25th July 1943. It was the first time 'window' was used. A thin metallic strip dropped in bundles from aircraft, swamping the German radar by producing a false echo - regrettably this idea was not so effective for very long.

Pip and I were sharing a training detail on the Oxford, working the beam. After an hour we swopped seats and Pip sat on the main spar between the instructor, Fg/Off Tidy, and myself. The hood was put over my head and I took off to fly a figure of eight over the beam as instructed. On arriving at the inner marker beacon, 100 feet above aerodrome level, I opened up the engines to overshoot when the starboard engine failed! Tidy yelled, 'I've got her!' and I let go of everything. He turned into the dead engine (not recommended at that height![4]) and then jinked about, lining the aeroplane up with the runway downwind. 'Pump down the undercart, Nobbie!' he yelled - the hydraulic pump for the undercart was on the dead engine! So I started to pump, every downward movement of the lever removing skin from my knuckles.

The undercarriage indicator lights were obscured from Tidy by the blind flying hood over my head and he was now getting desperate, holding off an aeroplane that no longer wanted to fly! He yelled, 'Can I put her down now, Nobbie?!' He sounded like a man dying for a pee! Our conversation became decidedly brusque. 'NOW?' 'NO!' 'NOW?'. I was as pleased as he when the green light flicked on and I yelled, 'NOW!' We touched down, ran a few yards on the tarmac, and turned off onto the grass. I took the hood off, pleased I hadn't had to watch that drama! Pip must have been a bit anxious too not having the benefit of a safety belt. Tidy had done a magnificent job. We were walking away when he said, 'Christ! I know what that was, we ran out of fuel, I forgot to turn the auxiliary tanks on!' Whereupon he went back

---

[3] - *More than a decade later I was proposing the toast of the guests at a Royal Auxiliary Air Force Squadron dining-in night. Air-Vice Marshal H.L. Patch, No 11 Group Commander was present. In my toast I took him back to Coningsby and to that dining-in night when he was tossed in a blanket. Sam Patch didn't take very kindly to the reminder. It was a pity, if only in memory of those aircrew who had taken part in the revelry and later failed to survive.*

[4] - *'Turning into the dead engine' - the good engine would tend to turn the aircraft into the direction of the dead engine. Overbanking into the dead engine would result in a potentially disastrous loss of height.*

into the aircraft and surreptitiously pushed the auxiliary fuel cocks down. The engineer's report said the fuel pump on the starboard engine had failed!

An AMO (Air Ministry Order) ordered RAFVR officers to remove the brass VR's from the lapels of their uniforms. None of us took any notice of it and continued to wear them. One evening in the mess the Station Adjutant came round asking those still wearing them to remove them and put them in a box he was carrying. The Air Force Journal said you would now be able to tell the difference between RAF officers and RAFVR officers by the two holes the latter wore in his collar lapel!!' This decision by Air Ministry seemed petty at the time, we were proud of our VR'S. After the war the Air Council decided those who had served during the war in the RAFVR could not wear the RAF tie. I was amazed; the same Air Council that had destroyed our individuality and made us part of the RAF now prevented us from wearing their tie. In a fit of pique and anger I burned the RAF tie I had become so used to wearing!

In a letter home I criticized the instructors at Coningsby[5] for doing their best to kill themselves and added, aggressively, if I stayed much longer I would punch one of them on the nose! Now I wonder what that was all about? It certainly affected my assessment: above average for Beam & 'Q' Code (Link); average for Receiver Operation and Application of Beam Procedure, and below average for Instrument, Cloud flying and Night Flying. My flying, 12 hours since Banff, must have deteriorated a lot!

My Mess bill for six days came to 16 shillings and 9 pence (85p). We were charged 7/-d for messing (35p), 2/6d (13p) for Mess Guests and 3/6d (18p) for maintenance (to pay for the splintered furniture when the 'Lancaster' crashed). Also included was a shilling for games (not specified!) and 3d for the library! Pip and I gave our 'gentleman's gentleman' ten shillings each (50p) - a fortune in those days!

I was posted to No 2 Radio School at Yatesbury as a Staff Pilot to fly Proctors and Dominies, I was sick. I didn't want to be a chauffeur to a bunch of WOP/AG's! Pip was posted to No 19 OTU (Operational Training Unit)

---

[5] - *Coningsby was the scene of a tragic personal loss many years later. Sqdn/Ldr Jack Jagger, a former regular adjutant of my Auxiliary Squadron tried to loop a Meteor 8 directly from take off, struck the ground and was killed. It was a tragic waste of a life. We had become great friends when we were POW. I went to his wedding and he was godfather to my daughter. He was a very talented young man. My family missed him.*

at Kinloss to fly Whitleys, I was green with envy. Then my posting to Yatesbury was rescinded, it was obvious those WOP/AG's didn't want me either! I was to join Pip at Kinloss. We stood two deep in the corridor of a train for the 18 hours it took to travel from Coningsby to Aberdeen. We left Edinburgh at dawn and saw the Forth Bridge in the half light, reaching Aberdeen at 08.00 to change trains for Inverness! Once at Kinloss I slept for 16 hours!

Kinloss was built during 1938/39 and with its numerous wooden huts, I don't think it was ever finished! It was the home of 19 OTU and 45 MU (Maintenance Unit), the latter preparing a wide variety of hardware for the RAF. The Station Commander was Group Captain F.R.D.Swain. In September 1936 he had flown a Bristol type 138A to a height of 49,967 feet - at that time the World Altitude Record for heavier-than-air aircraft. The influence of the Gulf Stream gave Kinloss good all year weather, we were told; the station would often stay open when others would be closed. Volume 7 of 'Action Stations', by David J.Smith (Publishers PSL), says of Kinloss:- 'Owing to frequent bad weather, high ground and worn out aircraft, 19 OTU had a higher than average accident rate, almost 200 aircrew being killed and 64 injured during its life.'(!) I recall when I was there, there was a lot of it about - bad weather, high ground, clapped out aeroplanes and accidents, I mean!

My assembled crew were all NCO'S: Sgt. E.M.Keep (Eric) was the bomb aimer, a dapper, well groomed young man from Huddersfield who had failed a pilot's course; Sgt Foster was the navigator, married, a pipe smoking serious man, at the age of 28 elderly by our standards; Sgt R.G.Thompson (Ron) was the WOP/AG, married and came from Manchester; and later, at Forres, we were joined by the rear gunner, Sgt D.W.L.Brown (Lloyd) from Canada and, the oldest member of the crew, the mid-upper gunner, Sgt E. Wilkinson (Ernie) from Bolton. I don't know how old Ernie was but, much to his annoyance, we told him he should have stayed at home by the fireside!

We were Course No 69 and spent the first two weeks at Ground School familiarising ourselves with the fuel, hydraulic and other systems on the Whitley and working 'Dry Swims' with the navigator (classroom navigation exercises with the clock moving at double time!) Synthetic Bombing and more cunning and confusing lectures made it all extremely hard work. In addition they made me Course Commander which meant I had to take the passing out parade. I had difficulty in stopping a bus, let alone halting a mob of bloody airmen in unison on the right foot.

We were then posted to Forres, a satellite of Kinloss, three miles to the west. We went to fly Armstrong-Whitworth Whitley MkVs. I arrived alone on a Sunday and was met at the entrance of the Mess by the orderly officer, a slightly built Flying Officer, who introduced himself as 'Shorty' Taylor. 'I am expecting you,' he said reassuringly, 'but I can't show you to your billet until I get some transport. In the meantime let's have a pint.' In the end we had a pint or three and I asked him where the toilet was. He directed me and I departed saying (as was the fashion), 'Keep an eye on my beer, Shorty.' Upon my return I raised the glass to my lips, and hurriedly put it back on the table! I peered into the glass and there, gazing back at me from the bottom was a glass eye! I looked at 'Shorty' who had a wide grin on his face and a twinkle in the only real eye he had! 'You did ask me to keep an eye on your beer!', he said! It transpired that he'd been flying a Blenheim when it crashed and he lost his eye. He was now the Air Traffic Controller at Forres. I eventually got out to my hut and Pip Hagues arrived later to share the room with me. The accommodation was widely dispersed but comfortable, the messing was excellent, all messes having their share of game sent into them by the local laird; we dined like kings.

No. 19 OTU Whitley N1412. It crashed on the approach at Kinloss and was written-off 9th December 1942 (Photo: RAF Museum ref:P17820)

Forres was a grass airfield and we joked that the wind had to be in the right direction to fly a Whitley out of it, it was always pretty tight. The Whitley V was a big aeroplane, and I am sure I wasn't the only 'sprog' pilot who feared he would never get this giant off the ground - and back down again. Compared with the Oxford, the wing span was 84 feet to 53 feet, the length 70 feet to 35 feet and the height 15 feet to 11 feet. The two Merlin X's of the Whitley developed 1145 h.p. each, the Oxford's Cheetah X's 370 h.p. No wonder it looked a monster! The cockpit was spacious and the layout tidy. All the flap, undercarriage, hand pump, and radiator shutter control levers were at the right of the pilot's seat, so were the elevator and tail trim wheels. The control wheel was large, like the half wheel of a bus! The brake lever protruded from the hub of the wheel and was operated by pressure from the thumb of your left hand. The engine controls were in the centre of the instrument panel, two throttles, a landing light dipping control lever, one mixture control lever and below them, something new to look after, two airscrew pitch control levers.

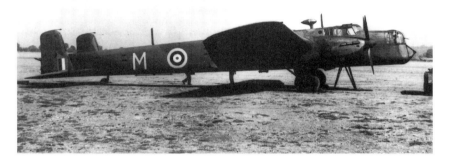

This Whitley, N1503, came direct from the factory to No.19 OTU in early 1940. It was converted to 3067M in May 1941. Aircraft designated 'M' were relegated to 'ground use only'. I wonder what had happened to this aircraft to cause it to be grounded? (Photo:RAF Museum ref:P570)

Like the Oxford there was the usual standard blind flying panel and a host of dials and switches festooned around it, only more so! Not the least was a series of extra engine instruments to take care of the in-line, liquid cooled engines. There was an auto-pilot, oxygen controls and countless other switches and dials. Looking at the Whitley pilot's notes nearly 50 years on I find it utterly confusing and incredible that I could have known where everything was, but I did, and the confusion was extremely well laid out!

The bomb aimer sat in the nose or in the front turret, unless he was assisting the pilot to fly the aircraft. The navigator's table was behind the pilot and he sat in the gangway with his back against the starboard side of the fuselage. In a small compartment facing the navigator sat the wireless operator. Every time the undercart moved up or down a thin jet of hydraulic fluid vented from a reservoir high in the roof and showered him and his log book! Ron used to get furious with it! Behind the Wireless Operator at floor level was a tunnel, the mainplane spar gangway which went through the centre section of the wing. In it was the emergency hand operated gear for lowering the undercart when the hydraulic system had completely failed. It was said it took about 700 turns of each handle before it came out and locked down! The tunnel led to the rear end of the fuselage. Here the Elsan toilet and the rear gunner in his Frazer-Nash 4-gun turret were situated. The pilots' notes says the crew entered by the rear door - I can't remember ever using it - the crawl through that tunnel was enough to give anyone claustrophobia! We used the ladder in the front hatch, the rear gunner used the rear door.

Whitley cockpit - Well laid out confusion! (Photo: Imperial War Museum ref:CH6376)

The Whitley was a docile aircraft to fly - providing everything kept working, which fortunately for me it always did! To take off, the throttles were opened fully with the brakes hard on. When the engines were developing full power the brakes were released, followed by a hard push on the wheel to get the tail up. It came up quickly which led to that worn out cliche that the tail gunner got more flying time in than the rest of the crew! She landed pretty solidly too.

It took me two sorties, ten landings, and 2 hours 20 minutes flying time to solo, I cannot believe I was that proficient. My instructor, Flg/Off E. Brunskill DFC, must have chewed his finger nails down to his elbows while I completed my two solo landings. Two months later, on 6th October 1943, that aircraft (LA792) crashed in the mountains near Boat of Garten; there were no survivors.

Day Conversion Training took ten days. I flew 8 hours 30 minutes and made 37 landings! For my efficiency I was made Aerodrome Control Pilot for the night and was stuck on the end of the flare path with a canvas windbreak for shelter and a coke brazier for warmth. It was a very cold night! Crew training then started in earnest. Our rear gunners had been one month late in arriving and I was allocated Sergeant Brown, a tall, quiet, shy Canadian of 20 years. We immediately started fighter affiliation exercises with Martinets and Spitfires as the attackers. My belated promotion to Flying Officer had now been gazetted - over three months late! September began with Eric dumping all the bombs on the grass as we were preparing to make a war load climb! He said he was checking the switches - I didn't hear what the armourers said! They reluctantly winched the bombs back into the bomb bays and we flew the sortie later, dropping two live 250 pounders into Spey Bay.

Night Conversion started. We flew to Kinloss and used their concrete runways for our night circuit and bumps, the final landing, aided by a floodlight, being made on the grass at Forres. I soloed in 5 hours 15 minutes after 15 landings. My instructor was then Flt/Lt E. Baldwin DFM[6]. An Aircraft Apprentice in 1932 he finally completed 145 operational sorties, and was awarded the DSO and the DFC. Once, flying from Forres, he landed a Whitley at Stornaway with engine trouble. Finding no one could help him, he took the engine cowlings off, repaired the problem himself and flew back home!

With night conversion finished, we took off for our first night cross-country. Flg/Off Brunskill, a 'screen' (an instructor), sat at my side. Our route was Base - Tiree - Gigha - Base. We had been flying a little more than two hours on the outward leg when, nearing our ETA for Tiree, I asked the navigator, Sgt Foster, for my next heading. To my astonishment he said he had been suffering from a migraine and hadn't got a line on his chart! I looked at Brunskill, expecting him to take over, but he didn't want to know and looked fast asleep anyway! I turned onto the reciprocal course and asked Ron to get me a QDM (radio code for a bearing) to base giving it a minor priority rating. I told the crew I intended to get home using QDM's to steer by until I picked up the Kinloss beam, on which I would let down, get into the Forres circuit and land. Fortunately it was as easy as that.

---

[6] - *Later to take part in the development flying of the Handley Page Victor.*

Brunskill came to life when the engines were switched off and, once outside the aircraft, put Foster under arrest. I didn't see him again as he was immediately posted away from the unit. I do hope he survived the war, he was a good man. The Kinloss ORB said of this sad affair:- '...and one crew was put back to No 72 Course to train a new navigator, the original navigator having decided he could no longer continue flying, when at the end of the Course.' The following night, for my sins, I was stuck on the end of the flare path again and, again, it was freezing! That afternoon, punch drunk from fatigue, I caught the Perth train to start two weeks leave. I was standing in the corridor of a first class carriage (the RAF liked their officers to stand in comfort) when someone tapped on the window and beckoned me into the compartment. An arm rest was pushed up and I was invited to sit down. Soon my head went between my legs (I could not lean back) and I fell asleep. I was woken gently, proffered a silver flask and invited to drink from it. It was brandy and I felt an inward glow as it went down. This gentleman then insisted that I took his corner seat. I woke as the train was grinding into Perth station. My benefactor turned to me and asked me if I was going to London. I said I was and he asked if I would care to join him for dinner. I said I would be delighted, but wondered where we would get dinner this time of the evening.

He was met on the platform by a top hatted gentleman, who raised that hat reverently and greeted him warmly. I gulped when I heard him say, 'Get this young officer a sleeping compartment on the London train.' As far as I was concerned only those with the rank of General had the nerve to ask for a sleeper. This 'young officer', I told myself, was surely going to spend an interminably long and cold night in the corridor! I was impressed when we were escorted to the dining room of the Station Hotel and shown immediately to a table; they had obviously been waiting for him. The service and the meal were immaculate which, for 1943, was really something. We rose from the table and were escorted to the waiting London train. To my surprise and delight I was shown to a sleeping compartment which my elderly benefactor inspected, approved and then bid me 'Good night'.

I was struggling with my suitcase as the train pulled into Euston when my benefactor greeted me and asked if I would like a taxi. Taxis at stations in those days were as rare as water in the Sahara desert. Extremely sceptical I said I would! He was again met on the platform by a top hatted gentleman, who raised his hat reverently and greeted him warmly. I gulped when he instructed him to, 'Get this young officer a taxi.' Again there wasn't to be any problem. I was immediately ushered to the head of a long waiting queue. He bid me, 'Goodbye and good luck,' as he closed the taxi door on me and

I moved off. I never discovered who my elderly benefactor was, he never volunteered a name, but was obviously well known to the LMS (London, Midland and Scottish railway). I have often wondered who he might have been and have never forgotten his kindness.

I met Dorothy between watches and we went to the theatre and saw Ivor Novello's 'The Dancing Years', there was an air-raid during the performance. On a platform at Kings Cross Station I proposed to my beloved Dorothy and she accepted. Now all I had to do was win over her father! She stood in a cloud of white smoke and steam as the train pulled away from the station for Edinburgh. I waved to her from the window until she disappeared from view. It took 19 hours to get back to Forres.

During my leave 19 OTU lost a Whitley (LA853) and its crew near Dishforth on the 27th September, it had gone out of control on a night cross-country. Back at Forres I met my new navigator Plt/Off R.J.('Kit') Carson RCAF. He was a tall, handsome, lanky chap with a quick smile and an even quicker turn of wit. He hailed from Toronto, Canada, I guess his age was about 22. The ORB said of him, 'No 72 course... one of the crews which had been added from a previous course had a navigator of well above average ability and that crew was put forward to No 71 course...'

Kit, Eric and Ron went straight off dicing cross country in the Anson, and me... I finished up on the bloody flare path at Forres again! I wrote to Dorothy at 3 am on 2nd October, 'I am sitting in a small canvas shelter on the end of the flare path writing by the light of a red Aldis lamp! All the boys have now taken off and I am eagerly awaiting their return so that I can tumble off to bed. What a night it has been! Firstly I have been soaked through to the skin but managed to dry myself off reasonably well. Secondly I have been frozen almost solid into a block of ice. In this state I fear I shall remain until the morning. I wish you could see me now, I bet you would laugh. I am dressed up to the ears in flying kit, my hat rests on the back of my head. On top of that I am smothered in dust from the old coke fire that is spitting away for all its worth. My hand is almost frozen to my pen. At least by writing this letter at this hour I shall catch the early morning post!'

I saw Pip take off and he gave me a wave as he opened up his throttles and watched him land safely some 6 hours later. During the night out of sheer frustration I pooped off a couple of cartridges from the Verey pistol at some seagulls trying to home in on my brazier. I missed them and the red flares bounded off into the darkness. Before I could say 'Reload!' the O.C Night Flying was out in his jeep and breathing down my neck. Fortunately in the dim light he could see I was more pissed off than he was and said nothing. I went off duty at 08.00hrs hours. While I was sitting out braving the elements, Lloyd had his 21st birthday party!

At Kinloss two nights later, at 00.45hrs, 4th October, Whitley Z9422 on a dual training flight failed to take off and ditched straight ahead into Findhorn Bay. There were no injuries and back at Forres the pilot, Fg/Off E.W.Smith and his pupils, Sgt K.W.Newton and Plt/Off A.A.Fraser, had us in fits of laughter when he told us what happened: They struck the water with an almighty splash and there was some confusion in the darkness, but they got the dinghy out OK. In accordance with the book the pilot sat on top of the fuselage and directed the crew into the dinghy. He told them to hurry as he expected the aircraft to sink at any moment. There were two remaining when a gust of wind moved the dinghy away from the aircraft as one was attempting to enter it. He missed and they saw him disappear into the icy water. He quickly re-appeared with the water only coming up to his chest. It was so shallow he was standing on the bottom!

On the 6th, the day we lost Whitley LA792 and its crew at Boat of Garten due to engine failure, Pip was posted to 1652 HCU (Heavy Conversion Unit) at Marston Moor for conversion on to Halifaxes. I was to miss him, we had been room mates for a long time. Now, I thought, he would soon be ahead of me on Ops. Actually he wallowed in mud for weeks on an Escape and Evasion Course before he was to fly again. He eventually flew Halifaxes as a pathfinder in Italy and completed 42 trips. For this tremendous effort a grateful Command let him continue to wear the pathfinder badge!

The end of September and October was to be a bizarre period in so far as accidents were concerned. No 69 Course lost two crews, one in an Anson and one in the Whitley (LA853) flying their last night cross-country on 27th September. Had it not been for the skill of Sgt Harrison, they would have lost another. Unable to maintain height on one engine he 'bombed in' out of the darkness onto the flare path. The pistons were protruding through the crankcase! An Anson from another course went missing never to be found.

I started work with Kit as navigator, I'd had a long break and was pleased to get back into the air again. We started off with two cross-countrys, from one of which we returned with the radio U/S. Kit got upset with me pushing past him to get through the tunnel to the Elsan at the back. Apart from pushing his beloved chart sideways I knocked all his beautifully sharpened pencils on the floor and bent them he said. It was obvious I would have to find an alternative hole down which I could relieve myself, which I did regularly once a trip. On the ground I looked around the aeroplane and found a suitable hole in the front - the camera hatch. It was a big hole and I couldn't miss finding it, or peeing through it.

We had been in the air sometime when I called Eric up from the nose to take over my seat. This he was required to do during the flight to give him flying practice. When safely installed, I went down the front and opened up the camera hatch. I proceeded to relieve myself, I couldn't stop, neither would the slipstream that came up through that hole and I finished up drenched! Kit continued to grumble when, later, I painfully pushed past him and crawled through that bloody tunnel to the Elsan at the back. To hell with it! I wasn't going to piss into the wind again for anyone!

F/Sgt Major, RCAF, was to fly with us for one sortie I was told. He would pass through Forres as a captain of a headless crew, getting a crew at HCU. He was to fly the aircraft with the exception of the take off and landing. I took off and handed over to him and returned to the seat for the landing. His flying was immaculate, unlike my flying, the needles of his instruments never wavered. Kit was elated and jumped up and down saying something about how it made his job much easier. As far as I was concerned this exhibition was going to make my job much harder!

I made a reasonable landing, which won me a few brownie points. I had forgotten the flight when the F/Sgt came up to me in the crew room and asked me how he should enter it in his log book. His total flying hours were 4000! He had been an instructor in Canada, no wonder those needles didn't move. I was to meet him in York some months later, but it was only a passing handshake and a quick enquiry how he was. He had his crew and had already flown to Berlin eight times. I hope he survived.

It took 5 days to complete the day cross-country syllabus and during that time I satisfied my curiosity by finding out what was in a hut where a sentry stood outside the door 24 hours a day. It harboured a *'GEE'* set (a radar navigation aid); only navigators were allowed to see it! About this time a flock of Horsa gliders (towed by Whitleys) arrived at Forres. They headed for the ground at an angle of 45 degrees and bounced awkwardly to a stop. They were then parked around the airfield for a week or two, presumably for the benefit of the high flying Ju 88's that came to have a look at us from time to time. Then the time came to tow them out and we said, 'There's no way, but no way, they are going to fly them out.' After a couple of aborted take-offs, the Whitleys barely getting off the ground, they decided to call it a day and the Horsas were dismantled and taken away by road.

The start of our night training heralded what must have been one of the most bizarre 'no casualty' accidents that ever happened at Kinloss or perhaps anywhere else for that matter. At 21.55hrs on 18th October, N1369 ('W'), piloted by F/Sgt J.H.Collins, started to roll down the runway for takeoff[7]. With the tail up and moving pretty fast they felt a bump. The 'screen' thought a tyre had burst, abandoned the takeoff, ran onto the grass and shut down the engines. The crew said afterwards they did not hurry out of the aeroplane, but the stench of petrol was overpowering. Once out they went to inspect the tyre and were surprised to see an Anson (DJ104 'K') perched on top of the Whitley! Fuel was flowing every where. I saw that combination in a hangar the following day, it was a hair raising sight. The Anson was eventually lifted off, repaired and flown again; the Whitley was written off.

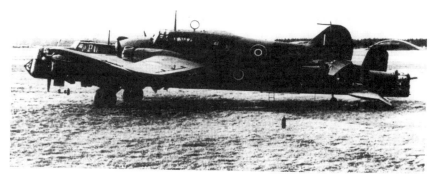

The morning after! Whitley N1369 and Anson DJ104 in collision 19th October 1943. Photo by the late Squ Ldr Beeby and property of the late Gp Capt R.C.Hockey. Reproduced by kind permission of the editor of 'Air Mail'

The weather took a turn for the worse. The OC Flying, in his anxiety to make up lost flying time and to get us airborne, would often have us sitting waiting in the aircraft, before cancelling night flying. Thus it was five days before we flew our first night cross-country sortie with Kit, flying down to St Abbs Head and then up the middle of the North Sea in a northerly direction for quite a long way. We were in cloud at 16,000 feet and it was always a struggle to get a Whitley any higher. Flying these aircraft with a full bomb load must have been a nightmare. I switched on the SBA (Standard Beam Approach) set, tuned into Wick and listened to the comfort of its signal in my head phones; then it happened! At first I thought we had been struck

[7] - *The Aerodrome Control Pilot later said he had not given 'W' a green light to move off!*

by lightning, but the flash was not accompanied by the usual clap of deafening thunder. There it was again, a silent flash like a giant spark from the front gun back to the turret. Then the tip of the starboard prop began to arc and then continued to outline its path in golden light like a giant Catherine wheel. Soon the port prop was also outlined in gold. Lloyd reported that sparks were flashing between his guns and that lightning was dancing between the aerial and the fuselage. It was a sight of great beauty and lasted about ten minutes. We later realised it was St Elmo's Fire.

We went to the cinema in Inverness and saw for the first time (but not the last!) that classic film 'Casablanca'. Back at Forres the mess gave a tremendous party, not the usual bachelor party with Shorty Taylor roaring around the mess with a pint of beer balanced on his forehead, but one with female company, tables laden with good food and an orchestra playing sweet music. It was unbelievable this took place during a war. The ladies were beautifully dressed and one in particular knew she was the *'belle of the ball'*. She stood in the centre of the ante-room surrounded by admirers, striking poses in which her bosoms led and the rest of her beautiful body followed. She held her glass daintily to one side which irritated Shorty no end, so much so that he took out his glass eye and popped it into her glass when she wasn't looking. She lifted her glass to her lips, saw the glass eye, shrieked and fainted. I can still see a shocked Shorty, both hands in his pockets, kicking his eye along the floor trying to get the evidence out of range, saying, 'Oh dear! Oh deary me!' It was 25th October and local night flying was taking place, our revelry was interrupted by Whitley LA881, piloted by Sgt H.R.Hagstrom, failing to take off. There was a loud thump and a tremendous fire on impact; reflected in the sky we could see the flickering shadows of the crew running away from the wreckage! Remarkably, there were no injuries. The party continued, we drank a little more than usual.

That same night, a Whitley out of Forres was flying night circuits and bumps at Kinloss. The 'screen' was our new O.C. Flying. He angrily reminded the pupil that there was an 800ft hill in the circuit and told him his last circuit was too bloody low and he was taking control. He said he would demonstrate how a circuit should be flown. Amid gales of helpless laughter the next day the crew told us the O.C Flying was flying down wind when the aircraft suddenly bumped a few times and ground to a halt! He had landed on top of the aforementioned 800ft hill. By great good fortune no one was hurt, the only casualty being the O.C.s pride! I cannot find reference to this accident anywhere, but anywhere. All details seem to have been destroyed other than the reference: 'Whitley EB386 Destroyed in Accident 25.10.43 NFD (No Further Details).' This must have been the aircraft that I saw sitting on top of that hill, it would have been impossible to have got it down and flying again and - I think I know who that 'screen' was!

Engine failure caused Whitley BD386, flown by Sgt L.C.Cronshaw, to ditch a half a mile off Peterhead the previous evening. Two of the crew in the aircraft were saved. The remaining 3 crew who had bailed out over the sea, were lost. Two days later we were sent to Kinnell for a Fighter Affiliation exercise with the Hurricanes of No 1 Combat Training Wing. The airfield was covered with low cloud so I flew out sea to make a safe let down. We found Montrose without any trouble and from there threaded ourselves to Kinnell, where we did a circuit and landed. I complained to the control tower that my progress was being impeded by a van and could they do anything to get it out of my way. I stopped and the van moved on. It was then I saw the sign at the back of it saying 'PLEASE FOLLOW ME!' When I reported to the control tower, they said they had telephoned Forres to say the weather was too bad to carry out Fighter Affiliation and would they stop the aircraft flying down!

The weather improved and we flew three routine night cross-countrys in a row. We had a bit of ice build up inside the aircraft on one when my cockpit window would not close properly. It was a change from having it build up on the wings which was par for the course. At the end of the month, in the foulest of weather, Whitley BD627 flew into the sea. Sgt Jones, the rear gunner and sole survivor, was picked up by the Trawler 'Emblem' after 24 hours in a dinghy. He was lucky to survive in such low temperatures.

I was at a loss what to write to Dorothy and asked Kit for advice. 'Tell her about that rotten landing you made last night,' was his retort. His favourite remark had now become, 'Navigation? What do you know about navigation? You're only the driver!' Nice guy!

The course appeared to finish abruptly and I found myself collecting signatures on a clearance chit. The OC Flying called me in to his office and handed me my log book. My flying assessment stuck on the last page was 'above average' for a Pupil Medium Bomber pilot - and so it should! I'd been at Kinloss a long time. I stood outside his door with 448 flying hours in my log book and a leave pass for nearly a month in my pocket. On 9th December we were to report to 1659 HCU (Heavy Conversion Unit) 6 Group RCAF, Topcliffe, North Yorkshire for conversion onto Halifaxes. In the meantime Bomber Command started its all-out assault on Berlin. I was still lucky enough to be out of the firing line, although I didn't think so at the time!

It was May 1985 before I returned to Forres, Dorothy was with me. It had been raining and the wet road surface gleamed. The little hotel in town, where we'd had so much fun, looked tired and dowdy - we would not be staying there as I had planned. We drove out to where I thought the airfield lay. It took me some time to find it, a post-war development had spread itself across my intended route. However, I found a familiar lane and turned off to where I thought Station Headquarters would be. The beautiful granite house had now reverted to a home and looked peaceful in its farmyard setting, beyond it was the airfield. I was appalled by the size of it. I asked myself how could we have got those lumbering, underpowered giants off? The green turf was being farrowed brown by a distant tractor towing a plough, the puny noise of its engine floating across the furrows. The farmer's son told me they were planting turnips in this hallowed soil, '40 years too late,' I told him. The parachute section was now a cattle shed and the doors of the fire station were bulging outwards and rotting. I could distinguish nothing else, there was nothing else but decay, rot and disrepair. There were no ghosts here, they had found a better place to go.

Forres 1986. Dorothy in front of the remains of the Fire Section.
Even the ghosts have found better places to go!

CHAPTER EIGHT

THE FINAL SELECTION

Schlaf, Kindlein, Schlaf,
am Himmel steht ein Schaf;
das Schaf, das ist aus Wasserdamf
und kampft wie du den Lebenskampf.
Schlaf, kindlein, schlaf.

Galgenkindes Wiegenlied.

Sleep, baby, sleep,
There's in the sky a sheep;
the sheep is made of cloud and dew
and fights life's battle just like you.
Sleep, baby sleep.

Gallows Child's Lullaby - Morgenstern

It had been a welcome leave. Dorothy and I met whenever we could, snatching a few moments happiness when the Air Force at Uxbridge set her free. Our frequent and brief encounters began and finished at Baker Street Station; we got to know it well. Pip was on leave and Dorothy brought a WAAF friend, Audrey Shepherd, out from Biggin Hill to meet him[1]. Together we went to see 'The Dancing Years' - Ivor Novello was becoming a habit! Pip introduced us to 'Maxims', a Chinese Restaurant in Wardour Street, later Dorothy and I were to eat and dance there quite often. In retrospect I wonder how 'Chinese' that food was! Whatever, we enjoyed it and relaxed in the atmosphere of the place.

[1] - *Years later I was to be best man at their wedding and, 40 years after, propose a toast at their Ruby wedding.*

Kit and I met early at Kings Cross to get a seat on the train to York, which we did by the skin of our teeth. Here I briefly met a Belgian who had been at Vereeniging with me. He said there were now many SAAF from those days over here. They'd gone a little further 'Up North' than they had expected!

Topcliffe had been planned as a Bomber Station in 1939. With its permanent buildings and huge 'C' type hangars it looked a paradise compared with the hutted and dispersed living sites of some of the units upon which I had recently served. Kit and I were billeted in a room in a married quarter, it was comfortable but bitterly cold; there being no fuel to light a fire. However, there wasn't any shortage of mud and the mess was a long way from our quarters!

An enormous Nissen hut housed the Aircrew Mess where all pupil crews, regardless of rank, lived. It was cold, uncomfortable, brash, noisy and lacked privacy. An inevitable radio blared full blast. The Canadian beer was awful and, as was the custom in North America, served cold enough to chill your back teeth. The fare wasn't much good either; pancakes with maple syrup seemed to be the staple diet. The Canadians would do nothing to improve conditions and for the very first time I felt I was expendable and that nobody really cared; it wasn't a comfortable feeling.

In the so-called lounge were six barrel stoves, surrounded by a tightly packed circle of chairs where we endeavoured to share the rarest commodity on the unit, heat! In an attempt to relieve the stark surroundings, the tin walls were decorated with life size murals; one depicted two scantily clad young ladies, one a pilot, the other an air gunner. In the background was a six engined aeroplane with as many guns sticking out of it as a porcupine has needles. The gunner was saying, 'Shot down 25 today, dear!' Underneath was a caption with the date, '1985'! At the time it felt like the war was going on for ever but happily, thank God, the prediction was wrong! There were others; a scantily clothed, curvaceous blonde was captioned 'Operational Breakfast'; another, 'Those famous last words'; others depicted gremlins, and prangs on the runway! I wondered how the time was found to paint them or for that matter why, they did nothing for me.

Nevertheless, I was pleased to be at 1659 HCU Topcliffe in 6 Group RCAF. The Group had recently been re-equipped with Halifax III's powered by four 1650 hp Bristol Hercules XVI engines, greatly improving its performance. I thought it would be great to fly one of those new high flyers on 'Ops' and started to take a keen interest in the activities of Bomber Command because it looked as though, at long last, we would soon be taking an active part in them.

The course started in the classroom with instruction on the fuel, hydraulic and emergency systems of the Rolls-Royce Merlin powered Halifax I & II. In an endeavour to boost our confidence in the Halifax we were told that it had six fuel cells in either wing as opposed to the Lancaster's three. This, they said, made the Halifax a better fire risk, it could also take more punishment! I had no desire to put these theories to the test! One thing was certain, the Messier hydraulic system on the Halifax was an ingenious one, it had one more way of getting the undercart down in emergency than the Lanc - we were clutching at straws!

The Halifax engineer's panel, situated just behind the pilot.
(Photo: Imperial War Museum ref:CH7398)

It was one year since I had received my wings and, in retrospect, the delay before that time had been fortunate. I had missed some of the the bloodiest battles of the bomber air war. However at the time I was more concerned with the immediate future - flying a Halifax. I would look up at it and think, 'Christ! What an enormous aeroplane. I'll never be able to fly that.' Who was the twit, I again asked myself, who said, 'If you can fly a Tiger Moth you can fly anything?' I consoled myself that after this course I would probably be posted to a Canadian squadron to fly one of the Mark III's, which were comfortingly rumoured to carry a marginally smaller bomb load, but to fly higher than a Lanc.

On 20th December we completed our crew with the addition of a flight engineer, another Canadian, Sgt. W.R.McBurney. We simply called him 'Mac'. He must have been in his late twenties when he joined us, making him, next to Ernie, the second oldest in the crew. Mac came from Alberta and before the war worked as a carpenter, constructing wooden grain elevators on the Prairies. It must have been a tough life and it showed on his rugged face. I can see him now, leaning nonchalantly against the crew room wall, his hands thrust in his pockets, his battle dress stained with oil and his forage cap pushed on to the back of his head. He said two courses had already passed through before I'd asked him to join us. He had been a fitter before he had taken his Flight Engineer's course at St.Athan and I was pleased to have him with his experience. He would talk the same language as the ground crews, as well as help us fly the aeroplane. At the time I think he was pleased to crew with us.

A letter home at this time says I'd asked a friend to remind me to straighten up whenever he saw me walking with my shoulders rounded. One day he reminded me in front of Kit who gave me a quizzical look, his eyes full of amusement. I turned on him and said, 'Didn't you know I'm developing my chest for the King to pin all my gongs on?' 'Look,' he replied, 'you're not going to win any gongs while I'm around. The only gong I want is for old age!' 'Oh!' I answered, 'You'll soon get that after you've flown one or two Ops with me', we both roared with laughter. Kit had been promoted to Flying Officer that day, 'Now, watch out!' he said. That evening we had a huge fire burning in the grate which made life a little more bearable. Kit made me chief stoker - saying it would be good practice for my after life! In the meantime I was swotting for an examination taking place the following day.

The morning of Christmas Eve was beautiful, the sky was crystal clear and a winter sun was shining for the first time for weeks. I was shaving in the bathroom with the window wide open, there was magic in the air, a vibrant hum, like some giant dynamo generating the very essence of life. I could see across the valley into the Hambleton hills beyond - the world was living and at peace. It was a remarkable experience at a time when the engines of main force bombers, on the ground, had barely grown cold. By the time I had left the house the sky had clouded over, the mood had disappeared and I wondered if it had really happened.

Christmas Day dawned with Kit and I suffering from a hangover, a self inflicted injury obtained the night before in Ripon. We were so bad we could only eat half our Christmas lunch. The camp band came into the mess to give a swing session, I remember the more they drank the better they played! I telephoned Dorothy, who was on watch at Uxbridge, and managed to get through to her in five minutes - I had expected it to take a couple of hours. It was the best thing that happened all day.

Now that Ground School was over, I was keen to get in the air again and wandered around the hangars looking at the aeroplanes. In retrospect, every aeroplane I looked at must have been absolutely clapped out and had probably completed more than 50 operational flights before they were junked for HCU use! We were lucky we didn't have to fly them all the time like the instructors. I was soon to find out what a wonderful job the Canadian ground crews were doing to keep them flying. Dorothy had her problems too, although we knew where we were going she had yet to tell her parents that she had become engaged to me. Her father, an old RFC type, took it well when I asked for his permission to marry his daughter. He said that I wasn't going to make his daughter an early widow and that we would have to wait until after I had finished my tour of operations before the wedding could take place. It was great having one's future father-in-law show such confidence in his future son-in-law's flying ability! Unhappily he was proved right in his wisdom!

January 1944 was to prove to be the worst accident month ever for the Conversion Unit. At least three aircraft were to be lost (two in one day) at the cost of 8 lives. I remember seeing, with some horror, the blood stained kit of two of the victims and avoiding the camp mortuary knowing that their bodies were there.

It was nearly two months before I started to fly again. From the pilot's seat of a Halifax I appreciated how Nelson felt, standing on top of his column in Trafalgar Square; it looked one helluva way down to the ground. Fortunately there were no pigeons in the cockpit - unbeknown to me they were to come later! After three hours dual I was judged ready to go solo but the aeroplane went U/S so I had to wait another day. After a further 25 minutes dual, Sgt Ken Tattersall and I flew an hour's solo each. During my hour I managed to scare him, myself and a gang of workmen at the side of the runway who were moving about with total disregard to landing aircraft. It must have been the same working party reported in the ORB that caused a nasty accident a few days earlier. The aircraft I soloed was Halifax, BB248, a B.II built by the London Passenger Transport Board at Leavesden and had been delivered to the RAF a year earlier. It had been with 77 & 78 Squadrons and then with 1658 HCU before it came to Topcliffe. It was to be written off in a landing accident at Topcliffe in May 1944.

It was about this time I started to arrange for Dorothy to spend a few days of her leave in Thirsk at 'The Golden Fleece'. I told her that I had borrowed Mac's bicycle, but in spite of that, it would be unlikely that I would be able to spend much time with her as it looked as if I would be busy flying. About this time the wife of Ron Thompson, my wireless operator, gave birth to a stillborn baby daughter. Naturally, he was terribly upset and we managed to get him off home on leave.

I read that 16 aircraft were lost on a raid to Stettin - on the night of 5/6th January - 4.5% of the force. It began to sink into my thick skull that I had been particularly lucky not to be participating in a deadly sequence of air operations where, in a period of three weeks, 202 aircraft were lost. The following day we went off for 3 hours circuits and bumps and local flying. I was surprised to see so many airfields in the area and very pleased to find we had an 'iron beam' to home in upon - a railway line that ran roughly 40 miles in a straight line from York to Darlington which would always lead us close to home once spotted. I only hoped that other aircraft using this convenient navigation aid would stick to the rules of the road and fly down it keeping it on their port side (the so-called left hand or portside rule). Fortunately most of the heavy aircraft were on the ground waiting for the next Main Force call.

Three days later brought us to 9th January. Three engine landings, dual and solo, had been completed and during one detail we had an air to air firing session. We fired off the coast at a drogue towed by a Martinet. We didn't shoot the Martinet down and presumably completed the detail successfully.

On the morning of the 10th, I scrounged my way on to the early detail as Dorothy was coming up from London by the afternoon train. I had booked a room for her at 'The Golden Fleece' and was very much looking forward to seeing her again. The early morning detail became late morning when the aircraft went U/S. I got off at 10.45, authorised for a 2 hour sortie which included air to air firing and a height climb to 22,000 feet. I couldn't believe any clapped out Mark II B Halifax[2] could reach 22,000 feet, even without a bomb load. At 10,000 feet I instructed the boys to turn on their oxygen; it was the last time I would do so although we did not know it at the time. I struggled hard to get her up there, she didn't like height and when we reached 22,000 feet she began to wallow horribly. Before she decided to fall out of the sky on her own accord I brought her down gently to go easy on our ears (mine in particular, which gave me no trouble). This was the highest we'd been in an aeroplane but, unfortunately, the panoramic view we had all looked forward to seeing never materialised, cloud covered most of the ground. We landed at 13.30, giving me just enough time to get to the station to meet Dorothy.

An early Halifax B.II series I DG245 of No.138 Squ. lost in March 1943.
An example of the many aircraft used at No. 1659 HCU
(Photo: Crown Copyright ref:138/HAL)

I told the Flight Commander where I was going and he reminded me to be back in time for the night flying detail. I hopped on Mac's bike and pedalled like fury to Thirsk, arriving at the station just in time to watch the only train of the day from London pull smoothly into the station (unbelievably on time). Before it had stopped carriage doors were flung open and people flooded on to the platform. Apart from the heavy breathing of the locomotive it was

[2] - *This aeroplane (DT560) was delivered to the RAF in August 1942 and finally scrapped in November 1945.*

quiet - I felt strangely quiet from within; Dorothy wasn't among those who had dismounted. I'd been jilted! Left waiting at the church! A porter strolled down the platform and with a rhythmic thump slammed shut the remaining open doors. The guard looked at his watch, then with an air of finality, slipped it into his waistcoat pocket. He looked up and down the train, waved his green flag and at the same time giving a shrill blast on his whistle. The engine disappeared in a noisy cloud of smoke and steam and the train began to move slowly out of the station.

I was stunned, there were no more trains from London that day. The guard slid skilfully into his compartment as the door came level with him. The engine strained under its load and the carriages began to gather speed and there, passing before my very eyes, was Dorothy - just gazing indifferently out of the window! Love is blind, of course, and although there wasn't much of the train left in the platform I raced for it, wrenching the door of the last coach open and hauling myself inside. The guard must have been watching my performance, judging by the look he gave me as I legged it past him down the corridor. I didn't wait to hear what category of fool he put me in. I arrived breathless at the compartment where Dorothy sat, blissfully ignorant of the drama she had precipitated. She looked up as I slid the door open and with a lovely smile, which could melt the hardest of hearts said, 'Hello, darling! And where have you come from?' 'From the ruddy station two miles back where you should have got out,' I replied through my teeth. I wasn't too happy, the Air Force did not take kindly to young pilots missing night flying details. It then occurred to my numbed skull that I had rarely seen Dorothy in civvies. With an air of new-found calm I sat down to enjoy the sight of the femininity that was revealed before me.

It transpired that Dorothy had just not realised that she had arrived at Thirsk, numbed as she was by stopping at so many stations on the way up. The next stop was Northallerton, some 8 miles further on, where I was relieved to find there was another train going in the opposite direction in 20 minutes. We crossed the bridge and decided to have tea in the Refreshment Room where, strangely enough, I met Dickie Barnard - a former school master. He was teaching in Northallerton and, as Dorothy and I were about to leave, he invited us to get in touch again and to go to his home for a meal, an invitation I later accepted and was rewarded not only with a wonderful meal but also with a dozen fresh eggs to take back to Topcliffe. It went some way to make up for some of the goodies I had been having out of Kit's parcels from home, he said.

I settled Dorothy in at 'The Golden Fleece' and then, having recovered it from the station, I pedalled Mac's bike like fury back to camp to prepare myself for an 18.25 take off. We took off on time and I was the pilot under instruction for the first session, Fg/Off McLaughlin was the instructor and Ken Tattersall waited in the engineer's compartment to take over from me. We flew for an hour, when par for the course, the aircraft went U/S. We got going again at 20.00 hours in the spare aircraft. Ken was now in the driving seat and I was lounging about in the engineer's compartment. After 50 minutes McLaughlin rose from his seat and told Ken and myself to shoot three landings each and then call it a night. He then disappeared through the rear hatch and out into the darkness. I sat myself next to Ken and away we went. There were no problems with his three landings and on completing his third landing he taxyed round to the threshold of the runway where we swopped seats. I strapped myself in and Ken set himself up in the jump seat beside me. I went through the vital actions and then flashed the aircraft letter on the downward identification light, signalling to the duty pilot that I was ready. From the caravan a green light returned my signal, I was free to go. I turned on to the runway and lined up with the flare path. Slowly I opened the throttles, Ken's left hand following behind mine to prevent them from closing. It wasn't a bad take off, I was ready for the swing and kept her straight, I got the wheels up O.K., and then the flaps. We had just reached safety speed (130 mph) when I noticed the starboard outer rev counter was beginning to wind up. The needle was travelling really fast around the dial. I shouted, 'Ken! the CSU's[3] gone on the starboard outer. Feather the starboard outer!' I shut down the engine and between the two of us we did just that! Probably not as simple as that, probably not without a tremor or two in my voice, but it happened just according to the book. I trimmed out the change in attitude of the aircraft as she yawed to starboard. There we were, established at 300 feet, the starboard outer engine nicely tucked away for the rest of the night, but we weren't gaining an inch of height!

For my next trick, I thought, I would catapult into Dorothy's bedroom window, hotly pursued by red hot gasses and a quantity of aircraft wreckage. We were then right on track for Thirsk and if the worst came to the worst I had the feeling Dorothy would again say, 'Hello, darling! And where have you come from?!' This time I could say that I should have got off at the station two miles back!

I turned the aeroplane gingerly to port and told the control tower over the

---

[3] - *Constant Speed Unit - enables both engine and propeller to operate at high efficiency by maintaining constant RPM. Failure of the CSU can result in the complete loss of engine oil.*

radio that I only had three engines. It didn't seem to bother them as much as it bothered me. For all I knew it was an every day occurrence and they were probably saying to themselves, 'Not another one!' There didn't seem any point in screaming 'Mayday' at them, it would have probably upset me more than it would them. In any case there was little they could do about it other than clear the runway for me. A laconic Canadian voice came over the radio telling me that we were clear to land. By then I had got us down wind and she still stuck at 300 feet and refused to climb an inch higher. Then I remembered when you put down the 15° of flap required in the down wind landing drill you pushed the stick forward to prevent the aeroplane from gaining height. So, I plonked down 15° of flap and pulled back on the 'pole' and we shot up like an elevator to 800 feet - the rest was easy.

Halifax cockpit (Photo: Chaz Bowyer)

To shut down starboard outer engine in flight:

(1) Pull back top right-hand lever (Throttle)

(2) Push down through gate lever below it (Airscrew control lever)

(3) Press right-hand feathering button in roof of cockpit

(4) Switch off starboard outer magneto switches (port switches can be seen above compass)

(5) Turn off fuel (lever behind pilot's head)

(6) If on fire press appropriate extinguisher button - situated to the left.

I got to bed just before midnight, it had been a long tiring day to say the least. In the air for 5 hours 40 minutes; up to 22,000 feet with a struggle and nearly down to earth with a bang; 20 minutes or more pedalling like mad on a bike; a death defying leap into the last compartment of a moving train; then spending 40 minutes or so journeying on two of them, and not the least of all of having one's mind kicked through all the emotions of bitter disappointment, elation, and fear. What a day!

One can never tell with a CSU failure, it could even have been the instrument playing up. Under the circumstances there wasn't much time or height to ask oneself which it could have been but, with a night's sleep behind me, I was anxious to find out and decided to have a look at that aeroplane. The early morning air was thick with fog, it clung to you like a shroud, a beautiful morning! It was so thick I could hardly see the front wheel of the bike I was riding. I found the dispersal where the aircraft stood with some difficulty, and the NCO i/c confirmed that the CSU had failed, also that the starboard outer engine was completely U/S. Ken and I had just caught that engine in time - at the very worst it could have led to the shedding of a prop or an engine fire.

It was with even greater difficulty that I found my way back to the flight offices afterwards. Flying had been cancelled and I asked the Flight Commander if he had any objections to my going to Thirsk. As he already knew the reason he readily agreed. Ring in early he said, as I was again on the 6 o'clock night flying detail. If the weather improved I would be flying at that time. I jumped on Mac's bike and pedalled furiously through the thick fog to Thirsk - strangely, I had no difficulty in finding my way! About midday it began to snow heavily and rather than look elsewhere Dorothy and I decided to have lunch in the hotel. Kit, Eric, Ernie and Lloyd joined us in the afternoon. Dorothy stoked up the lounge fire and we took tea in front of it, we all appreciated the unaccustomed comfort. The boys went back to camp and I telephoned in - night flying had been cancelled - it would be OK to sleep out of camp if I wanted too, telephone again in the morning to see what the form was.

For the want of something better to do Dorothy and I went to the cinema, a quaint little barn-like building with a corrugated iron roof. Nearly every seat in the house was taken and we found ourselves on the balcony in what was called a 'Lover's Seat'. A double wooden seat with the centre arm rest removed, it had a powerful spring and when you got up it folded back with a wallop! The film was one of those comedies much loved in the North and featured Jimmie James, Enoch and Ramsbottom. The audience rocked with laughter at the antics of Jimmie James flicking his cigarette ash all over the place. Fortunately I had Dorothy in our dual seat to keep me warm and my attention was suitably occupied elsewhere. All she can remember of the show was the seat was damned hard - so much for romance!

We returned to the hotel I asked the receptionist if I could have a room for the night, only to be told the hotel was full. I said that was a great pity since my fiancée was on leave and was staying at the hotel. I added because of the bad weather I had just been released from duty that night. Whilst my sad story made little impression on the receptionist it certainly made one on someone else! 'What a shame,' said a voice from behind me. I turned to see an elderly lady standing before me who must have been well into her late sixties - a great age through the eyes of a twenty year old! 'Would it not be possible to free my room by putting me in with my friend, Mrs......?' (regrettably I have forgotten her name) she asked. I politely refused her kind offer, but she insisted that the arrangement be made. At their age it must have been a great sacrifice for them both and Dorothy and I were truly grateful for their kindness.

We had dinner and afterwards sat in the lounge before a blazing fire with the rest of the residents. It was a great luxury for both of us since we both came from units where heat was at a premium. Apart from the two charming elderly ladies I can only remember two other guests, a Commander RN and his wife. I remember the Commander because he was knitting a pullover! Knitting was his hobby he said. Dorothy and I passed those two elderly ladies on the stairs as we went to our rooms. You could see by the look on their faces that they were very pleased with themselves.

Thick fog hugged the ground the next morning. Fantastic weather! I telephoned in as instructed to be told there would be no flying that day, it was so bad even the Link trainer was grounded! Would I check in later for the night flying detail. It didn't really matter as I was back in camp before night fall; Dorothy caught the afternoon train for London. I wrote a desperate letter on the day of her departure saying what a fool I had been not coming as far as York with her. Probably it was just as well, you can push your luck too far! I have the hotel bill for those three days before me. It totals £4.12s.6d or in today's currency £4.65p. It cost 9/6d per night for the room and breakfast (48p); dinner for two cost £1; tea and sandwiches for 6 persons cost 46p and the bill also included a 10% service charge. The hotel was part of the Trust House Group and as far as I know still is. Three days at a first class hotel for £4.65p how times have changed!

The day after Dorothy had gone the weather cleared and we got into the air with a vengeance. Two day sorties lasting 3 hours 35 minutes when we went up and down the iron beam on two engines during the first sortie and two at night lasting 3 hours 55. Towards the end of the second sortie my bladder again got the better of me. So I went through the rigmarole of putting Eric into the driving seat. By the time we had finished I was bursting and really had to leg it to the rear of the aircraft to attack the Elsan. When I had finished I thought it might be a good idea to leg it forward again this time to relieve Eric. Now legging it about from end to end in a Halifax isn't quite as easy as it sounds. It is quite dangerous and if in a hurry one must be particularly careful where you put your head and your legs or you were likely to finish the course as a bald soprano!

I remember asking myself where all those stars had come from! What was I doing on the floor with Ernie standing over me shaking my shoulder? What was he shouting above the engine noise - Was I was all right? I got to my feet and staggered forward to get back into my seat. I had a terrific lump on my head. Ernie said I had gone head first into the mid upper turret with such force that he had felt the thump. Looking down he had seen me lying on the floor, so he got down from his turret to see if I was OK. I didn't live that one down for a long time and it was suggested that I might in future take a milk bottle with me. That night after a brief period of dual we shot circuits and bumps for another three and a quarter hours.

I still kept in touch with a number of my contemporaries. Pip Hagues was still on the ground at 1652 HCU, Marston Moor after swimming in mud on assault courses. In a letter from No 4 Group Battle School at Driffield he said that he had ruined one pair of shoes, four pairs of socks and lost two finger nails. He had aching feet and an aching back. So far as he was concerned he was neutral and didn't care who blew the place up! (Shades of Jock Connell at Hemswell!) He was also suffering from the same malady as I - he'd seen Audrey in civilian clothes for the first time! He started HCU ground school on the same day as I had finished. He had gained nothing other than his aching back having been first to leave Forres in October. Dick Charlier, my co-pilot at 22 Air School wrote frequently. I last heard from him in India after a spell in hospital with jaundice in Cairo. While in hospital his Dakota Squadron No 117 left for India. When fit Dick chased after them only to be told when he caught them up that he was not wanted! Dick was hopping mad since he said he had left behind a very nice WREN! I think he later flew Yorks but I never heard from him again.

Johnnie Morgan used to write often from No 15 M.U. at Wroughton where he was a Flight Commander. Most of his letters were full of quotations from Rupert Brooke or Rudyard Kipling. He said he expected to stay in his job about ten months, he was getting plenty of flying. I met him once at Lympne after the war, he was flying Avro 748's for some airline or other; from his attitude it was clear he didn't wish to meet again.

Dorothy was my most prolific correspondent, a day or night rarely went by without her putting pen to paper. Reading through them, some 40 or more years on (they are all here!), I find them full of news, fun and humour. Mind you, I wrote nearly every day myself - so much so that it caused Kit to remark that I should have been an author![4] One letter to her I headed, 'Same bloody place.' She said, in reply, that the same day she had received a letter from Audrey Shepherd headed, 'Same super station!' (Biggin Hill!).

At that time Dorothy was an LACW teleprinter operator in the Signal Section of 11 Group Headquarters at Uxbridge. Their equipment was primitive compared with today's teleprinter operation - no VDUs or computers to assist the sending of their coded messages. They used to work eight hour shifts and were on duty 24 hours a day. Dorothy's show at Uxbridge was run by a married corporal called 'Spud' Murphy and the girls adored him. He certainly knew how to organise and discipline a bunch of extremely overworked 20 year old girls. 11 Group was in Fighter Command and rarely did she let me forget it. In fact the kisses at the bottom of her letters were always in finger four formation. Mind you at times there were so many you would have thought she had got the whole Group airborne! Dorothy rarely complained, although she did send this rhyme to me:-

The WAAF stood at the Pearly Gates, her face was haggard and old,
and timidly she asked the Saint for admission to the fold.
'What have you done?' St. Peter asked, 'to gain admission here?'
'I've been a Tele/Op,' she said, 'for many and many a year.'
The gate was flung wide open, St. Peter rang the bell
'Come he said and take a harp you've had your share of Hell!'

Dare I say it - she's been harping ever since!

Ron returned from leave on 17th January only to see Mac unwell and disappearing into hospital for treatment. They said I could wait for his recovery if I wanted; I said I wanted. In the meantime, having finished the course and just in case we were posted before Mac returned, we were given another flight engineer, a round faced Englishman, a really nice chap.

In the meantime we were sent on sea searches, looking for those poor

---

[4] - *Someone who read this manuscript commented, 'Why didn't he keep his big mouth shut!'*

unfortunates who were sitting in a dinghy in the North Sea. We took off at 14.30 hours and headed east out to the North Sea. For four and a quarter hours we meticulously carried out our square search over a very rough and dark grey sea. We saw nothing but an empty dinghy and a half submerged barrage balloon. We thanked our lucky stars we were able to return safely to base.

The following day we were briefed that out of 648 aircraft sent to Magdeburg the previous night (21/22nd January) 57 (8.8%) had been lost. After this hammering we were to be sent out again to search for survivors. This time I was to fly 'second dickie' to a Canadian pilot officer who had just arrived at Topcliffe, he was quite mad and irresponsible. Unbelievably, after 3 hours 15 minutes of the patrol, he said that he was bored stiff and would return to base. I couldn't believe my ears as we still had another hour to go. There may have been someone out there waiting and praying that someone would turn up and spot them. He wouldn't listen to me and turned back towards home.

We crossed the coast at a height less than that of the lowest hills and I managed to get him to fly higher, but we were in cloud which he didn't like, so he descended to have a look. He saw an airfield ahead of us, Wombleton, and did a quick circuit, saying he was going to land and chose a runway that had a lot of contracting equipment on it. To me our direction looked bloody dangerous and I said so; at least it persuaded him to open up and go round again. In bad visibility he was still flying dangerously low among surrounding hills so I suggested, as I knew the area well, perhaps he would like me to take over. Or, alternatively, get some height, find the Leeming beam, fly down it, break cloud over the flat ground and find our way to Topcliffe.

Some of the crew were getting a little anxious about his instability and insisted he listened to what I was saying. Fortunately he did and I found base for him and we landed. Eric my, bomb aimer and the only member of my crew flying with us, paid me a great compliment by saying with a grin on his face, 'Nobbie, if you hadn't come along today I would have been really scared!' The Canadian was sick and should have been grounded.

The following day we again flew out to the North Sea, this time for a 6 hour search. Mac was back on board again so we flew as a complete crew, it was quite an eventful trip. After spotting another barrage balloon drifting across the grey water we were near to the Yorkshire coastline when we saw some flares going up. We went over to have a look and there below in the water was a USAF B17. The crew had already taken to their dinghy and were waving their arms and pooping off flares as if it were the 5th

November (or 4th July!). There were numerous aeroplanes circling, so there wasn't any point in our hanging about. We shoved off to carry on with our search. At the end of our patrol we went back to have another look, the B17 was now lower in the water and the dinghy further away from it. Later, we saw an Air Sea Rescue launch pounding its way through the rough sea towards it. How that B17 got there I don't know, the USAF were operating in the Pas de Calais area that day.

We were all exhausted and glad when the weather closed in and we were able to rest. Half of the course had already been posted and unbeknown to us we still had a night cross-country to fly before we finished. Topcliffe was getting me down - I couldn't get away fast enough. I was frozen, there wasn't any fuel for the fire and the messing sickened me. Then, to my utter joy, we were posted to No 138 Squadron at Tempsford for Special Duties. Nobody seemed to know was this meant, someone remembered that one of the 'screens' had served on 138 and introduced me to him. I asked him what kind of a squadron 138 was. He refused to answer any of my questions and said I would have to wait until I got to Tempsford to find out - he wasn't going to tell me.

That night we flew our last cross-country, taking off at 1800 hours we were back just after midnight. There was a lot of air activity and I was surprised to see how interwoven the circuits of the airfields were. The 'Drem' lighting of some looking like giant clover leaves. We touched down smoothly at Topcliffe without the slightest suspicion of a bounce, just to show the boys I could really do it... if I tried.

Next day I packed my gear and found that all my shoes needed repairing! Then came the long walk around the camp getting signatures on my clearance certificate. My log book showed, as a Heavy Bomber pilot, my Flying Assessment was average plus (6). I had 496 Hours 20 minutes total flying. Sergeant Albert Stanley had 31 hours and 8 minutes (20 hours 28 minutes solo) pilot flying time when he went to France in April 1917 to join No 13 Squadron.

Topcliffe ORB says we were posted to Tempsford with Sgt. M.F.Radcliffe. I found no mention of Ken Tattersall who also came! He was later commissioned at Tempsford, served with No 161 Squadron and received the DFC. He once brought back a Halifax with a high tension cable wrapped round it! A sparkling performance! The ORB also said that they had taken us as part of an RAF intake, although we had a number of Canadians among us. So my dream of flying a Halifax MkIII with a RCAF Squadron never was on, but it was that dream that kept me going in that wretched place! It is interesting to note that 1659 HCU Topcliffe had on strength at that time 31

MkII Halifaxes and 2 MkVs.

It was raining hard when we drove into the cobbled market square of Thirsk. The ivy covered facade of the old coaching inn had not changed. The golden effigy of a limp fleece still hung high above the front entrance. A sign above it pronounced 'Golden Fleece'. The bad weather that predominated our last encounter was still about! I drove into the courtyard and parked. Dorothy and I walked into the hotel - the ghosts and the memories were unquestionably there. We obtained a room, dined and took ourselves to bed, it had been a long day. This time we slept in the same room! We had breakfast next morning and I paid the bill. Before leaving Thirsk we did a little exploring. The old cinema building was boarded up and looked in a very sorry state of repair. We drove off in the direction of the A1, stopping, at the main gate of the airfield. A notice board indicated the RAF had long since gone and that the Army had now taken over - I felt it was time that I went too, I had never been happy there.

CHAPTER NINE

R.A.F. TEMPSFORD, SANDY, BEDFORDSHIRE.

'Posted for Special Duties - Air and Ground conflict'

Low-hanging moon!
What is that dusky spot in your brown yellow?
O it is the shape, the shape of my mate!
O moon, do not keep her from me any longer.

'Out of the Cradle Endlessly Rocking' - Walt Whitman.

The journey to Tempsford was a nightmare, transport from Topcliffe to Thirsk was late and we found ourselves with a barrow piled high with kit, pleading with the station master to hold the train. He ignored our pleas and it departed without us. Hours later we took another train, it was running late. All 21 of us with over 50 pieces of kit changed at York then Grantham and finally ground to a halt at Peterborough. Here the RTO (Rail Transport Officer) said the next train to Sandy would depart the following morning! How we blessed that station master at Thirsk!

We left the RTO's office with the sergeant and the corporal arguing over an orange that I had left on the counter! We spent the night at Toc H. since all the hotels in town were full (probably with Americans)! Here, MacBurney, in his inimitable manner flattened someone for calling us a 'sprog crew'!

We arrived at Sandy the following morning. Powdered snow scurried across the car park like wisps of wind driven sand across a desert, it was bitterly cold. A crew bus waited for us and, inevitably, it was parked in the farthest corner! We lugged our baggage aboard and we moved off to RAF Tempsford. At a barrier on top of a hill we stopped, those in charge of it appeared to be very particular whom they let through. The rear doors of the bus were opened and an RAF corporal peered in, counted us and verified the figure from a piece of paper held in his hand. The barrier lifted and the bus moved on, stopping first at the Sergeants' Mess and then at the Officers' Mess. The camp was very widely dispersed! 'What a dump!' said Kit, reflecting my own thoughts.

We were told to report to 138 Squadron flight office and in the distance I could see Halifaxes at dispersal. They looked very black, their silhouettes accentuated by a background of sprinkled snow. They had four-bladed airscrews and were without mid upper turrets. They were Mk.V's with a Dowty undercarriage and one less emergency system for lowering the undercart! A cold wind swept across the airfield and I remember tucking my head deep down into the collar of my greatcoat. Kit and I reported to Flt/Lt Jaffe, the adjutant of 138 Squadron. He, in turn, introduced us to the Squadron Commander Wg/Cdr 'Dickie' Speare. He said we had been allocated to 'A' flight commanded by Sqdn/Ldr Cooke and then told us what it was all about. I remember how bitterly disappointed I was when he told us that 138 Squadron was not a Main Force Bomber Command Squadron. It was engaged on clandestine work dropping agents and supplies by parachute to the Resistance. Operations extended throughout Europe and were carried out at low level during the moon period. We would operate singly and navigate ourselves from pin point to pin point until we arrived at the DZ (dropping zone).

No. 138 Squadron badge. A Gordian knot, representing occupied Europe, being cut by the sword of St. Paul. The squadron was first formed May 1918 and disbanded February 1919. Reformed in 1940 and finally disbanded in 1962

(Photo:Crown Copyright ref:CH14437)

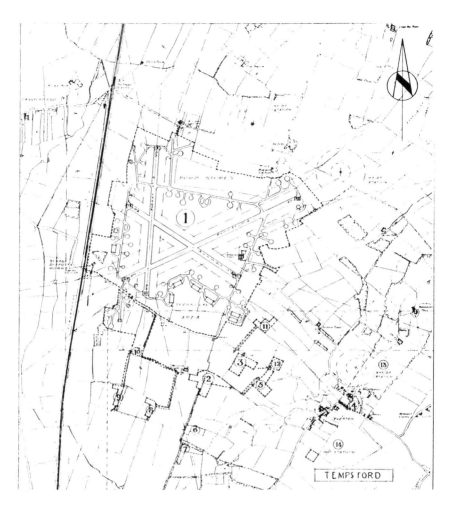

RAF Tempsford. The railway can be clearly seen and the
Great North Road (A1) was a little to the west (Plan: RAF Museum)

Our sister squadron at Tempsford was No 161 which, he went on to explain, also had a flight of Halifaxes ('B' Flight) used for the same purpose. In addition 'A' Flight flew Lysanders and 'C' Flt flew Hudsons - both of which landed in Enemy Occupied Territory. I was stunned by this piece of intelligence. All of the activities at Tempsford, he went on to say, were top secret and he could not overemphasise this fact. We were not to discuss our operations outside the limits of the airfield.

Tempsford from 3000 feet. The main railway line is on the left and the cooling towers are top left (Photo: RAF Museum ref:W8/2/6)

This interview depressed me and so I tried to look at it positively and count the credits. I could find none except that the airfield was only 40 miles from London! Low level operational flying at night, alone and deep into enemy occupied territory - a sobering thought rather than a credit! Although I had feared the high level work of Bomber Command might trouble my ears I had never considered the other end of the spectrum - how low level night work might damage my health!

They started to hack the airfield at Tempsford out of a marsh late in 1940, finished it in the late summer 1941, and No 138 Squadron arrived from Newmarket in March 1942. In mid winter January 1944 it was a bleak, desolate, muddy place. It had three concrete runways; No 3, on the west side of the field, was 1,600 yards (QDM 010 & 190) running roughly due north and south and almost parallel to the main LNER London to Edinburgh railway. At the northern end on the other side of the railway stood a small power station with one large cooling tower. If you hooked your take off going north it came into play and really scared the pants off you. I don't ever remember taking off to the south on this runway. The shortest runway, No 2, was 1383 yards (QDM 130 & 310) running roughly from south-east to north-west. Taking off in the westerly direction, the railway banking quickly loomed up in front of you looking like a mountain range. If a train had passed at the same time as you went over you could have finished up at

Kings Cross or Edinburgh depending which direction it was going! I never went the other way so I never knew what hairy surprises that held. The main runway, No 1, was 2,000 yards long (QDM 070 & 250) running roughly north-east to south-west. During my short tour at Tempsford we used this runway most of the time. It presented no problem in either direction.

Surprisingly, I found the Halifax difficult to taxy at Tempsford, she tended to weathercock into the strong winter winds that rushed across the airfield. Once off the taxy track you were up to your axles in mud, another sobering thought, especially at night if other aircraft were taxying out behind you. I thought Tempsford was a poor airfield, a dump, and I am sure No 3 Group Bomber Command must have been pleased dumping it onto a Special Duty Unit!

South of the triangle formed by the intersection of the runways stood the control tower. Behind it were a cluster of four black B1 type hangars and beyond, a conglomeration of buildings making up the engineering, headquarters, and domestic sites. I never knew where the infamous Gibraltar Farm was situated - a barn like building where agents were readied for dropping. Pilots of my rank weren't allowed near the place!

Construction work was still going on at Tempsford and it was said that 300 workmen from the Irish Republic were encamped on the airfield. I well remember a number of them taking a keen interest in the containers being loaded onto my aeroplane. With security being the watchword it gave me an uncomfortable feeling at the time. The Officers' Mess was a large Maycrete hut built of brick and concrete with an asbestos roof. The entrance, through a small wooden door, led into a hall where the floor was covered with a highly polished dark brown lino. On the left was a large ante-room and a door on the right led to the dining room. In the centre of the ante-room was a brick fireplace in which a fire blazed all the time. Wooden beams traversed the room from which struts radiated supporting the high roof. I remember those beams well. During a drunken party after the war someone was nailed to them by his braces. He dangled there gently bouncing up and down like a yo-yo!

In the left far corner of the room was a small bar and beside it stood an upright piano against the wall. Used not only by pianists but also, judging by the number of rings on its lid, by beer drinkers as a parking place for their glasses. Opposite the bar was the games room in which there was a billiard table and table tennis, both were very popular. Somewhere there was a radio and a gramophone, one or the other usually on full blast most of the time - saturating the atmosphere with the melodies of Glen Miller, the Ink Spots and the Andrew Sisters. In all the mess was a warm and friendly place.

In letters to Dorothy I enthuse about our food and living standards, anything must have been better than Topcliffe. Probably the promise of eleven days leave two weeks hence had much to do with my buoyant mood. I was more than pleased to meet two friends of mine: Gordon Hart, a navigator, we had been at school together; and Dennis Carroll, a pilot with 138 Squadron, who came home with me from South Africa.

It was four days before we were airborne; Plt/Off Pick took us up twice to have a look around. We dropped a few dummy containers and packages on a DZ laid out on the airfield at Henlow. As we circled Henlow, Pick suddenly said, 'Keep a bloody good look out for the chimneys.' There were dozens of them surrounding the brick-fields of the London Brick Company, each 150 feet high and looking like starved skittles. Six weeks before Sgt Williams, flying a Halifax from Tempsford, had knocked one over and nine lives were lost. We ran in at 500 feet, dropped and returned to base in time for tea.

Dennis Carroll had a car and suggested a few of us went out for a beer. I was happy to go, I hadn't been out of the camp since our arrival. In complete darkness, we parked in the square at Gamlingay, the village policeman recommending a pub a few yards away. At closing time the landlord said he didn't get many RAF in his house so we could make a night of it behind closed doors. He told us he was an ex-special branch London policeman. Later our 'bobby' joined us, had a pint and went off on his beat. We spent most of the night drinking and playing poker dice.

At an early hour we decided we'd had enough and weaved out to Dennis's car and he drove home though I don't know how! I do know I woke next morning with an appalling hangover! I often wondered if that landlord was still active in the Special Branch and had been put in that pub to keep an eye on us all. There were a number of RAF and USAF bases nearby.

Fg/Off Ashley took us on a night training sortie to Henlow. We were dropping on a DZ we could expect to see in enemy territory. It consisted of three or four white lights, approximately 50 metres apart in the shape of an inverted 'L'. Beside the first white light a red one flashed the site code letter. We flew towards the base of the 'L' and above the centre light we dropped the containers from a height of 500 feet. An agent would be dropped from 800 feet, it was all very simple. The trick was finding the site in enemy held territory! We were back in the mess within an hour. The following afternoon I found my name on the Operations Board flying as second pilot to F/Sgt H.F.G. Murray and his crew. We had our target briefing which was 'BUTLER 14' at pinpoint 47 37 24 North. 00 57 21 West. The DZ would be flashing 'Z' and our final briefing told us we would have perfect weather conditions. We were to be the only 138 Squadron aircraft operating that night.

At 21.02hrs on the night of 3/4th February 1944 we took off, flew down to Reading, thence to Selsey Bill and south towards France. At 22.15hrs at a height of 5,000 feet we crossed the coast at Pte la Percee (midway between Grandcamp and Port-en-Bessin, just west of the Normandy beaches). I remember it was a beautiful night, the light from the moon made it as bright as day, visibility was fantastic. We flew into the DZ area and arrived over the pinpoint at 23.30hrs and circled, but could see no sign of it. Murray was about to give up when I spotted the lights, they were very difficult to see in the bright moonlight. I pointed them out to him and we could just make out a red light flashing 'Z'. So we turned towards it, made our run in at 500 feet and dropped. Murray was annoyed to find although the packages had gone our containers had 'hung up'; around we went again and this time, to everyone's relief, they dropped out over the middle light. On the way back we dropped leaflets in the Laval area.

We landed back at base at 01.56hrs having been in the air 4 hours 55 minutes. It had been a text book trip; the weather forecast had been correct, the reception committee had been in place and the lights turned on at the right time. *'BUTLER 14'*, *'AUTHOR 9'* and *'BOB 78'* were the respective code names given to DZ's operated by those SOE (Special Operations Executive) circuits, or *reseaux* in French, working in France.

During my research I discovered that *'BUTLER 14'* was a site operated by the Germans! (In retrospect quite an introduction to my Operational career!) The twelve store drops on *'BUTLER'* sites, of which we were one, were intended to help disrupt communications between Brittany and the rest of France. The organisers had long been captured and the Germans operated these sites for 9 months. Regrettably Flt/Lt Johnson (a pilot of No 138 Squadron) was to drop two agents (J.T.J.Detal and P.F.Duclos) on *'BUTLER 12'* during the night 29th Feb/1st March; both were captured. On 7th March, one week later, two more agents (Marcel Defence and Octave Simon) were dropped on a *'BUTLER'* site and were to suffer the same fate. I can find no mention of this drop either in No 138 or No 161 Squadron records. In addition Francs 1,150,000 (then £5750) were dropped on *'BUTLER'* sites between December 1943 and May 1944. ('SOE in France' M.R.D.Foot. HSMO pages 335 & 345). Warrant Officer H.F.G.Murray and five of his crew were killed during a mission to Holland on the night of 1st June 1944, two survivors were taken prisoner.

The following night, 4/5th, I flew with Flying Officer Ashley and his crew. The primary objective was *'AUTHOR 9'* flashing 'C' situated at 45 05

17 North, 01 32 49 East. The alternative was *'AUTHOR 15'* flashing 'Q'; both sites were situated near Brive, in France. It was incredible to think that a coded message transmitted by the BBC during their normal French service would alert these reception committees. As we were taxying out, two black USAF B24's steamed down the runway. They must have on *'Carpetbagger'* (SOE) missions. Previous B24 missions had been recorded in Tempsford's ORB but these were not. We took off at 21.25hrs with 15 containers and 4 packages on board. Our route was Selsey, Pte la Percee, The Loire, Roullet, Perigueux, Brive and then to the pinpoint. The cloud was 9/10ths most of the way but obtained rare *'GEE'* fixes within 50 miles of the target area. We could not find any reception at *'AUTHOR 9'* so turned our attention to the alternative *'AUTHOR 15'*, where we arrived at 00.30hrs, and positively identified the DZ. We flew around for 25 minutes waiting for the reception lights to appear, they didn't - so we went home. We saw two Stirlings[1] on our way, one was coned by searchlights and being clobbered by flak, the other crossed our track 200/300 feet ahead and 200 feet above - it was as busy as Place Etoile![2] We dumped our F2 leaflets near Angouleme and landed at Tempsford with our undelivered load at 04.40hrs.

That night Flt/Lt Johnnie Downe's aircraft was hit by machine gun fire, catching it on fire in the nose and in the rear turret. Nonetheless he returned safely, his load undelivered! P/O Pick also had *'AUTHOR 9'* as his target. He arrived earlier than us and completed his mission. I expect the reception committee had had enough by the time we arrived and had gone home!

The next night 5/6th February, 138 Squadron sent seven aircraft to France, three to Norway and three to Denmark. I was still to take my crew on their first operation. With mixed feelings I stayed on the ground and watched the other crews go! The moon was just rising; they were using the long runway taking off to the west. In particular I remember the Stirlings, I wondered what the side effect of the cross wind had on them with that enormous tail. How ungainly and spindly they looked on the ground, not unlike a walking

---

[1] - *Two Stirling Squadrons, Nos 90 and 149, arrived at Tempsford to take part in these 'moon period' operations. No 149 was the only Stirling Squadron to have a crew member awarded the V.C. It also had the doubtful privilege of completing Bomber Command's last Stirling operational sortie on 8th September 1944.*

[2] - *Place Etoile - now Place Charles DeGaulle - a very busy road intersection in Paris in the centre of which stands the Arc de Triomphe.*

heron, but once in the air, like a heron, they took on a new dimension of beauty. When they poured on full power down the runway the centre of their Hercules radial engines glowed red hot! After seeing most of the effort take off I decided to go out for a beer and finished up at the WAAFs' dance. I didn't stay long and was soon in my bed.

Although our names were on the Ops. Board for the night of 7/8th and we had air tested our aircraft, LW276, our operation was cancelled. Only four 138 Squadron aircraft took off that night, the Squadron Commander, Wg/Cmdr Dickie Speare, 'A' Flight Commander Sqdn/Ldr T.C.Cooke, Johnnie Downes (his 5th sortie in 9 days) and Dennis Carroll. They all went to France, only one sortie was completed. Sqdn/Ldr Cooke DFC, DFM, whose target was *'JOCKEY 15'* was lost, he and his entire commissioned crew escaped from the wreck. Sadly my friend, Fg/Off G.O.Carroll, and his crew were killed, his target was *'JOHN 35'*. Unaware that he was already dead I missed him and prayed he was OK.

Halifax Mk. V similar to K-King. An aircraft of No. 644 Squadron used for glider towing and also for SOE supply drops. It has the same four-bladed props and the mid-upper turret has been fared over. (Photo: Via Phillip Jarrett)

I was given a brand new Halifax MkV, LL252 'K' King, - powered by Rolls Royce Merlin XXII engines. It was unusual for a new crew to be given their own aeroplane, let alone a new one. My ground crew said they had the last 'K' King for a long time. I said I earnestly hoped they would have this one a long time too! We took her up for a 15 minute air test with the full crew prior to the night's operations.

Sgt Eric Keep, the bomb aimer and 'Kit' Carson RCAF, the navigator; both sat in the nose. Eric was responsible for assisting me fly the aeroplane, map reading, guiding us in over the DZ and dropping the load. Low level map reading at night was extremely difficult and none of us had had any previous experience at it. Kit's table faced the port fuselage wall and now out of the way of any nocturnal meandering to the Elsan. At his right, to assist him with his navigation, were two RADAR sets. One *'GEE'* the other *'REBECCA'*.

Simply, *'GEE'* was an ingenious radio receiver contained in a small metal box about 18 inches long 9 inches wide and probably 12 inches deep. Within it was a cathode ray tube about six inches in diameter. When the set was switched on, radio pulses received from ground stations were displayed on a green screen. By manipulating control knobs the navigator moved a scale over the pulses and read off a series of co-ordinates. These co-ordinates were then plotted on to a special latticed Mercator chart from which the aircraft's position was fixed. Unhappily, enemy jamming rendered the set useless soon after reaching the coast, but sometimes, when miles into enemy occupied territory, one would get a freak fix.

'REBECCA' was not always fitted. It was similar in size and looked like a *'GEE'* set. The cathode ray tube in this set interpreted the distance and direction from signals received from a small radio transmitter (*'EUREKA'*) operated from a DZ. It was virtually impossible to jam and the signals received in the aircraft had a range of about 25 miles. Underneath the pilot's seat, facing forward, on the same level as the navigator, sat Sgt Ron Thompson, the wireless op/air gunner. He operated the radio equipment, a Marconi R1155 receiver, and a Marconi T1154 transmitter. On the 1155 he listened out for any Group broadcasts and, in conjunction with the transmitter, obtained radio bearings at the request of the navigator. He also obtained the BBC at the request of the pilot (although frowned upon) and, most important, wound in the trailing aerial before we landed in case we clobbered someone on the ground with it or broke it off (which negligence would make him very unpopular with the Radio Section).

The flight engineer's panel was directly behind me. Here Sgt 'Mac' McBurney RCAF, the flight engineer, stood facing aft, attending a multitude of engine instruments. He also kept an eye on the fuel consumption. When not employed scrutinising his instruments he kept his head in the astro dome searching the night sky for enemy aircraft. Sgt Ernie Wilkinson was recruited into our crew as a mid-upper gunner, but as 138 Squadron aircraft did not have mid-upper turrets, he was now the dispatcher. He was responsible, when over the DZ, for pushing out agents, packages and any other odd gear through a circular hatch in the rear of the fuselage. What Ernie did meantime I never knew. I do remember his cheerful face peering over my shoulder once or twice, but it must have been an awful bore for him. He was the only member of the crew allowed into Gibraltar Farm[3]. The removal of the mid upper turret obviously saved weight, increased our range, created more space for the packages, long range fuel tanks and all the other clobber they stowed in the rear of our aircraft. In spite of this there is no doubt in my mind that its added protection would have enabled us to fight back more effectively thus preventing many unnecessary squadron casualties.

The crew of K-King. Sitting, left to right: Ernie Wilkinson, 'Kit' Carson, self, Lloyd Brown, 'Mac' McBurney. Standing, Ron Thompson and Eric Keep.

[3] - *Unhappily I am unable to ask him what the place was like, he died a few years back. I don't think it was any more mysterious than an old barn with a few racks fixed to the wall for storing gear. Who called there to collect it is another story.*

Sgt Lloyd Brown RCAF, was the rear gunner, who sat in a Boulton & Paul turret nursing 4 x .303 Browning machine guns. We reported to the briefing room for our first 'Op.' during the late afternoon of 8th February 1944, we had waited a long time for this moment. Ten 138 Squadron crews were there together with the Halifax crews of 161 Squadron and the Stirling crews. It was basically a weather briefing, there was not, as in Bomber Command, a dramatic unveiling of the target and its route. It was the only briefing at which I remember seeing the Station Commander. He said nothing, no encouraging message of good luck, nothing, he leaned against the wall of the briefing room smoking a cigarette from a long cigarette holder. He usually spent the moon period at Tangmere with the Lysanders of 161 Sqdn which operated from there. Most of us thought he had little time for Halifax crews - we were small beer. He was obviously at Tempsford that night to receive a 161 Hudson operation, due to land dramatically early next morning.

After the main briefing, Kit, Eric, Ron and I went into a nearby room for our target briefing. We were going to France - our target, *'BOB 78'*, was south east of Orleans, near Chatillon-sur-Loire. We took off at 21.05hrs, and 37 minutes later we whistled down the entire length of Bogner pier at zero feet! Across the Channel to Cabourg, thence to Belleme, some Isles in the Loire, Sancerre and to Chatillon. We had made four runs at the target, and decided the fifth would be our last, when three bonfires and a non flashing red light were lit in front of us. We dropped our load at 600 feet through a heavy snow shower, visibility was down to 500-600 yards! We made haste for home the same way as we came in.

What a terrible night for a reception committee to be out! Apart from getting to the DZ to set it up, they had, after we had gone, to collect the containers and packages, dispose of them and the parachutes and tidy up the site for the next drop; all during a curfew and under noses of the enemy. These faceless persons were the true heroes of the hour.

Ten minutes from base, over the R/T, I heard the chatter of other aircraft asking Tempsford for a turn to land. It seemed a good time to reserve my place otherwise we would be out here all night. I switched on my face microphone pressed the transmission button on the control wheel and said 'Hello, Brasstray, Goldchain 'K' King, my turn to land please, over.' A cheerful female voice came over my headphones, 'Goldchain 'K' King this is Brasstray, your turn to land 4 out.' We had timed it nicely, the speed was down to 140 mph when we reached the airfield Drem lights and instructions came from the control tower. 'Goldchain 'K' King, your turn to land number one, over.' I acknowledged, checked with Ron that the aerial was in,

'Brasstray' - Tempsford's control tower showing runway 07 in use with fire tender and 'blood waggon'in attendance (Photo C. Annis via Ken Merrick)

reminded Kit, Eric and Ron to move out of the nose and take up their landing positions, Eric set up the jump seat beside me and strapped himself in. The main runway lights ran down the edge of the port wing tip and I advised 'Goldchain' that we were now downwind, and selected 'undercarriage down' which rumbled out of its housings beneath the inboard engines. A small light on an instrument in front of me turned from red to green. Mixture controls to rich and airscrew controls to fully fine - just in case I made a 'cock up' of the landing and had to go round again. Down with half flap, push the nose forward to counter the tendancy for the aircraft to gain height, all trims to neutral and turn into wind. The runway lights appeared, stretching out before me and the glide path indicator blinking green, beckoning me to the ground. Slowly back on the throttles, speed down to 100 mph, down with the rest of the flap. Over the runway threshold, throttles fully back, gently back on the pole. She bounced, protesting that the air was her domain, then settled, the tail wheel touching a moment later. We ran fast between runway lights, streaming white either side of us, and a touch of squealing brakes finally slowed us to a halt. I moved the throttles of the inboard motors forward, the inertia generated by the airscrews taxyed us down the remaining length of the runway. We turned off and I raised the flaps, pressed the button on the control wheel and said into the microphone, 'Brasstray, Goldchain 'K' King landed, goodnight.' 'Goodnight 'K' King' the WAAF replied.

We moved slowly between coloured taxy track lights, the aircraft gently bouncing on her hydraulics, the phosphorescent-lit instrument needles dancing as we ran over each bump, the engines murmuring. Two torches penetrating the darkness signalled me to come ahead. A change in the signal pattern instructed me to turn right. I pushed the rudder bar to the right, opened up the port outer motor and squeezed the brake intermittently to avoid turning on a static wheel. The aircraft slowly responded and amid protesting squeals from the starboard brake turned a half circle facing the direction from which we had just come. The torches signalled me to cut engines. I carried out the shutting down procedure, finally the fuel cocks are closed and ignition switches were flicked to 'Off' and the four-bladed airscrews rotated slowly to a halt. Above the unaccustomed silence there was the clatter of movement from inside the aircraft. I unstrapped myself, unfastened the last umbilical cords of oxygen and radio - I was free. Eric was already out of his seat. From its stowage bin I grabbed my parachute, made my way down the silent black hull and left by the rear door. A voice outside asked if everything was OK - I said it was. We had been in the air 6 hours 50 minutes and had landed at 03.55hrs. Apart from visibility problems caused by snow over the DZ it had been an uneventful and successful first Op.

We climbed into a waiting crew bus which took us back to where we had started - the briefing room door. We entered and put our flying gear onto a table. The station Padre welcomed us with steaming cup of coffee laced with brandy and a large wedge of fruit cake on a plate. He was always there to meet us crews no matter what time we landed. Once I told him how much it was appreciated and asked him why he did it. He said a mother lost her son and had written to him; he realised he had never known the boy. Thereafter he met every crew member on their return to make sure he knew them.

We were debriefed and completed an operations report giving weather details, any recommendations for improving the DZ, the height and direction the load was dropped, where the leaflets were dropped, if any enemy opposition, the route we took etc, etc. Kit and I were finally released to eat eggs (real not powdered!) and bacon in the mess - a rare treat in those days! When we finally got to bed at about 05.30hrs, Johnnie Affleck - a 161 Squadron Hudson pilot was still over an hour's flying from Tempsford.

2/9.2.44

B 86 78   V

2. 860

1st .... T/o Clark

3. ....
(a) ....   (c) Endurance 15.   (e) .... 8 - F12
(b) 8   (.. ....   (f) ......

4. ....
(.) ...... France
(.) ....
(.) .... not bought
(.) .... ?/2
(.) .... to deception

5. ...... of operation. (if not completed, state reason)

Completed.

(a) 2105
(.) 2345   hours to 0017   ....
(.) .... 0357 ....

(.) ....
(.) ....?   Yes
(.) ....?   DIR run from CHATILLON.

(a) .... as briefed.

(d) 0017
.... 0900 600 ft.
.... 145 - 150
.... (........ lights) Vis not good enough

(f) .... for return use

(.) Reception high ....
3 bonfires and 1 red light. No letter seen.
Bonfire after fourth run was made.

(.) .... SANCERRE, 4 47.41N 0132E
....

(x) ...... (...... ... ... and heights when ..... crossed.) BOGNOR at
2142 Lo 2000ft. CABOURG 6000ft. 2216 Lo: BELLEME
47.41N. 0132 E; SANCERRE: CHATELON: TARGET.
CHATELLON. SANCERRE 47.41N. 0132 E. BELLEME
CABOURG. 6000ft. 0217 Lo. BOGNOR 1500ft. 0256 Lo

194

8. If Load (or part of Load) Jettisoned:
   (a) Place:
   (b) Height:
   (c) Time

9. Report by Despatcher: *O.K.*

10. Enemy Opposition (state place, height & time):

11. Meteorological Conditions: *On route, fair. Some haze. Vis 3-4 miles. Over target Vis 5-600 yards through Shots.*

12. Captain's Personal Report:

13. Remarks by C.O. _____ Squadron:

[signature]

Officer Commanding,
No. _____ Squadron,

14. Remarks by Officer Commanding R.A.F. Station, TEMPSFORD:

Officer Commanding,
R.A.F. Station,
TEMPSFORD.

Operations report on the first Op. 'BOB 78' 8/9 February 1944
(Courtesy of the Public Records Office ref: Air 20/8478)

I did not intend to write about the exploits of the Lysander and Hudson pilots of 161 Sqdn. Deservedly a multitude of words have been written about them, not the least in Hugh Verity's book, *'We Landed by Moonlight'*. Understandably, they were faceless individuals to me in the mess at Tempsford and during the 'moon period' the Lysanders operated out of Tangmere. However, on the same night as my first Op, Johnnie Affleck had been bogged down in a Hudson for 2 hours in a field at Bletterans, some 48 kilometres east of Chalon-sur-Soane. With the aid of villagers, horses and oxen, sheer guts, determination, and extraordinary flying skill, Johnnie finally got off the ground. His passengers were Monsieur and Madame Aubrac and their son. A month before Monsieur Aubrac had been rescued by his wife from a van taking him to his place of execution by the Gestapo. We had been in bed an hour when, at 06.40hrs, Johnnie landed at Tempsford. Madame Aubrac, was rushed off to hospital to have her second child - a daughter!

Johnnie, a flying officer at the time with a DFC and a string of foreign decorations, was awarded an immediate DSO, I remember congratulating him in the mess. To put the Germans and anyone else off the scent, the newspapers said this French family were taken by train to Spain concealed beneath a railway coach.

There was yet another strange occurrence that night; a 161 Squadron Halifax, 'Y', flown by Flt/Lt Parker, went to two targets in France - *'CALANQUE'* and *'MIRAGE'*. At *'MIRAGE'* there was no reception, but at *'CALANQUE'* he dropped 4 agents, 9 containers and 2 packages. The agents were R.E.J.Alexandre, a 22 year old French aircraft fitter; an American called Byerley (his radio operator); a Canadian named Deniset, a replacement for Princess Noor who had already been captured; and an Anglo-Frenchman, Jacques Ledoux, whose duty it was to establish a new circuit *ORATOR* at Le Mans. As they landed they were captured. In Anthony Caves book, *'Bodyguard of Lies'*, he goes on to say that all of them were so inexperienced and ill-trained that their mission seemed to be sacrificial!

That same night, a Lysander, flown by Flt/Lt Leslie Whitaker, brought back a Frenchman named Dericourt from a field near Tours. Dericourt had been accused of co-operating with the Germans in Paris and was being recalled to London. I mention the return of Dericourt to London because of an interesting book written by Robert Marshall called, *'All The King's Men'* (published by Collins). There was also a BBC TV documentary, with the same title, produced by Marshall and broadcast on 1st May 1986. Briefly, the book tells the story how SOE was created against the wishes of Special Intelligence Service (SIS or MI6) and the rivalry that existed between the two organisations. It tells also of the malicious intent of one Lt/Col Claude Dansey, second in command of MI6, who considered SOE operations in Europe 'a damn nuisance'. Dansey was a powerful man and penetrated SOE headquarters, thereafter every SOE signal, whether incoming or outgoing arrived on his desk.

In 1942 Henri Dericourt, a French pilot, was recommended to SOE as a prospective agent - he had already been through the hands of Claude Dansey. In January 1943, Dericourt took up duties in France as Air Movements Officer of the SOE. As a double agent he started to feed SOE information to the German Intelligence at the same time reporting back to Dansey in London who it was said, was his true employer. As a result many Lysander landings were observed by the Germans and signals destined for London or Paris were shown to them before onward transmission. Far worse, the SOE network *'Prosper'* was betrayed and more than 400 Frenchmen lost their lives. It is alleged in the book the person responsible for this was the 'power sodden, powerful man' (it is said) Deputy Head of MI6, Claude Dansey, who had pledged himself to destroy SOE. It was known he was hostile to the French generally, a real square peg in a round hole if it is true. 'Or was he?' I ask myself. He employed Dericourt, it is alleged, as a double agent to feed information on the SOE to the Germans. A post-war court martial cleared Dericourt! It must be coincidental that SOE in Holland had been totally destroyed; radio messages from captured agents indicating that they had been compromised were ignored in London. Thus some Dutch agents were parachuted directly into the hands of the Germans; 138 Squadron and, presumably, 161 Squadron Halifax's were shot down as they approached Dutch DZ's. In Belgium the SOE was seriously crippled. Halifax aircraft were regularly attacked on their way to and from their DZ's. Did this add up to treachery? We will never know, all records on SOE activities in these countries have been conveniently lost or destroyed.

If true, it is incredible to learn that such happenings were due to the clandestine activities of an individual supposedly on our side. It is unbelievable to learn that not only the lives of our aircrew, but those of the reception committees for the DZ's and landing fields were put in jeopardy by this man. It smacks of political intrigue, Claude Dansey received a Knighthood on his retirement - a KCMG, undoubtedly approved by Winston Churchill who must have known what was going on.

It was a pity that the lives of aircrew and others should have been put at risk for such motives - whatever they were. Perhaps if all was known, this deadly charade was used to protect the Normandy Landings. On the other hand why should I whinge or complain? Operational aircrew were expendable for any reason whatsoever! But I digress!

I finally surfaced and reported to the flights in the late afternoon, there I was summoned before the Squadron Commander. There was no doubt we had done a good job and I surmised he was going to congratulate me on our first operational flight. I knocked on the door and Dickie Speare yelled 'Come in.' I went in and saluted him, he didn't look up from the papers in front of him. 'That's a pity,' I thought, 'that wasn't a bad salute.' His 'pregnant pause' was too long to be comfortable and when he eventually looked up his face told me that something was wrong. I waited for him to speak. That smug feeling with which I entered the room was fast disappearing. He spoke, 'Clark,' he said, it was a good start I thought, he's got the right person. 'Clark,' he said again, 'I've had a complaint from your ground crew.' 'What on earth could they possibly have to complain about me?' I thought. 'They say last night your aircraft was left in a disgusting state.' He went on, 'The wrapping paper from your crews flying rations left all over the place, empty tins of orange juice left lying about - you know the standing orders about that...' he paused for breath, 'what's more someone puked all over the floor!' He then looked me straight in the eye and said, 'It won't happen again, if it does you will clear the mess up, do I make myself clear?' 'Yes sir,' I said feebly. 'That will be all' he retorted. I saluted, turned on my heel and walked out of his office.

That wigging rankled! He had laid it on thick and heavy, I really didn't need him to remind me who was in command of the squadron! I'm not denying I should have been told about this breach of discipline, but I thought that perhaps my ground crew corporal could have said something about it. Normally I expect the Flight Commander would have spoken to me but, alas, he had been shot down three days previously. I spoke to my crew and told them what had happened. I never bothered to ask who was sick, but I was bloody annoyed about empty tins being left to roll around the fuselage floor and said so. They could have caused serious problems had they rolled into the control lines. There was no further complaints from the ground crew and we became great buddies. Our aeroplanes were always kept immaculate and it was my proud boast you could eat a meal off the floor of mine. Undoubtably the CO was right in so far as the ground crews knew that their complaint would be supported.

While four 138 Squadron aircraft out of a total of 26 aircraft went on Resistance operations on the night of the 10/11th, I went to the cinema and saw 'Yankee Doodle Dandy'. Afterwards I went to Gamlingay on a binge. Flt/Lt Mill was the only one to complete his mission. Another returned early because an escape hatch blew open, the other two returned due to bad weather. A Lysander pilot (Flg/Off McDonald) was lost, it was a filthy night.

We flew an air test the following afternoon in preparation for the night's operations. Four Squadron aircraft took off, we weren't among them. The weather turned foul and we had two days off. Those magical words came over the Tannoy 'Operations for tonight are cancelled', or, as our Bomber Command colleagues would so callously say, 'No frying tonight!' With flying cancelled a lunch time session drinking mulled ale got under way. Sleeping in his favourite armchair beside a roaring fire was an elderly Flight Lieutenant, a First World War veteran. Habitually, each day after lunch, he sat in this chair, lit his pipe, read his newspaper, and quietly supped a pint of beer. When he had finished he would knock his pipe out and, with the bowl uppermost, stick the stem into the front of his buttoned trousers and go to sleep. We spotted him and quietly crept to where he slept. Then someone, young enough to be his grandson, took a pint of beer and very, very carefully poured it into the bowl of the protruding pipe. The whole pint disappeared, we waited quietly, looking at each other nonplussed. It seemed minutes before he leapt from his chair and with a shout yelled, 'Christ! I've pissed myself!' He took the joke well but he never stowed that pipe in his trousers again and, as far as I know, we never again disturbed his afternoon nap!

On the 14th I received a Valentine Card and the news that we had been given 10 whole days leave, starting from 4.30pm on Friday 18th February. I wasted no time, I arranged to meet Dorothy at Uxbridge at 2 in the afternoon on Saturday! In the meantime, we had to work for our leave. The night of the 15/16th came and of the 48 aircraft on Resistance Operations, we were one of twelve 138 Squadron crews briefed to fly to France. We sheltered from the snow beneath the wing of our aircraft, wishing we could have another cigarette. I could not believe they would send us out on a night like this. It was snowing quite heavily and I waited for the red Verey cartridge from the control tower to burst into the air, to cancel the operation. We could see other crews sheltering under the wing of their aircraft, obviously thinking the same as us.

That red Verey light never came and we reluctantly climbed aboard 'K-King' to prepare ourselves for take off. At 21.55hrs we rolled down the runway. By now the snow was thinning out; but I was still seriously concerned about conditions on our return. At 23.00hrs I angrily flew low over Bognor and beat up the pier, hoping I would disturb those sleeping warmly in their beds below, and set course for France. Our target was 'TRAINER 120' near Bourg. The weather en-route was 10/10ths cloud, topping at 5,000 feet with a base of 3,000. It was a dark night and bad weather made it impossible to find either the bonfires or the white lights of our DZ. On our way back we saw some heavy flak coming up from Orleans. We landed with our load on an airfield clear of snow. We had been in the air 8 hours 25 minutes. Of the 12 squadron aircraft, 8 failed to complete due to weather. I was relieved to hear that two other aircraft on 'TRAINER 120' had also failed to find the target. One Stirling was lost.

Then the moon disappeared, the Stirlings disappeared and practically all the Squadron disappeared, I couldn't get home fast enough. In the darkness of the moonless nights, Bomber Command battled on - good luck to them. I had at last got them out of my system, my guilt complex had gone. With a squadron loss average of approximately 3%, as high as, if not higher, than most Bomber Command squadrons, I had a survival problem of my own.

Fortunately, Dorothy was able to get time off and we revelled in our good fortune. We saw Elizabeth Welch in 'Arc de Triomphe' and, being Ivor Novello fans, we lapped up every word. Whenever we could we dined at Maxim's in Wardour Street, now our favourite restaurant. Here in a cloakroom the size of a small cupboard sat the attendant working on a hand operated sewing machine; what she sewed we never found out! She was a dear old soul and greeted us warmly saying how pleased she was to see us again. 'As you can never tell these days!' she said. I knew the feeling well! To the tinkling of a piano we danced on the tiniest of dance floors, held each other close and sang softly to each other those wonderful love lyrics of our time. We ate *ersatz* Chinese food and wished that our mutual chums, Pip and Audrey could have been with us.

There were nightly raids on London by Messerschmitt 410's. They came in from the north, dropped their bombs and beat it fast for home. The local heavy Ack-Ack battery at Chadwell Heath now had a rocket launching site operated by the Home Guard. The noise when launched and the detonation in the air were deafening, the released pyrotechnical display was terrifying. I don't know what the German pilots thought of it all, or what success that diabolical machinery had, but it certainly frightened me. I was pleased to leave it all behind when the time came to return to the peace of Bedfordshire.

My leave had every appearance of finishing when I was caught off guard. It happened at Uxbridge when I was kissing Dorothy goodbye. I looked away from her eyes and for the first time I noticed the moon; it was huge. 'I should've been back,' I groaned, 'I've over stayed my leave.' She must have been mystified at my reaction towards such a beautiful moon, but she was unaware of what I was doing at Tempsford. I was now very anxious and said, 'I must telephone and find out.' I was pleased when someone answered the mess telephone, had there been any operations that night it would have been cut off, as it always was. The person answering the telephone said I was wasn't adrift and would see me tomorrow. I felt a bit of a Charlie.

CHAPTER TEN

MY SECOND FULL MOON

'The Moon is up: The Stars are bright;
The wind is fresh and free!
We're out to seek for gold tonight
Across the silver sea!

'The Moon is up.' - Alfred Noyes
Modern Poetry - Edited by Guy Pocock - J M Dent 1937

I met Mac and Lloyd at Sandy Station; luckily there was a truck at the station and we were able to get a lift to the airfield. It was a warm, beautiful day and the blanket of snow that had covered the ground had now turned to slush. Dragging my suit case, I returned to the Maycrete hut where I shared a small room with Kit. He had returned one day early and was furious about it, there had been no heat or hot water! His temper improved as the day went on. I wrote to Dorothy during that first day back and told her what a wonderful leave it had been. I said all that remained were tender memories and a smear of red perfumed lipstick on one of my handkerchiefs!

No 218 (Gold Coast) Squadron Stirlings had arrived from Woolfox Lodge and with them came an old Hemswell room mate of mine, Flt/Lt Chaplin. We were pleased to see each other, he had a DFC by then and, I think, a bar too. Although he had qualified for his flying badge long after I did he had served on 218 Squadron for some time. I didn't envy him. He showed me his Stirling and promised me a ride in it, but the opportunity never arose.

About this time all Halifax IIs & Vs (with Rolls-Royce in-line engines) were permanently withdrawn from Bomber Command operations to Germany. They were now only used operationally for glider towing, Coastal Command and Special Duty Squadrons like ourselves.

During my leave, on the night of 24/25th February, a 161 Squadron Halifax 'X' X-ray, piloted by Sqdn/Ldr Radcliffe, dropped 2 agents on *'PETER 16'* near Clermont-Ferrand without the aid of a moon (squadron records say 3 agents, but Yeo-Thomas says only two were dropped. 'X-Ray' was the only aircraft with agents on board that night). One was a saboteur whose code was Trieur (his first trip) and the other was Wg/Cmdr

F.F.E.Yeo-Thomas GC, MC. 'Travelling second class,' he called it! His primary objective was to rescue his great friend Pierre Brossolette who was imprisoned at Rennes. In less that a month Yeo-Thomas was betrayed before he could accomplish his mission. Bruce Marshall's book *'The White Rabbit'* tells of Yeo-Thomas's appalling experiences in the hands of the Gestapo.

The Squadron stood down on the night 28th/29th, although a 161 Squadron Halifax piloted by Plt/Off Caldwell parachuted 3 agents into France roughly 31 kms east-south-east of Chartres on DZ *'PHONO 4'* (a suspect DZ). They were J.F.A Antelme OBE (a Mauritian businessman known as 'Antoine'), his radio operator Lionel Lee, and his courier, Mlle Madeleine Damerment. Their reception committee was the SD (*Sicherheitsdienst* - the German Security Service). The Germans knew all about 'Antoine's' connection with the *'Prosper'* organisation (as did Dansey at MI6). All three were later executed in German concentration camps.

The view from a 'DZ' as a Halifax makes its drop (Photo:Crown Copyright ref:CNA3243)

During the short time (two months) I was at Tempsford 191 agents were dropped, 102 by the Halifaxes of 138 Squadron, 41 by 161 Squadron Halifaxes, 32 by Lysander and 16 by Hudson. In addition the Lysanders picked up 32 and the Hudsons 7 - a remarkable effort. No 161 Squadron also carried out two sorties to Germany during this period. It is officially recorded that SOE section F sent 393 officers to France (not all by air) of whom 119 where killed or arrested (only 17 survived German captivity)

(Nigel West - *'Secret War'*). It would appear that approximately 25 were arrested the same day as they were dropped. Although the exact number of SOE agents dropped is still disputed.

On Leap Year day, 29th February, eleven 138 Squadron aircraft went out. The only 4 engine night operation of the war to take place on this day, worthy, perhaps, of a mention in the Guinness Book of Records! Our trip that night was a 'doddle', we took off at 21.25hrs and were back home after 3 hours 50 minutes in the air. We must have been well tucked up in bed long before the rest of them got back. Our target was *'HARRY 24'*, some 50 miles inside Normandy near to La Ferte Mace from which we made a Dead Reckoning (DR) run into the DZ. We got a *GEE* fix right over the pinpoint, in a clearing in the middle of a wood, with the correct recognition light 'P' flashing, all as briefed. We did a quick circuit and Eric lined up the aircraft, opened the bomb doors and dropped 15 containers 400 feet over the centre light. We went round again and Ernie pushed out 10 packages through the hole in the rear fuselage. The reception was operating within a stone's throw of the enemy's heavy coastal defences, I wonder now if it was all too simple?!

I should explain that a container basically held munitions: Sten guns, Bren guns, rifles, pistols, ammunition, spares, magazines, plastic explosives, hand grenades, fuses, field dressings, anti-tank rockets; in fact a proverbial arsenal. They must have been extremely heavy and both the containers and the parachutes were usually removed and hidden by the Reception Committee on the night they were dropped. A package usually contained material specifically requested by radio and were carried inside the aircraft. They were delivered by a parachute attached to a static line and were pushed out through a round hole in the floor at the rear of the aircraft. Effective and efficient logistics concerning resistance operations must have been an enormous problem.

In the meantime Dorothy had asked me to send her a piece of tape the size of my finger, so she might buy me a ring for my 21st Birthday!

Ten Halifaxes and one Stirling took part in Resistance flights on the night 1/2nd March, we weren't among them. The next night the 2nd/3rd March, 44 aircraft were on and we went to *'BOB 55'* which we located in a misty valley in the Aignay-le-Duc area some 20 miles N.W. of Beaune. The DZ consisted of two red lights and a white light flashing a poor 'R'. We made a run at 600 feet and dropped 15 canisters; then the lights went out, we circled, they came on again and we were able to deliver our 6 packages. On the way back we dropped our leaflets (Issue F.18) in the Avallon area and headed for Sancerre. Here we intended to go north direct to Cabourg and then home.

At Sancerre, the turning point, I set everything up, the height, speed, direction, engine boost at +4 and, as was normal practice, put *'George'*[1] into gear to let him do the flying. I had a piece of parachute cord with one end firmly attached to the automatic pilot control cock lever (to give it its official title!), the other end was a loop which was firmly attached to my wrist. One quick jerk at the cord disengaged *'George'* and I had full control again. I was flying at 3,000 feet, at which height it was said we were out of range of both the light flak, which couldn't reach us and the heavy stuff which could not bring to bear and fire that low!

I was very tired and my mind was mesmerised by the lights of a large marshalling yard. I remember seeing ground detail quite clearly, tracks, rolling stock, locomotives, the lot. It was unbelievable that so much activity was going on under floodlights, in the middle of the night (at 12.41hrs to be precise!). Then some twit ruined my day dreaming or night dreaming whatever you like to call it. He, whoever he was, switched the marshalling yard lights off and another on, this time illuminating us. I pulled sharply on my parachute cord disengaging *'George'* and turned the aircraft into a screaming dive to starboard. The radar controlled searchlight held us and up came the large wavering orange balls of tracer shells. Slowly at first and then whipping past us at breakneck speed. Luckily they were as dim-witted as I was and didn't hit us, or at least that's what I thought! My final manoeuvre ducked under the light and it went out - it took some considerable time for my own light to come back on again!

I have since been to Orleans many times but never again, I am pleased say, to such an aggressive reception. In retrospect it was a stupid route back, we were cutting corners to get home quickly and it brought us close to trouble. I must confess my own contribution to the crisis was none too bright either. We landed at 03.00hrs, after 6 hours 10 minutes in the air, taxyed in, shut down the engines and got out. Mac wanted to look at the port outer, he had complained that the oil pressure had begun to get a bit low and the temperature had been wavering on the hot side. The Flight Sergeant produced a torch and waved the beam around the engine nacelle, it looked a bit wet and streaked with oil. The operations report said the port outer had been hit. Not hard enough, me thinks; that ground crew of mine must have worked really hard to get that aeroplane ready for operations the following night! Two myths were dispelled by that sortie, one: you could be hit by light flak

[1] - *George - automatic pilot.*

at 3,000 feet and two: I wasn't as fire proof as I thought I was!

Seventeen squadron aircraft took off on the following night of 3rd/4th. What a fine squadron effort this was. Our target was *'BOB 17'* near Rambervillers / Baccarat, we went via Sancerre. Baccarat is within 50 miles of the Rhine and a little over 25 miles south east of Nancy. We made three DR runs, but couldn't find the reception, although the operations report says we saw some lights at Menil (which I cannot now find on any map!). I remember making a really low run over them to let them know that the RAF were about! Although we were unable to make contact on this occasion it was another example of the dedication of Resistance Groups, this time operating within 50 miles of the German border, though it was later said that there were some German operated sites operating in this area!

I hope I didn't scare them too much, at least not as much as the bloody predicted searchlight (radar controlled) which held us for 15 seconds at Laigle and the fireworks that followed scared me. Fifteen seconds is a hell of a long time, especially when you are being shot at! How I wished we could have fought back with that non-existent mid upper turret. The fuselage blocked out the rear turret preventing Lloyd from returning fire. We were flying at 2,000 feet and I went for the deck like a rabbit down a burrow! We were 17 minutes from the coast and 14 miles east of track, what we were doing there I don't know. Perhaps having been in the air 7 hours 45 minutes when we landed had something to do with it. Fg/Off W.C.Kingsley and his crew failed to return that night. He and 4 of his crew were killed, two survivors were taken prisoner. Their target was *'JOHN 23'* in France and it was only their second operational flight.

On the night of the 4/5th we were left at home while 12 squadron aircraft went out as part of a total effort of 76, so the records say, which is unbelievable - that's a lot of aeroplanes, No 38 Group must have been working overtime! The new 'A' Flight Commander Sqdn/Ldr W.M. Russell DFC & Bar carried out his first 138 Squadron operational flight. We complained bitterly among ourselves that we were 'on' again so soon! On the night 5/6th there were a total of 66 Resistance sorties, 12 from 138 Squadron. Our target was *'BOB 77'* which was in the same area as our last abortive trip. For the second time within a few days I was given 'A' Apple (LK743). It was a pig of an aircraft to fly and probably had a twisted airframe, the result of either it being built into it on the production line or of an unreported heavy landing; no one liked flying it. I swung her badly to the left taking off on the short runway and really thought we were going to finish up inside the control tower. I straightened her up by closing the starboard motors and opening them up again. For my next trick I thought I was going to put us into the railway embankment. She clawed herself free of the ground, but the margins were very small!

We went via Sancerre again (makes you thirsty doesn't it!) and made 3 DR runs from Luneville, about 18 miles S.E. of Nancy. No reception lights were seen, but we picked up a *REBECCA* signal 8 miles out and, as instructed, dropped into the DZ when the signal collapsed on the cathode ray tube. The load was seen to fall alongside a wood which we identified as the pinpoint. We also had 'S' phone on board which was a short range radio transmitter/receiver with which we were able to take messages from the ground. Unhappily we didn't make contact. We landed 'A' Apple back at Tempsford after 7 hours and 55 minutes in the air. I remember some wag asking me why I hadn't left her behind in France! Two months later she was a burning wreck on the ground at Great Barford, which is about 3 miles west of Tempsford, the crew escaped.

It had been a bruising night for the squadron, over Belgium both Sqn/Ldr Wilding (dropping 3 agents) and Flt/Lt Johnson were attacked by fighters and Flt/Sgt Baker was hit by flak, as was Flt/Lt Ashley over France. We felt absolutely knackered, doubtless other crews felt the same. 'K' King had had engine trouble so we gave her a quick fifteen minute air test prior to taking her out on the night 6/7th. Ten squadron aircraft were on the Ops. Board and to his eternal credit, Dickie Speare, the Squadron Commander, was down to take 'A' Apple.

At briefing we were advised that a Bomber Force would be attacking the marshalling yard at Trappes. Although they had been bombing marshalling yards and other targets over France, this was the first time we had been given prior information. It particularly interested me since we were going in that direction. We took off early at 20.15hrs, our target, *'DICK 54'* was in the woods near two lakes, Etangs de Hollande and Etangs de St. Hubert about six miles north of Rambouillet which, in turn, was about 25 miles south-west of Paris. I would have cause not to forget the shape of these lakes and the target area.

In retrospect, Kit and I chose a stupid route to the target area but we were trying to avoid running straight over Paris in a west to easterly direction. We decided to approach Rambouillet, from the south via Sully. Taking our fix from Rambouillet, we could make our DR run to the target. Thus, if we overran the target we would keep out of harms way, Paris would then be far off to our right. The expected cloud cover at 6,000 feet over the coast did not materialise, it was a clear night and there was a brilliant moon. The first light flak gun opened up on us, probably from Ouistreham, to the right of track, the shells burst at 6,000 feet. A light flak train stationed at a railway junction at Mezidon joined in a few minutes later. We were still at 6,000 feet and so were the shells; it was a great start to an operation. Ground detail was so clear we could easily identify where our antagonists were lurking. Fortunately their shooting wasn't too accurate and I made a rapid dive for the ground.

As we approached Belleme another blighter had a go at us with a machine gun, we were down to 500 feet and I could clearly see the guy hosing tracer at us from the top of a building. They were too bloody close and I remember looking over my left shoulder to see where they were going! I warned Lloyd in the rear turret that if the cheeky bastard continued to fire at us as we went over him he was to knock him off his perch with a sharp burst or two. However, it was a wily bird that sat on the perch on top of that building; as we went over, and the rear guns came to bear, not a cheep came from him, he didn't reveal his position! Maybe he heard what I'd said to Lloyd! We weren't doing very well, there we were, still on our first leg and they had got at us three times already. I was feeling a bit uncomfortable to say the least.

We turned at the islands in the Loire and made for Sully where we turned north for Rambouillet. It was a difficult leg and I nagged Eric up front to get us a pinpoint from his map. Kit got fed up with my bullying and told me in no uncertain terms to dry up and leave him alone. I should have saved my breath. Two predicted searchlights coned us and I was blinded and shocked as the tracers came at us. I screamed in panic to Lloyd to shoot the bloody lights out. We were so low, I am sure if I had put the wheels down we could have landed on Mondesir airfield (5 miles S.W. Etampes) where we now found ourselves! I weaved the aircraft madly to avoid the tracer which snaked towards us.

My mind rolled my body into a tight ball, I tensed myself waiting for the inevitable hit. A long burst of gunfire came from the rear turret and one of the lights swung crazily around the sky and went out. The action stopped as soon as it had started, I sweated - as I do now, some fifty years after. I tried to settle back on to the course Kit had given me, groping with my dazzled eyes in the sudden darkness for the instruments that would re-orientate me. This was a classic attack which we could have repulsed sooner with a mid upper turret. Kit said over the intercom we were coming up to Rambouillet and gave me the new course that would lead us into the target area. I set it upon the compass and continued to run on the directional giro for a few minutes until Kit said, 'OK to turn'. We turned, the time was about 23.30hrs.

I had never seen a target marker before, but there was no doubt in my mind what it was. It burst on the ground in a cascade of colour just beside us and yet another. 'Christ!' I thought, 'we're over Trappes just as Bomber Command are doing their stuff!' I called to Kit to come up and have a quick look which he did, by now the heavy stuff was coming down. 'At least we know where we are,' he grumbled, 'Don't ever ask me to have a look again, I don't want to know!' With that he disappeared down into the darkness of the nose of the aircraft, among his charts and his pencils.

We found Rambouillet and made two more runs which took us over the lakes, identified our pinpoint, circled but no one was there. I turned for home via Belleme, Trappes burned behind us. I throttled back and put down flap and Ernie carefully parachuted out 15 pigeons in their containers. The squadron parachuted many of these birds out of our aeroplanes. We reasoned some of them found their way onto French dining tables, but a number of them did return to their lofts in the U.K. The information given by the French and carried by them more than compensated for the care we took to pitch them out.

We landed at 01.47hrs, I wrote DNCO (Duty Not Carried Out) in the authorization book and the flight time as 5 hours 30 minutes. I remember thinking at the time that we would be very lucky to complete a tour of operations at this game. This was a real hairy trip and probably reads like fiction. If it wasn't for the operations report I would probably think so too, but I distinctly remember those lakes so vividly. A new dimension had entered my life: fear and apprehension. I got out of bed at 5.30 in the afternoon and announced to Kit that today was the third anniversary of my joining the RAF. I don't know what I expected him to say, perhaps, 'Congratulations, have a Hertz bar,' but he didn't. All he said without the slightest interest in me was, 'Surely there must be an easier way of making a living!'

The morning newspapers said the Eighth Air Force had taken 730 bombers to Berlin, covered by nearly 800 fighters. It was an expensive mission, 69 bombers failed to return, a further 3 were scrapped and 102 had major damage. The fighters lost 11 and claimed 81 destroyed! We had a B17 base at Thurleigh, approximately 6 miles to the west of us. It was the home of four B17 squadrons, the 306 Bomb Group, eventually the oldest Bomb Group in the 8th Air Force. We used to watch them forming up for a mission and straggling back after, some showing much battle damage. I peeped into Thurleigh once during an air test; they were landing after a mission. Their flying discipline was fantastic, one aircraft turning off the runway, another one halfway down, and the third just touching down - a nice tidy operation, not easy with a big aeroplane like the B17.

MOST SECRET
REPORT ON OPERATIONS UNDERTAKEN BY
138 SQUADRON NIGHT 6/7 2.44

Name of Operation: DICK 54

No........ 'K'

2. Aircraft: Hal.

1st Pilot F/O Clark   W Operator   Despatcher
2nd Pilot   A/Gunner
Navigator

3. Personnel & Equipment Carried:

(a) Personnel   c) Containers 15   (e) Leaflets 4-F25
(b) Packages   6   d) Pigeons 15 to scatter (f) Coffee

4. Instructions to Captain if A/C:

(a) Area: France
(b) Pinpoint:
(c) Alternate Pinpoint:
(d) Action if pinpoint not located:
(e) Reception arrangements:
(f) A/c's Recognition Signal to Reception: C/C

5. Result of Operation (if not completed, state reason).   Not completed
    to reception

6. Times:
(a) Time off: 2015
(b) Over target area from 2326½ hours to 23.45 hours
(c) Landing: 0147
(d) Action taken on landing away from Base:

7. Captain's Report:
(a) Was exact pinpoint found ? Yes
(b) How was pinpoint identified ? found detail B.R. on far
    bank of Routchillet

(c) Estimated dropping points:

(d) Time dropped:
    height above ground:
    Course:
    I.A.S. in m.p.h.
(e) Description of Target Pinpoint (apart from lights):

(f) Recommended ___ for future use
    Not Recommended
(g) Reception Lights. Report by Captain indicating suggested improvements:

(h) Leaflets dropped:
    Pigeons   " :   Coming to Belhone & Isle en Lorne
    Coffee   " :
    Chocolate   " :

(k) Routes (state place, time and heights when crossing coasts).
    Bognor 2100 Base. Coming 21.37 low ft. Some 30 K
    Belhone. Isle en Lorne Jully. Rouchillet △
    Return Rouchillet. Belhone. Coming 0033. low ft.
    Return Bognor 0107 low ft.

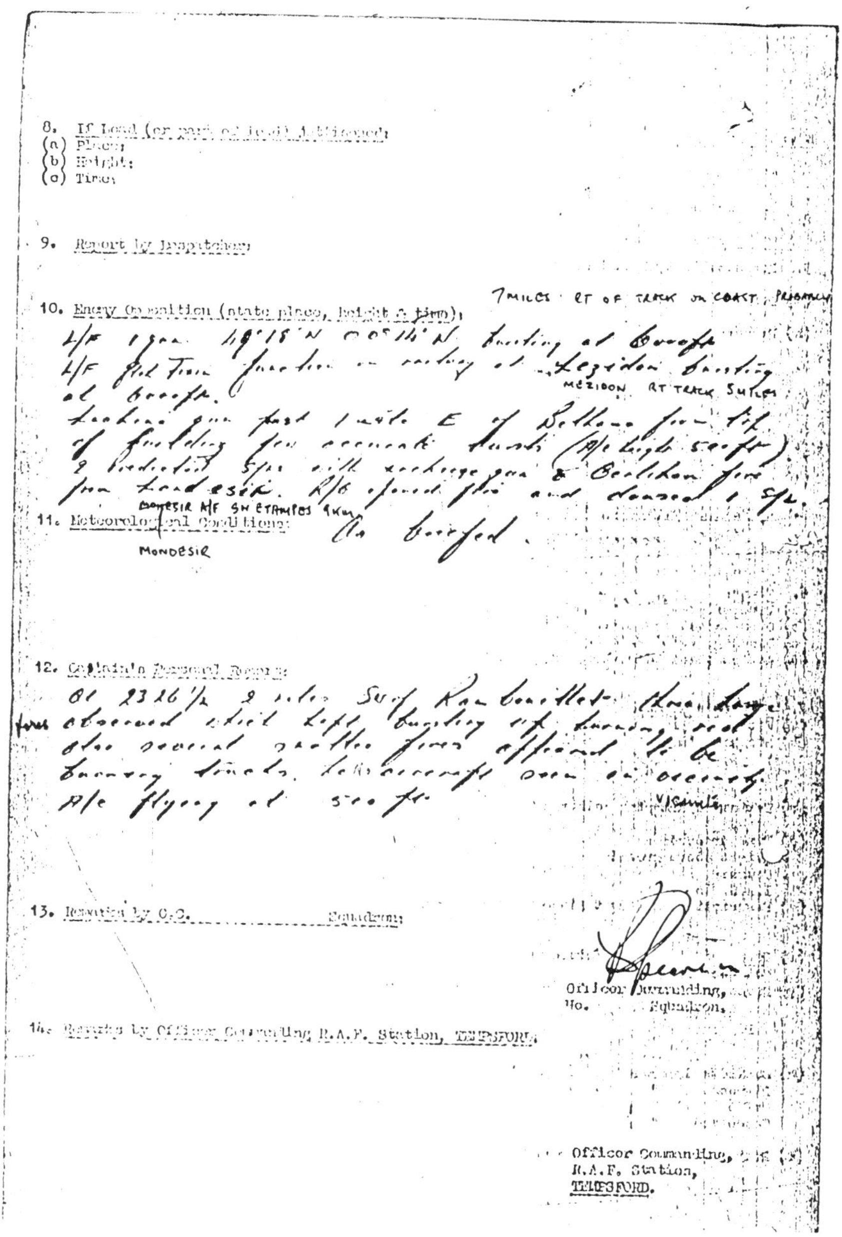

8. If Lost (or part of load) (1) Missed:
(a) Place:
(b) Height:
(c) Time:

9. Report by Despatcher:

10. Enemy Opposition (state place, height & time): 7 MILES RT OF TRACK ON COAST, PROBABLY

[handwritten, largely illegible]
M/F 1 gun 49°18'N 0°54'N ... at Beuzeville
M/F flak from ... at ... Lezioton ...
at Beuzeville. MEZIDON RT TRACK SULES
... one post 1 mile E of Bellene for ...
of building few accurate bursts (Height 500 ft)
2 predicted 5/m with exchange gun & Oerlikon fire
from Fond-esik. R/G opened fire and dowsed 1 S/L
ETAMPES M/F SW ETAMPES 9Km
11. Meteorological Conditions: As briefed.
MONDESIR

12. Captain's Personal Report:
At 2326½ 2 miles S of Rau bouillet three large
fires observed while left, buzzing ...
also several smaller fires observed ...
Enemy tracks. No aircraft seen or ...
A/c flying at 500 ft.

13. Remarks by O.C. _____ Squadron:

[signature]
Officer Commanding,
No. _____ Squadron.

14. Remarks by Officer Commanding R.A.F. Station, TEMPSFORD:

Officer Commanding,
R.A.F. Station,
TEMPSFORD.

Operations report 'DICK 54' 6/7th March 1944 see next page for detail
(Courtesy Public Records Office ref: AIR 20/8478)

The report reads as follows:

'L/F (light flak) 49"18'N 00"14'W bursting at 6000 feet. L/F flak train junction on railway at Mezidon bursting at 6000 feet. Machine gun post 1 mile E Belleme from top of building few accurate bursts (A/C height 500 ft), 2 predicted S/Ls (search lights) with machine gun and Oerlikon fire from Mondesir (airfield). R/G (rear Gunner) opened fire and doused one search light.'

We were bombed by the RAF at Trappes, the DZ wasn't operating and we brought back our load. We had a very bad night.

Two P51 Mustangs landed at Tempsford and I went down to have a look at them. They were highly polished and looked really smart. One of them had two Swastikas painted just below the hood. They were piloted by Americans and I asked one where he had got his victories. He wasn't interested and ignored me so I asked him again. He turned on me and said brusquely, 'Over Berlin!' I said to him that he had better check his brake fluid before he left because most of it was a puddle on the tarmac! His attitude changed, he was grateful that I had noticed it and thanked me. He became more talkative, and from what he told me single engine combat over Berlin was not for me! He was visiting Tempsford to see an American friend who was serving in the RCAF, which was interesting, but I never found out who it was.

On the night of 7/8th it is recorded that 51 aircraft went on Resistance Operations, 11 went from 138 Squadron. I was pleased to stay on the ground and was given a few hours leave. My original plan was to fly a Halifax down to Fairlop, which was close to London, and closer to my home. I received permission from the OC Flying and I told the lads in my flight what I intended to do, saying if they had a pass they could come too. Quite a few said they would do so, however, Fairlop[2] Flying Control told me to stay away since they were flying Typhoons operationally from there and they didn't want any unfamiliar aircraft cluttering up their airfield and wasting their precious man-hours attending to it. We fortunately had time to catch the early train to London.

I met Dorothy in London and we had dinner at Maxim's where we

<hr>

[2] - *All flying ceased at Fairlop on 15th March, one week later 192 Squadron moved to Thorney Island.*

embarrassed one of Dorothy's 'watch mates' who was also out of camp without a pass! On my return to Tempsford I flew 'King' on a quick air test and a 55 minute Special Training Flight, showing a new pilot the ropes at Henlow. There were no ops on the night 9/10th and according to letters home we had one helluva party in the mess. I expect, as usual, Johnnie Johnson, the Squadron Training Officer, belted away on the piano. He wore spectacles and we called him our 'Blind Flying Instructor', he also wore the DFC. He would play his signature tune, 'Good night, Padre', to warn the Padre that the songs we were about to sing would offend his ears. He always left in good humour wishing us an enjoyable evening as he went. I stayed up late and got drunk with the rest of them. I am surprised how dependant on tobacco and alcohol we were in those days. However, it should be said that we never ever drank when there was the likelihood of flying (the limit for alcohol on a Flying Officer's monthly mess bill was £5).

Lloyd had a swollen face and we treated him like a leper - we thought he had mumps! They took him off to hospital and on the night 10/11th March I flew with a Fg/Off G.H.Ash DFC occupying Lloyd's seat in the rear turret. I was flattered when I asked him if he would like to come along with us and he said, 'I'll fly with you any time, Nobbie.' What I liked about it was he sounded as if he meant it. They told us at briefing it was to be a maximum effort. All 13 aircraft of 138 Squadron were going down to Maquis country to a target coded 'UNION 3', situated in the mountains about 65 kilometres due west of Dijon. We were told to drop on any triangle of bonfires we could see and it was possible that we would have the aid of REBECCA. It was the nearest thing to a Bomber Command operational take off I had experienced, we were all to take off at the same time. I assume they wanted us over the DZ's and out quickly, thus protecting them from being pinpointed by the enemy.

We were bunched up, taxying one behind the other, slowly moving into the vacant space left in front as an aircraft turned onto the runway, received the green light from the caravan and took off. We were using the long runway in a westerly direction. There was a fairly high wind and 'King' kept weather-cocking into it. I remember the great difficulty I had keeping her between the taxy-track lights and was acutely aware that if I got one wheel off the track we would be up to our axle in mud. The brakes were squealing, huffing and puffing, perhaps I should have made more use of the outboard motors for taxying, but I didn't. I had been so preoccupied that when the green light flashed instructing me to turn onto the runway and take off, it came as a surprise. I turned slowly on, lined up with the runway lights and pulled on the brakes to stop the aircraft. Nothing happened, we kept moving forward. I looked at the brake pressure, it was showing zero! It was like waiting at the first tee until it was your turn to tee off and finding that you had left all your balls in the club house - except in this case I couldn't get back to the club house for more air! Both taxy-tracks either side of the runway were full of aeroplanes waiting for us to go - so we went!

Instead of the luxury of opening up the throttles with the brakes hard on, releasing them, pushing the tail up and correcting the swing with the rudder, I had to dribble half the power on one side to correct the swing until I had all the engines going full power, got the tail up, and then picked up enough speed to get us off the ground. Fortunately I'd had practice on my previous hairy take off in 'Apple', although this time I did send up a silent prayer to the great Station Master above to keep all his trains off this part of the track as we lifted over the railway embankment. He must have heard me, there were none! Once airborne I was relieved to see the brake pressure soon build up.

We got over the French coast and at reduced speed gently bailed our 10 pigeons out at one minute intervals. We pinpointed Dijon and made our DR run in the mountains to a Lake Bourge where we hoped to have a sighting or pick up a *REBECCA* signal. I have recently searched for this lake on a large scale map but could not find it any more than I could 50 years ago. The only difference is that 50 years ago it must have been there, though since then they might have filled it in or drained it! In the operations report I say that the aircraft passed over two rows of fires just before receiving a *REBECCA* signal. I can only assume we were looking for a different DZ.

There was still plenty of snow on the ground which obliterated ground detail and made pinpointing difficult. We didn't spot the lake and continued our run. The operations report says that Kit estimated our position to be over Moutier when we turned back. This I cannot believe since Moutier is a long way inside Switzerland. We had already pinpointed our position at Dijon and the wind couldn't have changed so much in such a short time. Perhaps the Intelligence Officer must have misheard the name of the town. However, as we turned back we picked up a *REBECCA* signal and circled for fifteen minutes trying to decode it. Then through a gap in the cloud we saw a triangle of fires in a valley, near a railway station and made our drop. I couldn't climb out of those valleys in the mountains fast enough.

Nearing the English coast, as required, I switched the R/T over to channel 'D' Darky, an emergency channel on which one could call the Royal Observer Corps and get one's position. As we flew on the R/T set picked up a wailing noise which screamed into my headset and over the intercom. It was not unlike an air raid siren only the frequency of the noise was much wider - a blood curdling sound like I imagined a banshee would howl! A none too steady voice came over the intercom echoing my thoughts, 'What the bloody hell is that, Nobbie?' it asked. We were tired and edgy, the last thing we needed was this unholy row blasting our eardrums. I searched my exhausted mind for the answer. 'It's *Squeakers*[3],' I replied, and then my brain heard what my mouth had said, 'Christ! IT'S *SQUEAKERS*!' It came to me as if I had been struck in the face with a flat hand. *'SQUEAKERS!* It's Squeakers!' I yelled, 'We're running into the bloody balloon barrage at Portsmouth!' In a panic I pulled down on the wheel, pushed hard on the rudder and turned the aeroplane through 180 degrees back the way we had come. I settled down on the new course that Kit gave me and landed after exactly 8 hours in the air. It hadn't been a very good trip.

Later it was said an aircraft had violated Swiss airspace and had parachuted containers into neutral Switzerland! The navigation experts said they had 'back tracked' our airplot and there was no doubt in their mind that we were the culprits. Unhappily, before charges were brought to bear and presumably a court martial convened I was residing in a prison far worse than the Tower of London! The forecast winds must have really been up the spout!

It is strange to relate five 161 Squadron Halifaxes that night went to individual targets in France and one, F/Sgt Brangden, went to Germany (I wonder what that was all about?!) and France - *'ELM'* and *'BOB 153'*, but bad weather prevented him from completing. A previous sortie to Germany on 7th/8th January was flown by Lt Hysing-Dahl[4] (a charming Norwegian). He had two targets; *'EIGER'*, where he dropped 2 agents and one package in the *Schwarzwald* (Black Forest) near Stuttgart; and *'MENEGER 2'* reporting 'No reception'.

Two days later our new 'A' Flight Commander, Sqdn/Ldr Russell, asked me to collect his crew from Wigsley in Nottinghamshire, 7 miles west of Lincoln, a bleak spot and home of a Stirling Unit - 1654 HCU. I took 'K-King', my crew and my old friend Chaplin (I never did get that Stirling ride!). We had no trouble in finding it and on the way I had another peep at Lincoln Cathedral, looking in the afternoon sun so majestically white on that

---

[3] - *'Squeakers' - the code name for a small radio attached to the balloons transmitting on 'Darky' frequency warning crews they were approaching the barrage.*

[4] - *This was the final operation of his first tour with No. 161 Squadron. On the 3rd March, just two months later, he commenced his second tour flying Lysanders.*

hill in the centre of the City. We landed, were directed to a hard-standing on the far side of the field and shut down the engines. We got out and took a few welcome puffs on a cigarette. Before long a crew bus came out loaded with six chaps and their luggage which we quickly stowed in the aircraft. They were all commissioned and only two of them did not wear either the DFC or DFM and in one case both. We were waiting outside the aircraft when a Hillman staff car drew up and out got the Station Commander. He was a Group Captain and wore a hearing aid. I remember seeing a large microphone protruding from the breast pocket of his battle dress. A wire led up to a single headphone that covered one of his ears. It must have been the prototype, the granddaddy of today's unobtrusive hearing machines. He greeted each of my intended passengers warmly, bade them farewell and wished them good luck on their next tour at Tempsford.

In the meantime I had a problem, the ground crew attending my aircraft told me they didn't have a starting trolley with the same size plug as my aircraft. The Group Captain overheard the conversation and said it was ridiculous. There must be a compatible starting 'ack' on the Unit and to prove it he would go and get one. After apologising to me, he got back into his car and went off. He was away a long, long time and I began to wonder if the ground crew weren't right.

The Halifax pilot's notes did not recommend starting engines on the internal aircraft batteries because it could damage them, so it said. I ran my mind over the aircraft's electrical system. The Halifax had three 24 volt 1,500 watt generators, fitted on the port outer, port inner and starboard inner engines. As the engines were still relatively warm I concluded that if we got a quick fire on the port inner engine, without turning the prop over too many times, we could get away with it. Moreover, the port inner would give us the added advantage of working the pneumatic pump and immediately building up the brake pressure.

I had a chat with Mac and we decided to have a go. I told everyone what we intended to do and as none of us relished the idea of staying the night at Wigsley, they seemed relieved that an effort was being made to get away. Mac and I got aboard and set up the starting procedure. With my left hand on the port inner magneto switches and my right on the throttle, to catch the engine at the slightest sign of it firing, I told Mac to push the appropriate button. He did and the prop turned over very slowly at first and then with a puff of smoke from the exhaust, she burst into life. Mac and I looked at each other and grinned. A roar of approval came from passengers and crew alike. With a generator now running there was no fear of damaging the internal batteries and we had no trouble starting the remaining three engines. After testing each engine I had a 'thumbs up' from the ground crew and without more ado taxyed out towards the end of the runway for take off.

I was congratulating myself as we bounced along the taxy track when I saw a Hillman car coming towards us. It approached not unlike a happy dog greeting his master, its tail wagging its body. Its progress certainly wasn't in a straight line. The driver of the vehicle saw us coming and pulled off the tarmac onto the grass to let us go by, the door opened and the driver got out. There was no doubt, by the brass on his hat, who it was. He stood with his hands on his hips as we went by. There was a 'trolley ack' lashed with a piece of rope to the rear bumper. I didn't know quite what to do as we passed him, I wasn't sure if one saluted when wearing a flying helmet. Not wanting to upset him any more than he already looked, I ignored him!

As though by way of divine retribution, my landing at Tempsford was unforgettable. The tail wheel struck the ground first and thereafter it was one enormous bounce. The rear gunner was shot into the roof of his turret and cut his head! I guess I had other things on my mind. I reported to Russell who was pleased to have his new crew in one piece and he rolled up when I told him my story. I asked him to apologise on my behalf when he telephoned the Group Captain. This he did and he told me they both had a chuckle. Sadly S/Ldr W.M.Russell DFC & Bar (Acting Wg/Cmdr) was shot down on 17th May 1944; neither he nor any of that crew I brought from Wigsley survived. His French target was 'CITRONELL 1'. His crew were Fg/Off D.Brown DFC (Nav); Fg/Off B.P.McGonagle (B/A); Fg/Off J.A.Armour DFC DFM (WOP/AG); Fg/Off A.F.Bryce (AG); Fg/Off N.Simster DFM (AG) and Plt/Off G Cable DFM (F/Eng).

On the night 13/14th March we found ourselves flying towards 'DICK 71', taking the long route out, trying to avoid known flak areas. At 00.51hrs we had reported seeing the reception lights of 'HARRY 27' laid out port of track, one of 161 Squadron's targets. The Squadron ORB credits me with dropping 15 pigeons, my operations report doesn't mention it. Makes you wonder if there was a racket in pigeon pie going on! It was standing joke among us that each crew member shot down wore two watches and carried two thermos flasks, so that this number could be written off against deficits in the inventory!

Our DR runs to the target started from Joigny (about 50 Kms S.W.of Troyes) and the weather was perfect, visibility being about 5 miles with a little ground haze - better than forecast. At the end of the first run we found ourselves 3 miles to the port of track so we continued to St. Julien-du-Sault from which we made a further 2 runs identifying the pinpoint each time. We then made a run from Troyes again passing over the pinpoint, situated to the east of a road bordering a wood. Having spent 30 minutes over the target area and not seeing any reception lights, we turned for home at 02.28hrs.

Date NITE MARCH	CAPTAIN.	AIRCRAFT	A/LET	OPERATIONS.	COUNTRY	SoE SIS	C	N.C	REASON FOR N.C
138 SQUADRON									
13/14	F/O... Mullen	HALIFAX	L	FEMUR P/O	France			N.C	No Reception
	F/Sgt Williamson		P	TRAINER 1/3	FRANCE			N.C	.. ..
	F/L Ashley		M	DICK 73	FRANCE			N.C	.. ..
	F/O Clark		K	DICK P	FRANCE			N.C	
13/14	F/L Jamieson		M	DICK 73.	FRANCE			N.C	No Reception
	F/Sgt Mackay		V	TRAINER 169	FRANCE			N.C	No Reception
	F/Sgt Jones		S	DICK P	FRANCE			N.C	No Reception.
	W/O Rodgers		F	STATIONER ..	FRANCE.		C		

161 SQUADRON   * 'C' = COMPLETE

							C	N.C	
13	F/Sgt Landers.		L	PLAYER/BULLET			C		
13/14	F/L Parker	HALIFAX	Y	STATIONER 3R	FRANCE			N.C	
	Capt Hayle		V	BOB 139	FRANCE		C		
	F/Sgt Broadley		X	DICK 70	FRANCE		C		
	F/O McGregor		U	HARRY 27	FRANCE.		C		
	F/Sgt Taylor Bell		T	DICK 70	FRANCE			N.C	Engine Trouble. Ret'd Early.
	F/Sgt Smith		W	TRAINER 198 / SHOPKEEPER & WENCE	FRANCE.			N.C	No Receptions.
14	F/O Hart	HUDSON	N	ARNOLD				N.C	No Contact
14/15	F/Lt Fitzpatrick	HALIFAX	X	GOVERNOR 4	NORWAY		C		
16	F/Lt Clayton	HUDSON	N	BULLET/PLAYER.			C		
13/14	F/L Abecassis	LYSANDER	D	LOUISE.	FRANCE		C		

A strange night - a wasted effort. A copy of the Operations Record Books of No.138 Squadron and No.161 Squadron for the night 13/14th March 1944. The difference in success is very marked! We were getting to the DZs but there was no reception committee for us (Courtesy Public Records Office ref:AIR 20/8459/8460).

We still had our wretched leaflets to scatter, four bundles of issue No F25. We were coming up to Sully, our first turning point, when I suggested to Eric that he guided us in and give the OK to Ernie when to drop. I heard a howl of laughter from Fg/Off Ash in the rear turret and asked him over the intercom what that was all about. He said that the string of one of the bundles had failed to break and in the bright moonlight he had been able to follow it down. It had hurtled into the main street (I sincerely hope it did no damage!). I told Ernie to take more care otherwise next time he would find himself putting them through the letter boxes!

We landed at base having been in the air 6 hours and 5 minutes. Out of 8 squadron aircraft the only successful sortie was flown by W/O Yardley on

'STATIONER 41'. The rest reported 'No Reception'. I wondered why the Squadron's operations that night had been so unsuccessful. It was probably London failing to transmit radio instructions - a strange night, a wasted effort.

Two squadron aircraft went to Norway on the night of 14th/15th March. On that night, just before midnight, the Tempsford ORB reports 'Air Raid Red many hostiles overhead.' This was the third similar report during the time I was at Tempsford. Two took place in February, one on the 13th at 20.55hrs, the other at 00.50hrs on the 19th when I was on leave. We had another false alarm when someone taking off yelled 'Bandits!' over the radio and all the runway lights were switched off. Once airborne he had the decency to apologise but by that time we who were waiting to take off were gibbering idiots.

I recall one night, during one or other of these 'red alerts', I happened to peep out from wherever I was hiding and saw a parachute flare burst into life over the solitary cooling tower on the north-west side of the field. Its brilliant white light lit up the airfield and the surrounding countryside for miles around and cast swift moving shadows of low flying aircraft turning south towards London. Next day it was reported in the newspapers that low flying Me 210/410 aircraft had attacked London. It was obvious they used the cooling tower as a pinpoint to turn south and then flew down the 'iron beam' direct to London. The report did not say whether or not they were delayed by signal failure!

The 15th/16th saw 6 squadron aircraft out, we stayed at home. Letters home say Frank Sinatra was blasting my ear drums in the mess with 'Pistol Packing Momma' and that I was suffering from an illusion that I might fly an Oxford down on leave to Fairlop. I cannot remember an Oxford on the Unit but I suppose there must have been. We had a terrific farewell party in the mess, given to someone in our flight who had completed his tour of operations, my active participation in it helped to ease the pain of having heard that my leave had been cancelled. The massive hangover I suffered the following morning was no illusion.

Of the 8 aircraft out on Resistance operations on the night of 18th/19th, 138 Squadron supplied 6, all to France. We'd had a great 3 days rest and Lloyd was fit again to rejoin the crew. Our target was *'WHEELWRIGHT 61'* a pinpoint in the great forests south of Bordeaux. On our way in, at 23.27hrs, we reported a very large explosion in the Bergerac area, some 85 kms due east of Bordeaux. Thirteen aircraft of 617 Squadron were bombing an explosives factory; no wonder that bang was big! We commenced our DR run from Marmande on the River Garrone about 80 Kms S.E.Bordeaux. It was a text book operation, at 3,000 feet we picked up a *REBECCA* signal 20 miles out. At 23.58hrs we ran over the pinpoint and the lights were switched on with the correct letter flashing. We turned and dropped from 700 feet, our IAS (Indicated Air Speed) being 150 mph. On the way back just south of Angouleme we saw a square of lights in the middle of nowhere, possibly a prison camp. We saw them again on another trip but never found out what went on there. We landed after 6 hours 20 minutes and found that one container had 'hung up' which was a pity.

The following morning I got a raspberry from the OC Flying for keeping my aircraft on the runway too long during the previous night's take-off. It was a stupid thing to do. Apart from over-stressing the undercarriage there was the point that had a tyre burst there would have been the most spectacular prang ever. After that my day improved - I was told my leave had been reinstated.

On 20th March Dorothy and I wrote to each other, she telling me how wonderful it was to be home on leave and how disappointed she was not having me with her. I wrote to her saying my leave had now been reinstated and how I wished everyone would make up their minds! That night 9 of us took off, 6 from 138 Squadron. Our target, *'JOHN 59'* was south of Lyon and we crept down there via Cabourg, The Isles in the Loire, Sancerre, Dijon, Roanne and Condrieu, which is on the Rhone, roughly 50 kms due south of Lyon. From there we intended to make our DR run but we couldn't find it, the cloud base being 3,000 feet and 10/10ths cover. We finally found a pinpoint N.E. of Valance and started a 30 minute search for the DZ - which we couldn't find. 'No lights of any description seen en route. No joy from the *REBECCA*, aircraft set working OK,' says the report. Cloud conditions remained the same over the target area, 10/10ths, base 3,000 feet. They were very low and it was bloody dark! At touchdown we had been airborne 7 hours 25 minutes. During debriefing I was shattered to hear that Plt/Off Pick, also on *'JOHN 59'* had completed his mission. Hopefully he found it first and the reception committee afterwards packed up and went home. It helped to know Sqdn/Ldr Wilding, 'B' Flight Commander, jettisoned his load due to bad weather!

We had not been on the ground long before scooting off on 5 days leave and 'K' King went into the hangar for inspection. The squadron was out twice while we were away.

CHAPTER ELEVEN

PETER FIVE

Der Stern Licht am Mond zerbricht,
Doch dich zerbrach's noch immer nicht.

The starlight pales before the moon,
Will you yourself be paling soon.

Bundeslied der Galgenbruder / Chorus of the Gallows Gang

Galgenlieder - Christian Morgenstien

I returned from leave on 25th March, as usual it had been all too short. Dorothy had given me a gold signet ring for my 21st birthday which was two weeks away. It was obvious I would not be home in such a short time to celebrate the event. It had my initials engraved on the face of it and the name Dorothy engraved inside it, I'm still wearing it - 50 years later!

In a letter to Dorothy I said Kit and I had to walk to camp from the station and that evening we had our 'usual house warming party' which was an after-leave party to celebrate 'the gathering of the clans'. I said this was going to be my last for some time. The weather was fine and warm, Spring was there at last, the sun shone and the heat shimmered on the ground. My resolutions not to drink until my twenty first birthday went for a 'burton' when someone in the flight became the father of a son. Lucky man in more respects than one, I said, he will also finish his operational tour next week.

'K-King' came out of the hangar but wasn't fit enough to fly so we decided, as a crew, to go to Sandy that evening for a party. Mac took some photographs of us before we went. Weatherwise it was another perfect day - a little fog about, otherwise a clear blue sky. It must have been quite a party, I fell off my bike on the way home; it also showed how weak willed I was!

The following morning I was two minutes late for breakfast and the doors of the dining room were slammed in my face, it annoyed me. I seem to remember these same doors causing quite a fuss on a previous occasion when a queue had formed waiting for them to open. It was our usual custom, we were all young men and hungry by the time meals were served. However, there was much shouting and waving of arms by a senior officer telling us not to form a queue, he said it was unbecoming for an officer to do so etc. It was all rather petty.

Our names appeared on the Ops. Board for the night 26/27th March so we flew a 35 minute air test on 'K'. She started to vent glycol badly from the starboard inner engine and when we landed I told 'Chiefy' (the F/Sgt) of the problem. He took off the cowlings in double quick time and his head disappeared inside the cavity after which he straightened his back, looked at me and pronounced the aircraft U/S - so back she went to the engine fitters. They gave us the spare aircraft LL276 'F' Freddy[1], and a quick air test found her OK.

Our target was *'JOHN 71'*; another 138 Squadron aircraft was also that night on a *'JOHN'* DZ. A total of 4 aircraft were on Resistance operations. We got off at 20.24hrs and made a long detour before arriving at Roanne. At a height of 3,500 feet we picked up a *REBECCA* signal 16 miles out. The DZ lights were very dim and we had to make three runs over them before I was satisfied we could make a safe drop; it was an uneventful run home. We saw an *Occult* (a white light on the ground used as a navigational aid or, above it, as an assembly point for night fighters) flashing PT in the Belleme area - the enemy were in the air too. We landed after being away 6 hours 40 minutes. It looked as if my new talisman, my new ring, was going to work well with my old plastic owl (to help me see at night!) and the black cat (for luck!) both of which were still attached to the strap at the back of my helmet since my EFTS days. With them the future looked bright, there could be no more trouble for me!

On 30th March Fg/Off 'Mac' McMullen, a great friend of mine, an Australian who wore the dark blue uniform of the RAAF, said he wanted to fly to Waterbeach to meet some friends. Mac couldn't have been any older than I and if I remember correctly, wasn't very tall. He had a mop of black curly hair on top of a small round smiling face. We could take the unit Tiger Moth, he said, but reminded me it was considered a 'jinx' and anyone flying it usually got the 'chop'. I remember retorting, '*"Jinx"* - don't be bloody daft!' He flew it there and at Waterbeach we had tea among his friends and I flew it back. Neither of us had flown a Tiger for over two years and my landing back at Tempsford was a memorable one. I held off about 20 feet up

---

[1] - *This aircraft, flown by Plt/Off J.P. Callagher, failed to return on 1st June 1944.*

and Mac said I nearly parked it on top of the aerodrome control pilot's hut, which caused a bit of panic. I pump-handled the throttle to get some air underneath the wings and finally came to a halt when we ran out of bounce! Luckily the undercarriage remained in one piece. I remember we both thought it highly amusing and got out of the aeroplane roaring with laughter. That night Bomber Command lost 95 aircraft in bright moonlight over Nuremburg, its biggest loss ever - they should never have gone out on such a bright night.

That same night 138 Squadron sent out 5 of its most experienced crews to Belgium. Sqdn/Ldr Russell, the new 'A' flight Commander, Flt/Lt Ashley, Flt/Lt Mill, Plt/Off Baker (newly promoted from F/Sgt), and W/Off Gregory. Their targets were *'TYBALT 11', 'OSRIC 7', 'OSRIC 27', 'OSRIC 32',* and *'TYBALT 22' / 'BALTHASAR 1'* (2 targets for W/Off Gregory) respectively. It has since been recorded by historians that as high as 30% of the loads dropped in Belgium fell directly into enemy hands. Nevertheless Sqdn/Ldr Russell dropped 15 containers and 1 package; W/Off Gregory completed both targets and dropped 3 agents, 15 containers and 3 packages. Flt/Lt Ashley and Plt/Off Baker reported 'No reception'. They dropped 155 pigeons between them! The large number dropped suggests that there was something seriously wrong in this sector and information was wanted.

Flt/Lt Brian B. Mill crashed in the Wester Scheldt and 3 of the crew were lost at sea, 5 others, including Flt/Lt Mill, were taken prisoner. During the 2 months I knew him he had flown 12 sorties, only two failed due to bad weather. He had dropped 7 agents, 117 containers and 51 packages and was one of our most experienced pilots.

I received a wonderful letter from Dorothy saying no matter how long I was away from her she would never cease to love me and would keep me forever in her heart. I wondered why she said that, I didn't think I was going anywhere, we were already talking about what we were going to do during my long leave in June. Besides, we had already fixed our wedding date for the 9th September.

The following afternoon McBurney and I were looking at the Operational Fuel State Board. The chalked figures on it indicated the number of gallons of fuel each aircraft would be carrying on Ops. that night. We weren't supposed to be so inquisitive, but the gallonage usually gave you some idea how far you were going. Mac commented that we were down for a long,

long trip[2]. It looked like Norway, which would make a change, apart from being tiring and a probable landing at Kinloss on the way back; if the weather was OK they were usually uneventful. I was all for ticking off an easy trip against our tour total.

It was good to see 'King' back on its flight 'banjo' ready to go. We had air tested it again two days back and pronounced it fit. I had duly signed the Form 700 saying so, which pleased 'Chiefy', my ground crew and myself no end. Later that afternoon Kit, Eric, Ron and myself presented ourselves at the large Nissen hut for the collective briefing. Ernie went off to Gibraltar Farm to see what they were putting inside the aircraft. However we had only got inside the door when we were ushered into a small room. I remember the sense of urgency about it all. A chap in khaki leaned against the wall taking it all in. 'What the hell was he doing here,' I asked myself? It was then revealed that we were going to do something special that night in the region north-west of Chateauroux, so much for our 'easy' trip to Norway. I hoped that we weren't going to lug all that fuel to France!

Our main target was 'ORAGE' where we were to drop 2 packages and 6 containers on a triangle of lights. A red and white light would be at the apex, the red would flash 'F' in answer to our flashing 'D' to reception. We were not under any circumstances to drop unless all these conditions were met. One of the packages would be marked with a red cross. This was the important one we were told. I never knew what was inside it but I had a hunch it contained specie[3].

On the way to 'ORAGE' we were to incorporate in our flight plan another DZ, 'PETER 5', on which we were to drop 9 containers and 6 packages. If we didn't get it on the way out, perhaps we could catch it on the way back. We were then given our take off time, weather briefing and radio frequencies. It seemed an easy trip, we would be home and tucked up in bed before most of the others. There was one snag, we were informed that our normal routes into France were now forbidden. Entry via Cabourg was out, in fact the whole area along that coast was now a 'prohibited area'. The

[2] - *A Halifax could hold enough fuel to drive a small car at 30 mpg approximately 54,000 miles!*

[3] - *Specie - money in coin form.*

order was signed by an American[4]. In retrospect I do not see the logic of prohibiting us from flying over this area since our operations had been checking in and out of France with the German Radar at 6,000 feet over this point for years. It presented us with a problem, we were now forced to fly over routes where flak areas were virtually unrecorded.

Kit and I sat down to work out our routes, I cannot remember precisely what they were except we decided to give the residents of Bognor a quiet night by not running down their pier at zero feet! We would leave by way of Selsey Bill. We were going in and out of France near the Cherbourg Peninsula and this would take our outward route over the secondary target on the way down. If we failed to see it we could sweep across to the primary target at Chateauroux, if OK, drop and then return back for a second go at *'PETER 5'*. These tactics would bring us pretty close to Tours on the way back and there was a railway bridge to the west of the town which would give us a good pinpoint over the Loire. There were no flak areas marked on the master map.

An hour before take off the normal routine would begin: I would counter-sign the authorization book which permitted us to fly on 'Operations as Ordered' and went to my locker in the crew room to change into flying kit. Long Johns first, then large white socks over stockinged feet stuffed into flying boots, a dark blue woollen polo-necked jersey under the battle dress blouse[5]. Yellow life jacket (Mae West) next, bow tying the tags between the legs. Parachute harness next, clipping the shoulder straps into the quick release buckle, the two crutch straps wagging behind like a dog with two tails (to avoid acute discomfort or possible injury!). To complete the ensemble, gloves (if a cold night all three pairs - silk, woollen and leather). Into the parachute section next door, plugging the helmet into a tester to see if working OK, then collect a chest-type parachute, checking the release pins were not bent. Finally, collect flying rations, probably a flask of coffee, a tin of pure Californian orange juice, a bar of chocolate or two and perhaps a sandwich.

We all dressed thus. The navigator took special care to leave his sextant

---

[4] - *This area was, of course, where the 'D Day' landings were to take place and, presumably, the powers-that-be must have thought unnecessary traffic should be kept out of the area.*

[5] - *Our smart white one had been withdrawn, 'Too conspicuous if trying to evade capture,' they'd said.*

in his locker. This he did in spite of the Navigation Leader's plea that he was finding sextants in the lockers of missing navigators! We didn't understand what all the fuss was about, they were of little or no use at low level anyway. We left the warm comfort of the crew room and a crew bus took us out into the cold darkness where our aircraft stood on its hard standing. Leaving the bus I would hurry over to the small Nissen hut where our ground crew were waiting. Entering, I would be greeted warmly, as always, in the fug and blinding light. The Form 700 would be pushed in front of me informing me the daily inspections had been done and what the fuel state was. I would check it and sign it confirming that I was satisfied and accepted the aircraft. I would always leave, to shouts of, 'Good luck! Safe trip!' and I would step out into the darkness with the ground crew. Mac and I would then complete the outside check of the aircraft - she always looked so very big in the dark. The probing beam of Mac's torch caressed each engine, searching carefully for a tell-tale drip or slick of oil, an unfastened clip or cowling button. We would check the covers were off the engines and the pitot head, inspect the tyres for creep, check undercarriage pressure from gauges in the inboard engine nacelles, and finally that the starting accumulator was in position and plugged in. We then joined the others standing in the darkness at the rear of the aircraft for a last cigarette.

We were then alone, seven battle experienced aircrew, the ultimate tip of the iceberg. Somewhere, someone had planned the operation; the orders had filtered down; mechanics had pried, inspected, topped up, filled, cleaned, wiped and fussed; armourers had loaded, fused, harmonised and tested. Each tradesman to his task. Messages had been transmitted by the BBC warning of our coming and reception teams would soon be leaving their homes, defying the curfew and the enemy. The stage had been set, now in darkness, but later in the spotlight of the moon the drama would be enacted. We were the principal players, machine the expedient, man the expendable.

Perhaps we were luckier than those sitting in a slit trench or freezing in salt water! In the darkness a nearby motor would burst into life shattering the peace and our complacency. I would look at my watch and say, 'We'd better get started.' A shower of tiny sparks were shed as unfinished cigarettes were extinguished. Parachute harnesses were adjusted, the dog tails disappearing, our masculinity emphasised around our crutch by the tightened straps. My parachute would be pushed through the rear hatch and I would clamber after it into the darkness of the hull. Mac following me, the beam of his torch lighting the way as we made our way forward, checking as we went each neatly packed package was stowed with parachute packs uppermost.

Reaching my seat, I would hang my helmet on the control wheel while I stowed my parachute, then unlock the controls and stow the locking gear. This done, I climbed into the seat, switched on the cockpit lights and adjusted the brightness. A mass of silent fluorescent green instruments would stare blandly at me, watching my every move. All around in the darkness there was the noise of activity. Pulling my helmet onto my head had a feeling of comfort - we had flown a lot of time together. I connected the oxygen system to the face mask and plugged into the intercom and radio circuit. Strapping myself in, I was now part of the aeroplane - the brains - God help it! I would grab the controls moving the wheel left and right, pushing hard forward and pulling back. Pushing hard left and right with my feet on the rudder bar, the brakes would hiss back at me. There was no resistance to any of my actions - the controls were free. Eric would now be seated at my side in the jump seat and strapped to it. Kit, having stowed his gear up front, had now retired to his take-off position on the bench in the rear. 'OK, Lloyd?' I enquired over the intercom, 'OK, Nobbie,' came back. I checked with the rest of the crew one by one, 'OK, Ernie?,' 'OK, Ron?,' 'OK, Mac?', 'OK, Kit?', 'OK, Eric?' They all replied in the affirmative.

Checking the undercarriage lever was in the 'down' position, the flaps up the lever in neutral, and the bomb doors shut. I would move switches to 'ON' and then say to Mac, 'OK, Mac let's start the port inner.' 'Ground/Flight switch to ground,' would come the reply. He then selected the appropriate fuel cock and closed the radiator shutter. I would check the vacuum pump was selected to the port inner to get the gyro instruments working (I would check the pump on the starboard inner later). Moving the port inner throttle slightly forward, and pushing down the mixture control and supercharger lever, the airscrew lever would be moved up into the 'fully fine' position and the ignition switched on. Sliding the cockpit window open I would peer into the darkness, and seeing a white face below staring back at me I would yell at it , 'Clear for starting?!' 'Clear!' would come back from the face in the gloom. 'Start port inner!' I would yell and in the darkness I would discern a hand raised with a thumb up. An unseen body would prime the engine while another operated the external starter.

Internally the starter magneto was switched on and the starter button was pressed. The heavy four-bladed propeller would turn slowly at first and then gain momentum. The engine would protest noisily before bursting into life with a roar and a puff of smoke emitting from the exhaust. The tip of the airscrew would blend into one continuous yellow circle. The instruments in front of me were jerked into movement, surprised, as if they had been kicked in the backside. Their attention now diverted from me to their own individual actions. I would move the throttle slightly forward to have the engine running fast enough to prevent the plugs oiling up. Three times more Mac and I would repeat this procedure, the noise increasing. Finaly the ground/flight switch would be confirmed switched to flight.

The aircraft would now be vibrating with energy, our 'iron bird' had come to life. The pitot head heater and the navigation lights would be switched on. Orders to keep navigation lights on over UK were new - there had been overzealous, so called friendly, RAF trigger-happy night fighters around! I hoped I would remember to switch them off again at the coast! Check the DI (direction indicator) was synchronised with the magnetic compass and uncage it and see that 'George', the auto pilot, was sleeping but ready to wake.

The engines were warmed up, during which time I lowered and raised the flaps which checked the hydraulic system, then each engine would be opened up individually and the constant speed airscrews checked through fully coarse to fully fine. In turn I tested each magneto, checked the engine boost, the oil pressure and temperature. Finally, I checked the brake pressure, there was a loud 'psssssst' of escaping air as each wheel brake was tested. At last we would be ready to go and I would wave 'chocks away' from my window, a body would disappeared beneath the port engine, return and watch another unseen body under the starboard side. He would straighten up and raise his thumb, indicating all chocks clear. 'Test your guns, Lloyd' and his acknowledgement would be followed by a noisy burst of machine gun fire from the rear as Lloyd cleared his guns into the sand butt beside the dispersal. 'Guns OK, Nobbie.'

Two torches in front of the aeroplane beckoned us forward, 'OK, here we go,' I say and tension would mount as the brakes were released; the two outside throttles moved gently forward and the increased power began to move us forward. One torchlight remained steady; the other continued to beckon, I was to turn to the right. Touching the brake there would be the familiar protesting squeal and the 'psssssst, psssssst' of the air brakes. We would slowly turn onto the taxy-way where dim coloured lights marked the snaking way to the beginning of the main runway.

Arriving at its threshold I would go through vital actions for take off. T.M.P.F.F., the pilot's magic formula! T - Trim, the elevator trim wheel two divisions tail heavy, rudder and aileron trim in neutral. M - Mixture fully rich, control down. P - Propellers, pitch fully fine levers fully up, F - Fuel, 'Cock setting OK, Mac?' 'OK, Nobbie.' F - Flaps, press the lever down until 20 degrees registered on the dial, Mac confirmed the radiators were shut. Flash 'K' on the recognition lights and, from the glass dome at the top of the ACP (aerodrome control pilot's) caravan, an Aldis lamp would send out a green ray of light. It was directed at us and flashed 'K'. Turning the aircraft slowly onto the runway, its bright parallel lights converging into the distant night, an illuminated finger pointing the way. Another flash of green light from the ACP. 'Turret turned to port, Lloyd?' I queried (to make his exit easier, should he be left dangling on the broken end of a wrecked aeroplane). 'OK, Nobbie.' 'Never says much,' I would think to myself. 'Keep a good look out, Lloyd,' I would say, and added for the benefit of the others, 'Here we go.'

I would tightened the throttle nut and push the throttles slowly forward with my right hand, moving the port throttles ahead of the starboard to counteract the inevitable swing to port. Eric, beside me, followed behind the four levers with his left hand to prevent them from falling back. The engines responded loudly, lovingly, the airscrews spun into an invisible arc. The brakes, released, hissed back at me like angry snakes. We moved forward, slowly gathering momentum, forward pressure on the stick brought the tail off the ground. Needles moved across dials until engine revolution counters and boost gauges reached their peak and the airspeed indicator slowly recorded our increasing forward speed. The directional gyro remained steady - we had the making of a good take off.

Outside the runway lights, passing slowly at first, now flashed by. We were straining to get off the ground. The air speed indicator needle was pointing to 105 mph. A slight backward pressure on the control column and the rumbling mass had become a bird. A touch of brake, to stop the wheels rotating. With Mac's finger on the solenoid, should the lever fail to move, my right hand went down beside my seat and I pulled the undercarriage lever up. Two green lights on an instrument in front of me turned red indicating that the undercarriage was on the move. They went out, the undercarriage doors slammed shut. I raised the flaps and throttled back. The speed built up as I moved the aeroplane into a climbing turn. Behind us twinkled the parallel lights of the receding runway.

Eric stowed his jump seat and moved into the nose, Kit came up from the rear and grinned at me as he passed by. The team settled down to work. At 3,000 feet I straightened up on our course to Reading and made the necessary engine adjustments to maintain height. The instrument panel settled down like an audience after an overture, the curtain raised and the first actors appearing on the stage. The first act of this irreversible drama, orchestrated in secret places, had begun. The first pawn had been moved silently into place, without a word spoken between command and commanded.

At Selsey, its outline now clearly defined in the moonlight, I switched off the navigation lights and pushed us nearer to the sea. I hoped our new track would find another gap in the German radar chain as we had probably found at Cabourg. The night was peaceful, our way illuminated by the brightness of the moon, casting our moving shadow on the water below. Kit said we were approaching the coast and it was time to climb to 6,000 feet. Although I had my doubts about this manoeuvre it hadn't so far caused us any problems. Many months after, Mac said he once saw a night fighter pass right over us when we were crossing the coast at this height. I am sure I would have made some comment on this in an operations report had it happened - there is none.

Eric made a visual pin point of our position as we crossed the coast - surprisingly *GEE* was still working, as yet unjammed. He passed on the map reference and the time to Kit. I pushed the nose down and sought comfort from the nearness of mother earth. Relaxing in my seat I released my safety harness for more comfort. We trundled on our way over farms and villages making our presence below heard by a crescendo of noise as we passed swiftly overhead. We pinpointed our position on the Loire - a ribbon of reflected light in the moonlight. A change of course from Kit directed us towards the first DZ, *'PETER 5'*. On ETA we searched for the telltale lights and its flashing identification signal. There was no sign of them which, under the great difficulties they had to face, was not surprising. Kit and I decided not to hang about and he gave me a course to the next target *'ORAGE'*. We would have another look for *'PETER 5'* on the way back.

The site at Chateauroux came up with surprising suddenness. We could clearly see the triangle of burning fires and I circled while Ron flashed the call sign on the Aldis lamp. Ernie disappeared into the rear of the aircraft to prepare the special delivery for them. There was no response to our signal and I flew away to give them a few minutes to think and then went back. We signalled again and still there was no reply. Our instructions were quite clear, we were not to drop unless we received the correct response. We must have been making a lot of noise in the night and it was pointless to put those on the ground at risk any longer. Why hadn't they given us the letter? Reluctantly, I asked Kit for a course home which would also give us a second shot at *'PETER 5'*.

From out of the darkness there was a flash of white light. It was on the port side of the aircraft and to my mind quite deliberate. We were at the DZ's ETA and I said I was going to circle and investigate. Kit moaned, 'For Christ's sake, why don't you keep on the present course'; he was not too happy with my nightly meandering. 'Navigation was difficult enough,' he always said, 'without the pilot pissing about!' Nevertheless I turned to port and asked Eric to keep a look out in the nose and Mac to keep his eyes peeled from the astrodome. I turned through 360 degrees but saw nothing of the DZ and finally lined up my compass with the course we had previously been steering. Possibly it had been a farmer opening his back door or a friendly flash of light waving us on our way, but on second thoughts it was far too late into the night for such niceties. The wind had now played its part in our deadly drama. During that turn, unbeknown to me, it had shifted us a mile or two to the east and we were now flying parallel to our old track. This pawn was about to be taken by the rook.

Although it wasn't the first time I was still confused when that blinding light illuminated us. It was the suddenness of it all. There was no finger of probing light, searching, warning us of the impending danger. It was as immediate as an electric light being switched on in a dark room but brighter, much, much brighter. I could see into the inner most darkness of my instrument panel. The altimeter was reading 300 feet. I instinctively turned away from its beam; our belly now an easier target for those below. Then it started. How smart those gunners were, how alert they must have been, how accurate their aim.

The Boulton Paul Mk I rear turret of a Halifax containing the firepower we need but which Lloyd could not bring to bear (Photo: Chaz Bowyer)

The tracer came up slowly at first and then the coloured fire balls rocketed past. The searchlight stuck to us, like a leach sticks to flesh. Lloyd was unable to bring his guns to bear to give them a taste of their own medicine. My kingdom for a mid upper turret! The tracers were no longer missing us, they were no longer rocketing past as near misses. A new sound filled the air not unlike stones rattling on a tin roof. We were being hit. The light went out as abruptly as it had come on. The rattle of hits ceased. I quickly checked with everyone to see if they were OK; surprisingly no one had been hit.

The port inner engine was on fire, flames were streaming out of the exhaust and curving over the wing. 'Mac, I am going to feather the port inner,' I said; I am sure my voice wasn't as calm as these words sound. I pulled the airscrew control fully back through the gate, closed the throttle, hit the feathering button, switched the engine off and then pressed the fire extinguisher while Mac turned off the fuel. The propeller slowed down, its four huge blades thickening as they turned into the direction of flight and stopped. The flames ceased to stream out of the exhaust ports of the engine but a more ominous sight appeared as the flames were now burning fiercely at the rear of the engine nacelle. 'Mac, go back and see if the flames are burning behind the fireproof bulkhead!' I yelled.

Mac reported it looked as if they were. It was pointless to stay with the aircraft any longer. The wing looked as if it was being cut through with an acetylene torch. I pulled the nose up to gain height. It was going to be tricky bailing out at this height I thought. 'Parachute, parachute, prepare to abandon aircraft,' I ordered, 'Wait until I give the order, we've only got 1,200 feet.' A shaky voice came over the intercom; it was Lloyd, 'Nobbie,' he said, 'I've released my parachute in the aircraft!' It didn't really matter, I was caught between two stools, the port wheel had now dropped out of its housing and there was no response to the controls as I tried to pick up the dropping wing, we were describing a nose down arc towards the ground. There was little to do but pull back on the starboard throttles; the aircraft responded by lifting its wing. We were now very close to the ground and I was temporarily in control. I flicked on the landing light switch and pulled on the landing light toggle. Before me spread a wide beam of light illuminating the ground ahead and in the middle of our path - a tree. I wished I had not released my safety harness. I heaved back on the wheel and closed the remaining throttle. We staggered over the tree and hit the ground, bounced and ran forward for a about a hundred yards. My feet came off the rudder bars and went into the air behind me. I held grimly to the control wheel which deposited my face onto the instrument panel as we slithered sideways to a halt. I waited for the fire ball - it never came. The wing was still burning fiercely. I took off my helmet and, by habit, hung it on the control wheel. I can still see my lucky owl and black cat gently swinging from the rear strap.

I was now in a panic to get out of this burning wreck and reached up to the roof for the release lever of the escape hatch above my head. To my relief it worked and I was able to fling the hatch open. 'This way out! I've got the hatch open!' I yelled. I felt a restraining hand tugging at me, preventing me from climbing through the hatch, it was Mac. He pulled me down and led me through the gap where, just by the engineer's position, the nose of the aircraft had broken away from the rest of the fuselage. In my panic I hadn't seen this enormous hole just behind me. We got out and were shortly followed by Ernie.

We ran away from the wreckage expecting it to blow up at any moment. Shouts coming from the rear of the aircraft arrested our attention. Lloyd had traversed his turret to escape, but could not get out. Mac ran over and beat his bare fists against the jammed turret doors. With Lloyd pushing from the inside the doors flew open and Mac pulled him free. All four of us stood at a distance looking at the burning wreck. The flickering flames played tricks with our shadows in the quietness of the night.

There had been no fear in my heart, neither had there been a moment of truth, no flashing of one's past through one's mind, nor any thought of death. The action had been too short, too inconceivably quick, and I had been far too busy for any such thoughts to cross my mind. I stared at the burning wreck, incredulous that I could have survived it, that anyone could have survived. The sight reminded me of a Phoenix from the ashes of which nothing would ever rise again, my hopes and youthful aspirations were burning before me.

It was very quiet. There was movement within the wreck, the sound of an obstruction being pushed aside, of footsteps moving slowly each step echoing as if breaking a large twig. From out of the wreck staggered Kit, his head bleeding, his right arm horribly twisted and broken. I was shaken from my self-pity, and ran back to the aircraft where I went inside through the gap from which I had left, through which Kit had just appeared. Perhaps someone else would be in need of help. I quickly searched, I could find no one. There was no discernable trace of Eric or Ron in the mass of wreckage that few moments before had been our aircraft.

Then I remembered the package. My instructions under these circumstances were to destroy it. From its rack I took the incendiary bomb to be used for such a purpose. Removing the safety cap I struck the plunger home and, aiming carefully, threw it near the white package with the red cross. Then I fled in terror from the wreckage, not believing my good fortune that she hadn't exploded during the few minutes I had been inside her. We waited and watched for the searing white light of burning magnesium to illuminate the wreck internally, signifying the ignition of the bomb. Like the initial expected ball of fire, it never came. We had to assume that the bodies of the two missing members of the crew were either under the wreckage or inextricably entangled within it.

That is all I know of how my two very good friends, Sergeant Eric Keep, bomb aimer, and Sergeant Ronald Thompson, wireless operator/air gunner, died. The time was just after midnight, 1st April 1944. The place Vallee de Cosse, Vernou-sur-Brenne, France. It took many years to purge myself of the nightmare of their death. I went over my actions which led to it a thousand times until the healing of time said, 'Enough'. In retrospect, we who survived were extremely lucky.

Sergeant Ron Thompson (WOP/AG) who, with Sergeant Eric Keep (bomb-aimer), was killed in 'K'- King 1st April 1944. Ron was 22 years old and Eric just 21.

That night 138 Squadron's effort was 15 aircraft. One to Denmark, four to Norway, where our piano-playing, blind-flying instructor Flt/Lt Johnson DFC dropped three agents. The remaining ten went to France, where, notably, W/Off Yardley brought his agent back, as a car was seen on the road. Flt/Lt Pick, newly promoted from Plt/Off, had no reception, F/Sgt MacKay returned due to bad weather and was also hit by flak and Flg/Off McMullen completed. One aircraft 'K - KING', Flg/Off F.B Clark went missing.

A panoramic view of Vallee de Cousse. 'K'-King crashed beyond the top left of the picture, plowing its way through the vineyards of Fernand Thierry and Maurice Rougebec (Photo Editions Valiore)

As was the custom, I expect my photograph in the Flight Commander's office was decorated with a red halo and beneath it pinned the red skeleton made from pipe cleaners, one hand of which held a blood dripping chopper! A telegram was sent to my parents, it read:-
PRIORITY-CC MR S H CLARK DEEPLY REGRET TO INFORM YOU THAT YOUR SON FLYING-OFFICER S.B.CLARK 135098 IS MISSING AS A RESULT OF AIR OPERATIONS AGAINST THE ENEMY ON THE NIGHT OF 31ST MARCH/1ST APRIL 1944 STOP PLEASE ACCEPT MY DEEPEST SYMPATHY LETTER FOLLOWS ANY FURTHER INFORMATION RECEIVED WILL BE IMMEDIATELY COMMUNICATED TO YOU PENDING WRITTEN NOTIFICATION FROM AIR MINISTRY NO INFORMATION SHOULD BE GIVEN TO THE PRESS = OC 138 SQUADRON

The wreck of Halifax LL252 'K'-King being dismantled by the Germans.
I have trod that path many times since (Photos Courtesy The Resistance)

The telegram must have been dictated over the telephone by someone who had a lisp. Both my father's and my own christian name begin with an 'F'! It must have caused great distress both to my parents and to Dorothy. I often wondered what my Australian chum, Mac McMullen, must have thought about our ride in the 'jinx' Tiger Moth; young airmen were highly superstitious in those days. I never found out, Flg/Off H.H.McMullen and his crew were presumed lost at sea on 8th May 1944. He was flying Halifax

An extract from the Operations Book showing those who flew on the night 9/10th April. The top half is No.138 Squadron and the lower part No.161 Squadron
(Courtesy Public Records Office ref:AIR 20/8459/8460)

Date	Name		Letter	Target	Country	Remarks
9/10	F/Lt Lawrence		C	Stationer 53	France	N.C No Reception
	F/Sgt Hayman		P	" 134	France	C
	F/Sgt Jones		H	" 36	France	N.C No Reception
	W/O Palmer		N	" 52	France	C
	P/O Baker		O	Wheelwright 51	France	C
	W/O Gregory		R	Stationer 43	France	N.C No Reception
	F/Sgt Williamson		V	Pimento 78	France	N.C
	W/C Yardley		D	Wheelwright 73/Premoonle France		N.C Wireless Equipment c/s
	F/Lt Ashley		A	Wheelwrkht 90	France	N.C No Reception
	F/Lt Johnson		M	Scientist 52	France	N.C No Reception
	F/Lt Stiles		E	Harry 28	France	C
	F/Sgt Mackay		K	Pimento/Australia France		C P.78 N.C.N.R.
	S/L Wilding		J	Stationer 238/Tarwemi France		C St.33 N.C.N.R.
	F/L Ack		F	Tom 35	France	N.C No Reception
	F/Lt Thomas		Q	Tom 51	France	C
	F/O Mc Mullan		L	Dick 7	France	N.C No Reception
9/10	P/O Caldwell	Halifax	U	Temple // Peter 38	France	C
	P/O Smith		W	Pack 60	France	C
	Lt Pilfingsrud		X	Tom 42	France	N.C No Reception
	F/Sgt Tattersall		T	Stationer 144	France	C
	F/Sgt Bramsden		Z	" "	France	C
	F/Sgt McGibbon		Y	Syringa // Dick 8	France	C
	Sgt Benier		Y	Stationer 50	France	N.C No Reception
	F/L Hale	Hudson	M	Author 31	France	C
	F/O Ibbot		P	Davidstowe	France	C
	F/O Ferris		N	Stationer 116	France	C
	F/Sgt Merril		R	Bob 165	France	N.C No Reception

LL192, his target *'TABLEJAM 46'* in Denmark. Sqdn/Ldr 'Greg' Holdcroft, the Senior Administration Officer at Tempsford, was very kind and sympathetic when tidying up my affairs with my parents. He had been an observer in the First World War. We corresponded until his death. He once wrote to me saying how proud he was to have served at Tempsford. There was little doubt that he felt each casualty as if it were his own. I found a letter in a book he had sent to me - *'Moon Squadron'* by Jerrard Tickle. Greg had signed his name inside the book and his letter said it was a spare copy. He was delighted, he said, to have collected his post war credits amounting to £140! I mourned his death. It was the loss of a good friend. I wished he had written that book about Tempsford which he had often threatened. Of the 93 aircraft (16 from crashes) which were known to have been lost by 138 Squadron (the ORB for its early operations is incomplete), 74 were Halifaxes. The crews of 11 were known to me. Squadron losses were approximately 3.00% which was just about par for the course when compared with any Main Force Bomber Squadron. By the very nature of our low level operations, and from my own experience, it is doubtful whether many crews had time to take to their parachutes to save themselves.

This is a photograph of the operations board in the control tower at Tempsford. The information shown is based on an operation which took place on the 9/10th April 1944 (see extract from the Operations Book on preceeding page). The differences are: W/O Gregory was flying the aircraft attacked by the fighter, W/O Yardley had the radio problems, F/L Hale was flying a Hudson that night and F/Sgt Morris has been left out. No lights u/s, no Woodbridge landing and no oil leaks. The pundit for Tempsford flashed TE or TQ. I ask myself why was this picture allowed to be taken? It shows the name of almost every Halifax pilot at Tempsford. The WAAF using the chalk is Sgt Lintott (Photo: C. Annis via Ken Merrick)

In retrospect Tempsford was a mystery, an enigma. On the surface it was a secret, high security minded base where we were forbidden to discuss our activities outside the limits of the base; within it we were not allowed to discuss previous sorties, albeit to our mutual advantage. Yet No 161 Squadron Lysanders, complete with large overload tank and boarding ladder, were parked outside a hangar close to the railway for all passing rail passengers to see. Irish workmen lived and worked in the confines of the airfield and certainly took an interest in our activities. Photography, other than that of crews, was strictly forbidden and yet a photograph was taken of the operations board which showed the names of practically all the Halifax crews on the unit (I wonder who authorised it and where that photograph went to?). Why were Bomber Command so reluctant to advise us of their French targets? and ... that bloody awful airfield? But in the final analysis the aircrews were a brave lot, the Officers' Mess a fun loving bunch and the ground crews hard working and conscientious - I was privileged to serve in such company.

Endnote:

Flg/Off Nigel.L.St.G Pleasance joined 138 Squadron on 18th May, six weeks after I was shot down. On 18th July 1944, flying Halifax LL387, he failed to return from *'SHIPWRIGHT 9'* a sortie in France. His name and that of his crew are carved on the RAF Memorial at Runnymede, where those Airmen who have no known grave are remembered. Opposite his name is that of Flg/Off Brian.S Leuty, my room mate at Vereeniging, missing on 27th August 1944 whilst flying Lancaster LM225 on a bombing sortie to Kiel. Flt/Lt James F.Muir DFC, a room mate of Nigel's at Vereeniging, was killed whilst flying a 207 Squadron Lancaster about that time. Also Flg/Off Norman Brockhouse and his navigator were killed flying a Beaufighter at No 54 OTU Charterhall (the Unit where Richard Hillary lost his life). Norman was at Hemswell with me and in South Africa with us all. You will recall we were all posted to CFS at Bloemfontein, but insisted on coming home.

CHAPTER TWELVE

LA BELLE FRANCE - I MEET *'LOISEAU'*

'Is there anybody there?' said the Traveller,
Knocking at the moonlit door;

The Listeners - Walter De La Mere
The Oxford Book of English Verse - Oxford University Press - 1930

When the shock had diminished it occurred to us that we must quickly leave this disastrous place, there was little point in hanging about. The obvious way was south, but the Loire presented a formidable barrier. We would need guidance to cross its guarded bridges and deep flowing waters. Firstly Kit needed urgent medical attention to his wounds, we had to get him somewhere where he would be cared for, a farmhouse perhaps. We went north in the hope this direction would mislead our would be captors, allowing us time to find shelter for Kit, and for ourselves to make contact with the resistance.

Our movement was restricted by a row of wire which appeared to be either side of a path, we did not know we had crashed into a vineyard! Once free of this hindrance our progress became easier but Kit became very distressed and our priority was to find somewhere where he would be cared for. Eventually a barking dog led us to a farmhouse and we pounded on the front door and left him. Although he survived the war, albeit with a stiff arm that needed further medical attention, I have never seen him or heard from him since.

Behind us the burning wreck still gave off flames that flickered in the distant darkness. We went noisily through a wood, unseen twigs cracking loudly beneath our feet, branches scratching our faces and beating our shins. The wood cleared and we looked down from a high bank. We couldn't tell what was below, a stream or a road. Mac leapt into the air to find out, his spread-eagled body and the foul language that came from it left us in no doubt it was a road. Eventually we stumbled across a small white hut and tried the door which opened easily. It was darker inside and appeared to be some kind of a tool shed. It seemed a good place to rest; by now we were all very tired.

The vineyard where 'K'-King crashed. The wires pulled us up short of the edge of the cliff. The tree we just cleared is in the top right-hand corner and we came to rest at the bottom of the picture.

Dawn revealed the hut was a tool shed and was situated just below the brow of a hill. Bright white in colour, it could hardly have been more conspicuous in its green environment. It was at the edge of a vineyard and, nearby, we could hear a railway engine labouring its way along an unseen track, a steam whistle shrilled warning of its approach. Someone produced a map printed on silk from an escape kit, provided to assist us to evade capture! Its small scale rendered it virtually useless and gave me the impression that perhaps we weren't wanted back! From it we assessed our position somewhere to the north of Tours, which we knew anyway without referring to that damn irritating map. We decided it would be best if we sheltered in the hut during the day and moved out that night. We knew from briefings at home that the classical German search would be within a 5 mile radius of the wreck the first day, a 10 mile radius the second and 15 on the third. If we survived that we had a good chance of contacting the Resistance. Food and water at that moment were a secondary consideration.

It was Mac who first heard voices and motioned us to silence. He looked out of the unshuttered window and saw two persons walking by in deep conversation. It was now or never, we had to take a chance sometime or other. So I opened the door and Mac called after them. They both stopped,

The small white shed where we hid.

turned and looked at us. We made sure that they could not fail to see who and what we were. To our chagrin, in spite of taking a very good look at us, they looked at each other and, without another word, turned and walked away!

It was pointless for us to move, they would either be back with friends or the enemy. We spent a number of anxious hours expecting the *Wehrmacht* to appear and take us away. In fact the two Frenchmen eventually returned, entered the hut and questioned us; the answers we gave seemed to satisfy them. We asked for food and water and they told us to wait and they would be back. When they returned, after what seemed an eternity, they were four. They interrogated us further, one had been to Canada and questioned Mac about Quebec. His reply in his Canadian accented French satisfied them. They knew about our aeroplane, but had to make absolutely certain we were part of the crew. They said the Gestapo in such circumstances had been known to dress in Allied uniforms and ambushed members of the Resistance as they came to help them. They must have reconnoitred the area carefully before coming to see us again. They said we were near a village called Villedomer, about 7 kms to the north of our wreck, and that we were to stay there until it was safe to move us. Food and drink were brought and a bundle of hay spread over the floor of the hut to give us some kind of bedding. The nights were still very cold but at least we had made a text book contact with the Resistance!

We stayed in that small hut two days before they came to move us. As we were about to leave I found that Dorothy's ring was missing from my finger. Selfishly I said I would not move until it had been found. Fortunately it didn't take long, otherwise I might have come to an early demise there and then! They threaded us down the side of hedgerows, our presence never once exposed to prying binoculars that may have been scouring the countryside for a sight of us. It was a lesson in fieldcraft, these men knew what they were doing and one wondered by their stealth and expertise if they had a nearby DZ to look after, or better still, a landing ground. We were taken some way to an old barn standing in the middle of a field, to which we advanced singly and with caution. It was a great relief to be in such spacious and comfortable quarters. There was plenty of room to walk around and plenty of hay to sleep on. It was here that the stress and emotion of the last few days overcame me, I broke down and openly and unashamedly wept.

The old barn in the middle of the field.

The barn was probably more than a century old, the roof was rippled like a gentle undulating sea across high timbers, each tile clutching precariously to the next as if in fear of being swept away. The huge oak doors had so warped that they now formed an integral part of the building, had they been opened the roof would surely have collapsed. Into them a smaller door had been cut which opened with well oiled ease and when shut fitted snugly into the overall decrepit scene. There was no sign of nearby habitation, unless the stone lean-to at the end of the barn once housed its original custodian. Otherwise the building was completely isolated, standing by itself alone in a field.

At night, on a floor carpeted with thick hay, we slept in an infinity of peace. Before retiring an unknown benefactor brought us a basket of bread, meat pies, wine and fruit; providing us with a sumptuous but only meal of the day. I never knew who this brave man was - he would never give us his name. At dawn, as the sun rose, we cautiously crossed the field one at a time to hide in a nearby cave - our haven for the day. Lying on our stomachs, looking through the undergrowth that concealed its entrance, we passed the time watching a farmer plough his field, the plough was drawn by a pure white horse. We wondered if he knew we were there. At dusk we returned to our barn.

- 'Loiseau' -
Lieutenant Roger Pincon

Eight days after the crash we met Roger Pincon - 'Loiseau' as the resistance called him - a pun on his own name Pincon, which was almost the name of a bird of the finch family. He was a short, thin, wiry sort of man, with a round face and sparkling eyes that gleamed from behind gold rimmed spectacles. When he removed his beret his head was quite bald and his face took on the appearance of a hawk. I thought his code name was very appropriate. He was dressed in black and wore a black beret pulled over his left ear. His appearance gave him an air of mystique, an air of cloak and dagger. There was no mistaking he was French - and proud of it. At that time he was a Lieutenant in the FFI (Forces Francaises de l'Interieur) and 48 years old. We were going to Tours, he explained, where we would stay at his house. A horse and cart had been brought to take us part of the way and civilian clothes were produced and a small haversack into which he insisted we put our uniforms. We didn't look elegant, but we looked the part, that is, if no one saw our flying boots protruding from under our trouser legs! The four of us clambered over the tailboard and settled ourselves among the farm produce. Loiseau took his seat beside the driver, who slapped the reins on the horse's rump and off we jogged. The journey proved uneventful until we came to a level crossing near the village of Montage where we were asked to make ourselves scarce under a pile of sacks. Two men driving a cart must have been an everyday occurrence in the countryside, it was a good enough ruse to cover the real purpose of our journey. Eventually the cart stopped and we got down. It was getting late and the farmer had to get back home before the curfew. We were to go the rest of the way on foot.

I found it difficult to walk in flying boots especially at the speed Loiseau was going, but he never let up until it was quite dark. He then said we had gone far enough. We would cross the Loire by a footbridge (Pont Suspendu Saint Symphorien) at dawn when the guard would be off duty. The nerve of the man! We huddled together to get some warmth at the foot of a churchyard wall and tried to sleep. It was a long and bitterly cold night.

At dawn Loiseau roused us. In the half light, after threading our way past a few houses, he led us over the rickety planking of the footbridge that spanned the fast moving Loire. I remember in the middle of the Loire the bridge crossed a small island and here I felt very conspicuous, imagining that a thousand eyes must be watching us! Fortunately it was not so and once across the river we were swiftly conducted through the back streets of Tours. We crossed the tramway tracks of Boulevard Heurteloup and then moved silently into Rue du Rempart. Loiseau opened a small iron gate at No 115 and led us down a narrow path lined with a high wall. A row of concrete steps led up to the entrance of the house. The door opened and we were quickly ushered inside.

No.115 Rue du Rempart.

Inside the house we were met by a tall elegant woman, Madame Janine Pincon. Her black hair was tightly curled and piled high above her saint-like face giving the appearance of a halo. She smiled at us and welcomed us in. It was a smile rich in fun and good humour, not a trace of fear shadowed it. Unbeknown to us we were to become firm friends for another 40 years until she died. I was to be taken into her family as her second son, 'The son,' she used to say, 'who fell from the skies!' We were motioned into a warm kitchen, where Loiseau stamped his feet and briskly rubbed his hands implying that we were all very cold, tired and hungry. I turned to Mamie Pincon, as much later I was to call her, and said, 'Aujourdui, je suis un homme!' She looked at me puzzled and in answer to the query on her face I said, 'J'ai vingt et un ans aujourdui!' She positively beamed when she understood. This day was my 21st birthday. Mamie was 47 years old when she took us in.

'Loiseau' in front of his house.

I never cease to wonder at these moments, four strangers taken into a home, given food and shelter in a country occupied by an enemy, where the penalty for discovery was death or, perhaps worse, deportation to a Concentration Camp in Germany. We made 21 Allied airmen that had passed through her portals, 17 USAF airmen had been here before and passed down the escape route. Apart from the unseen dangers there was the practical difficulty of feeding us. We watched as fresh eggs and vegetables were emptied onto the kitchen table from a small haversack that Loiseau had been carrying. Soon pots were boiling and into a large frying pan went at least two dozen eggs to make the largest omelette I have ever seen or will ever see! It was a wonderful meal. At the end of it Mamie enquired if we would like some more. 'Enough, enough!' I said, not having room for another morsel. 'Ah! une oeuf, une oeuf?' she replied and before I could stop her another three eggs were frying merrily in the pan!

Madam Janine Pincon
My beloved 'Mamie'

Later that day, 'to mark the occasion', he said, Loiseau disappeared into his cellar and produced two bottles of wine. He had a standard ritual for pouring a bottle of wine. First, with the bottle held between his knees the cork was removed with an ancient corkscrew with a gnarled wooden handle made from the wood of a vine. The cork removed, a small quantity of the golden liquid was poured into a glass held up to the light. A taste, a swill round his mouth, a swallow, and the verdict given in a low growl '...pas bonne.' A quick circuit of the other glasses, the bottle was emptied. In spite of this habitual ritual and identical verdict the wine always tasted marvellous[1]

That night the air raid siren sounded off. Its high and low notes were longer and created a more menacing sound than that of the English siren I had been accustomed to. Mamie assured us there was nothing to worry about - a single aircraft, it happened all the time, she said. We relaxed and continued to play cards on the kitchen table. I was concentrating on the game and oblivious to anything else going on around us. The first explosion was enormous, the shock wave rocked the house, a mirror fell off the wall. My knees trembled and my body shook from the total unexpectedness of it all. It was as if someone had exploded an enormous fire-cracker just behind me - a childish prank, but this was far more deadly. I waited for the window

---

[1] - *I should mention the method of producing white wine in the Loire regions in those days is different to that of today. The vintage of this time would mature with keeping, it was a deep golden colour. Dorthy has had a Vouvray bottle of wine dated the year of her birth (which I daren't disclose!) and in 1992 I was given a 1944 vintage!*

glass to cave in - it didn't. Mamie put the light out and the darkness was illuminated by the pathfinder's cascading pyrotechnics and the flash of exploding bombs. We were quickly ushered downstairs to the cellar. The attack by 180 Lancasters from 5 Group on the railway yards at St Pierre des Corps had begun.[2]

In the cellar we cheered with foolish bravado as each bomb thumped onto the target. In the dim light you could see a thin shower of dust descending upon us as each explosion opened up the cracks in the floor boards. Bottles and tins rattled on shelves adding to that cacophony of hell. Each thump of a 'cookie' striking the ground was terrifying. We couldn't have been very far from the aiming point. Mamie was becoming extremely upset and our laughter and cheers froze. She told us that somewhere beneath that bombing Loiseau was working in the railway shops, repairing Focke-Wulf 190's. I silently thanked God that I didn't have to fly them after the Resistance had been tinkering with them! My thoughts sobered considerably when I asked myself what would become of us if anything happened to him? The all clear sounded followed by silence; we left the cellar. It was 10th April the day after my 21st birthday.

There was a tearful reunion when Loiseau came home the following day. He told us that much of the marshalling yard and buildings had been destroyed. Later we were to hear that there had been very few civilian casualties and very little private property destroyed. Miraculously some workmen sheltering in a tunnel running beneath the marshalling yard had been rescued alive. He commented that RAF bombing was more accurate than that of the USAF who had previously straddled Tours with bombs.

Our stay at Rue du Rempart lasted 10 days. I remember little detail of it as I tried to keep any firm impressions from my mind should I fall into the hands of the Gestapo. I never knew the address until I returned after the war. We spent most of the daylight hours in the attic. A small window gave us a limited view of the town which shimmered in the spring sun. Time passed slowly, our diet consisted mainly of potatoes and haricot beans, supplemented by eggs and the occasional rabbit brought home by Loiseau from the country. There was always plenty of bread and I found out years later that the local baker had been instructed by the Resistance to make sure that plenty was delivered. With such meagre rations as the French had in those days and with such a large family under her roof to keep, I don't know

[2] - *I was to find out much later that Bernard Kent, who subsequently became a friend, was above me in a Lancaster that night.*

how Mamie did it. It must have been a terrible strain on her and her resources. The house wine I recall came from a barrel in the cellar. A funnel into the neck of a bottle, a tap turned on and the bottle filled, not a drop wasted. We were never short of cigarettes.

During the few daylight hours we spent downstairs I could see from the kitchen window that beyond the garden wall there was a coal yard. Covering the loose coal were two planks which led to the firm ground beyond. From the garden to the top of the wall was another wooden plank. I assumed they could not have been put there by accident, but could not fathom out why they were there. Years after I discovered why and will explain it later in my story.

Mamie was a hairdresser and we saw little of her or Loiseau during the day and we remained obediently in the attic during their absence. She once told me that whenever a German officer came into the salon for a manicure they closed the windows and switched the hair driers fully on. Dressed in their high necked uniform the heat produced caused them great discomfort!

The weekend we were there the door bell rang and my heart flipped and I feared the worse, especially as we were downstairs and not in the attic. Before the door was opened we were ushered into the kitchen and bidden be silent. It proved to be an unexpected visit from friends. We saw their shadows through the frosted glass of the dividing doors and heard their animated conversation. They stayed a long time and a lot of wine flowed before they went. It was an eternity for young men to remain silent!

Robert Pincon,
We still meet.

Loiseau's son Robert came home from the South of France where he had been serving with the Maquis. The Germans wanted him for failing to report for work in a Labour Camp. He was a well built, handsome man with a high forehead, close curled black hair and a dimpled chin. I found out much later his good looks were such that they turned the heads of young ladies! I was envious - it never happened to me! Robert brought with him a bottle of clear white spirit from the mountains called *'L'eau de Lidoire'* - a breathtaking firewater, a liquid dynamite!

Loiseau said he was off to Paris to arrange for the next stage of our journey. Our escape packs contained a small quantity of Dutch, Belgian and French currency which we gave to him. He wasn't too happy when he returned; he told us the Gestapo had broken the escape route. However, he said we would be leaving in a few days. We belatedly produced the passport photographs of ourselves wearing civvies, taken at Tempsford, as part of our escape gear. He was upset that we had not produce these before he went to Paris. It would have helped him to get us some false papers, he said. I felt we weren't to know.

On 17th April Loiseau told us we would leave the following day by rail to Dax. Here we would pick up a *'Contrebandier'* who would smuggle us into Spain. More civilian clothing was produced - not a very good fit! At this time there couldn't have been many elegantly dressed Frenchmen in this part of France - shoes and clothes must have been at a premium. Hopefully they would fit us well into the scene. Contrary to instructions received in England, Loiseau insisted that we took our uniforms with us - wrapped in a paper parcel. The following morning we said our goodbyes to Mamie and Robert and departed early. It was good to be out walking again in the fresh air and morning sun. We went straight to the station entrance without deviation. However I do remember somewhere on the way seeing trams rocking their noisy way down Boulevard Heurteloup. They have now gone and the track has given way to a garden.

At the station I quaked on seeing my first German uniforms. Although the *Wehrmacht* were dressed the same as in the instructional films shown us in England I was not prepared for it, it was totally unexpected. I should have been prepared but it had never occurred to me and the sight of them shook me! The railway station at Tours was spacious and the sun streamed down through the high roof giving it a light and airy appearance. The forecourt in front of the platforms was then clear of the conglomeration of buildings which now clutter it. The view of each platform entrance was unrestricted. Large black locomotives could be seen hissing wisps of steam - a scene not unlike that at any English mainline station, except the locos were much larger and the presence of German uniforms, in colour and not black and white as those instructional films!

Loiseau went off to get the tickets. He must have had documentation of some kind to get them, or perhaps a sympathetic Resistance friend behind the station facade. Keep together while he was away, he said. He was gone some time and I turned my back on the others not wishing, for appearance sake, to be too close to them. To my discomfort a smiling young man was walking towards me. There was no doubt he was coming towards ME! ME?? From one side of his belt hung a green tin which held his respirator, from the other hung a bayonet. Both slapped his thighs in unison with the steps his short black jack boots made as he strode towards me. To one side of his fair hair he wore a forage cap on the front of which I could clearly see the badge of an eagle holding a Swastika. On the buckle of his belt that embraced his green *Wehrmacht* uniform, I could read the motto *'Gott Mit Uns.'* He had a rifle slung over his shoulder.

It was his smile that stopped me from running; in any case there was no where to run. He held a cigarette in the fingers of his right hand and, halting in front of me, raised the cigarette to his mouth and politely asked in French if I had a match. I fumbled in my pockets and withdrew a box of matches, they must have been French although I don't remember how I came by them, and replied, 'Oui, Monsieur.' My accent would never have fooled a Frenchman. I took a match out of the box and struck it into a cupped hand and by its flame lit his cigarette. My hand, I am pleased to say, was as steady as a rock, whilst inside I felt like a gibbering idiot. His blue eyes looked directly into mine as he pulled on his cigarette and exhaled the smoke. 'Merci, Monsieur,' he said and turned on his heel and walked away. I sincerely hope that smiling soldier survived the war, he could not have been much older than I.

Loiseau returned from the ticket office with five tickets in his hand, just in time to watch this charade. He thought it would only be a matter of minutes before the four of us were caught. Many years later he told me how pleased he was with the way I handled the situation, 'Without a tremor,' he boasted to his friends (if he had only known!). He added he was alarmed when my hands went up to the cigarette with the lighted match. He thought the game must now surely be up since my hands were pure white from the lack of sun. 'The hands of a woman,' he said, devoid of corns or callouses, and I, acting the role of a peasant! He made sure no one was watching us, came over, and led us to the platform where the train would leave for Dax.

I remember little of that journey south, tickets were inspected once or twice, but no problem arose. He sat to one side on his own, we had no papers, it was obvious he did. We arrived at Dax in the early evening when it was getting dark and almost curfew time. From the station we were led to a nearby piece of waste land and in the gathering dusk I could make out a number of rusting chassis of long abandoned vehicles, tall weeds had grown between the metal skeletons. We stopped before the red rusted corrugated body of a small Citroen van, remarkably the rear doors were intact and opened with noiseless ease. We were to stay here the night, he said, while he went off to find a *'Contrebandier'*. He said he'd be back in the morning. I was under the impression that he had been there before and my confidence in him rose even higher. It would obviously not be long before we were over the border and into Spain - how simple it all would be!

On the floor, a little straw and a few pieces of paper showed signs of previous habitation. Some other fugitive perhaps, either from the law or the

Germans. The four of us clambered inside and sorted ourselves out. There was little room for us to move and once again we found ourselves facing a long, cold, sleepless night. Each movement to ease the stiffness in our limbs created protesting creaks and groans from the small metal tomb in which we were incarcerated. The noise caused by our frequent twisting and turning, I was sure, could be heard for miles in that clear silent night. I began to fear that any moment the doors would be flung wide and unfriendly hands would drag us out.

At dawn the doors were cautiously opened and into the semi-darkness Loiseau peered at us through his spectacles. He had brought food, drink and bad news - the Gestapo had got down as far as Dax and he could not find a *'smuggler'*. It was impossible to go back to Tours, he said, but he would take us as close to the border as he dared. Then he would leave us to cross by ourselves! In the meantime he had discovered that identity papers were not checked on the local trains from Dax to Bayonne and so there would probably be no be trouble passing through the ticket barrier. We caught the early morning slow train out of Dax for Bayonne - it was packed with civilians and military alike. At Bayonne the train came slowly to a halt and like all other trains that have reached its destination a multitude of doors were flung open and people flooded out on to the platform. We passed through the ticket barrier and walked to Biarritz. It was a beautiful, clear, warm morning. At the outskirts of Biarritz we took the road to Ustaritz but soon turned off and made our way in a southerly direction. At a guess we were just over 30kms from the frontier.

We came upon Bassussary, the first village, quite unexpectedly. It was full of *Wehrmacht*, dressed in shirt sleeves going about their morning tasks. One of a crew cleaning a half track took a good hard look at us. My legs turned to jelly, but he decided we were harmless and resumed cleaning. We had passed through the next village, Arcangues, when my enjoyment of this lovely spring morning was brusquely brought to an end by the gesticulations of Loiseau. The look on his face showed he had spotted danger. What could it be, I asked myself. Swiftly and silently he moved us off the road and pointed into the distance. Coming out of the woods that fringed the road a line of troops could just be seen. Battle ready, in single file, wearing steel helmets, *Schmeisser* machine pistols slung across their chests. I wondered how on earth he had spotted them. 'Eyes like a hawk,' I mused, 'like *un oiseau*.' It was then I saw what he must have seen. There was a reflection of sunlight on the silver gorget (worn only on duty) that hung from the neck of the leaders throat. *'Feldgendarmerie'*,[3] whispered Loiseau hoarsely, whereupon he bent his body into a stoop and motioned us to follow him deep into the nearby woods to wait for them to pass.

It was time for him to leave, he said, he could take us no further; besides, he had to get back before the curfew! The frontier wasn't all that far away, he told us and gave us a Michelin map of the area, showing us our position. He warned us to wait for the evening patrol which would come down a nearby road. When that passed, he said, we were to make our way down to the frontier and cross. It sounded all too easy. We were heady with our success of the past two days and had come a long, long way in a very short time without any problems. We were in the woods bordering a road about 3 kms north-east of St Pees, the frontier being about 10 kms due south at Danchama. Nothing could surely stop us now. Over the border tonight and into Pamplona and the British Consulate tomorrow - easy!

Loiseau took his leave of us, shaking each of us by the hand and wishing us *'Bon chance'*. Then, pulling his black beret firmly over his eyes, he disappeared into the trees; it was to be a long, long time before I saw him again. We settled down to wait for dusk. We had plenty of food but our immediate problem was water. Mac came to our rescue. Disappearing into the undergrowth he returned carrying some spring water in the rubber bag provided in our escape kit. We drank the clear water, waited, and dozed in the warm sun. It was the sound of singing that shook us from our dreams, a marching song; a song that kept in step with marching boots and clanking equipment. We heard it first a long way off, it became louder and nearer until it, and they, went by in unison, not a step or voice out of place. The notes of the song drifted across our hiding place, the words sounded like 'EYE EE EYE OH!.' There was no doubt about it, this was the patrol Loiseau told us about. We decided to give it another ten minutes after they had gone by and we would up and go, making use of the remaining half hour or so of light to get us further south on our last dash to freedom. We left our hiding place and climbed the embankment onto the road. There wouldn't be much daylight left now, the shadows were already growing longer.

At first the command didn't register, its significance did not enter my brain. 'Halt!' the word was clipped and, I now realised, menacing. There were about 8 of them, all walking beside bicycles, all very quiet, so quiet we had not heard them coming, unseen until they were on top of us. 'My God!'

---

[3] - *Military Field Police - Wore a silver gorget around their necks suspended by a flat link metal chain. Known within the Wehrmacht as 'Chain Dogs' because of it.*

I thought, 'a second patrol and a silent one at that!' How could we have fallen into such a simple trap? As they approached they swung their rifles from their shoulders into their hands, the bayonets were already fixed and flashed briefly in the setting sun. 'No machine pistols,' I observed. They weren't particularly aggressive but you could see they were alert and ready for trouble - if there was to be any. One of them took a step forward and held out his hand and demanded in guttural French, *'Papiers'*. I tried to bluff it out, 'I have left mine at home,' I replied, I wasn't even sure the French I used was correct, but he appeared to understand. From a map case at his side he produced a large scale military map of the district and asked me where I lived. I looked over his shoulder and traced my finger down the road to a row of houses, pointed, and said, 'La!'

He then turned his attention to the parcel which I had placed on the road. 'What's in the parcel?' he demanded. 'Some food for my mother,' I said. Whereupon he put his bayonet under the string and tossed the parcel high into the air. All eyes were on it as it soared upwards, at the top of its trajectory, the string cut by the bayonet broke and the parcel snapped open and the contents, describing a blue arc, plunged to the ground. The brown paper wrapping followed, floating down to earth like a dead leaf from a tree. 'UNIFORM!' he yelled as my battledress hit the ground. Eight rifle bolts pushed eight bullets into eight chambers, the noise was almost in unison, almost as on parade. They moved back a pace or two as if they had found a colony of lepers. Their rifles levelled at us from the hip and made us raise our hands above our heads. The charade was over. They opened the remaining three parcels finding the other uniforms!

We had been marching for some considerable time, the moon had risen. A nail in the sole of my ancient shoe jabbed painfully into the flesh of my foot. Our guards had fenced us in with their bicycles. The butt of their rifles lay on the saddle, the muzzle on the handlebars. The bullet passed close to my right cheek, I swear I felt the heat of it as it went past. The shock of the cartridge exploding made my reflexes react like a spring released. I felt the blood drain from my face and Mac, who had been talking to me at my side, reacted the same way and leapt sideways to protect himself. There was shouting in a language we did not understand, an animated conversation, followed by loud laughter - for them, it had been a great joke. We continued on our way. He had slipped, so he said, his finger closing on the trigger, the bullet released by accident! I was unhappy in the thought that I knew he was lying. I began to wonder what flattened town in Germany he and his family had come from. The pain in my foot disappeared.

A sentry opened an iron gate and we staggered up a driveway to a darkened chateau, silhouetted against a night sky. We had come a long way that day. It looked a foreboding place in the moonlight - a house without sympathy. Then what sympathy could one expect in our situation? We were ushered into a room, lit by an unshaded bulb. A *Wehrmacht* officer sat behind a desk, he was sure of himself. He had an air of disdain about him, we were obviously beneath his status. He was impeccably dressed and had probably just finished dinner. His tunic was buttoned up and the hooks and eyes that held the green cloth close to his throat were undone. The silver wire epaulettes on his shoulder with two small pips informed me his rank was *Hauptman* (Captain). Protruding from a tunic button hole was displayed the red white and black ribbon of the iron cross. His elbows rested on the desk, the long thin fingers of both hands touched his chin. It was his manner and his impeccable uniform that took all my attention so I am now unable to describe his features.

He spoke, his heavily accented English was bad. 'You are a saboteur,' he said, 'vere are your vire cutters? I vill haff you shot as a saboteur.' For the first time I gave, in reply, my name rank and number; it was to be by no means the last. He continued to ask where my wire cutters were and to call me a saboteur. The interrogation never wavered from these two points. It was ridiculous. It would have been funny had it not been totally without humour and so deadly serious. It gave me strength. He finally finished asking his stupid questions and I suspected he needed another after dinner cognac!

He called for the NCO who had commanded the patrol. From a drawer he produced a bottle of *Schnaps* and removed the cap. To my astonishment and with some back slapping and laughter he then began to pour the contents of the bottle into the soldier's mouth. I can see that guard now, standing rigidly to attention, wearing his steel helmet, his rifle still slung over his shoulder, half the liquid going down his throat, half down the front of his tunic. I thought what a bastard that officer must have been - a real paper tiger! The guard didn't seem to mind, his reward for catching us was two weeks leave in Germany - a privilege not otherwise given. The chateau was in the village of Ustaritz.

We sat glumly at the bottom of an open truck that bounced us through the night to Bayonne, surrounded by guards. There wasn't a paper tiger among these chaps, festooned with military hardware, they created a terrifying image; machine pistols hanging from straps about their necks; stick grenades hanging from their belts. It was an image of invincibility to one like myself who was cold, hungry, tired, of low morale and very apprehensive of the future. I did not envy our own soldiers who, one day, must meet them face to face.

We were taken to an old fort in Bayonne which served as the local jail, searched and told to put on our uniforms. I was glad to see the back of those civilian clothes. Our personal belongings were taken from us. From me they took my watch, a pen, a pipe and a beautiful silver cigarette case given to my father by a German officer in the First World War. I remember it had eight cigarettes in it. There was little else because, as ordered, our pockets were emptied before we flew on Ops. They asked me to remove Dorothy's birthday ring from my finger. I made a great show in trying to do so (although it slipped off quite easily), they said leave it as it obviously wouldn't come off. They put the rest of my belongings into a brown envelope, sealed down the flap and wrote my name, rank and number on it and I said a silent goodbye to the contents. We were then put into a cell, given blankets and allowed to sleep. It was 20th April, 21 days from the time we left Tempsford.

Loiseau returned safely home to Tours. Not long after, in the late evening, they came for him. The pounding on the door was unmistakable, he told me many years later. The bolts had held long enough for him to make his escape into the garden, up the plank, over the wall, onto the planks covering the loose coal on the other side and away through the coal yard. An escape route he had so carefully planned. Mamie had been in the kitchen, Robert in the attic. They had stormed through the house and Robert got out of the attic window and clung to the roof, but a powerful light picked up his spread-eagled body. They wanted him alive, but left him in no doubt that they would shoot if he failed to come down.

The Gestapo at Tours were notorious for their brutality and have long since been brought to justice. During Robert's interrogation he was beaten and given the water treatment. That is, drowned in a bath of cold water, revived, drowned again, revived and so on. From there he went via Fresnes to a concentration camp at Neangaman, working every day waist deep in water. Today there is no hatred in his heart.

I have never been told what they did to Mamie, I don't think I would want to know, but she was finally deported to Ravensbrook. She returned home bent double like an old woman and was unable to walk for two years. The Americans awarded both Mamie and Robert the Medal of Freedom. The French, of course, were equally generous with their awards. The British Government gave them a certificate signed by Montgomery!

In retrospect there was little else Loiseau could have done, the escape route having been cut. His instruction to take our uniform was unusual and contrary to what we had been taught. I am sure it was made with the failure of his mission in mind. He had been to Dax before, he knew where that wrecked van was, he took us straight to it. I am sure he saw someone at Dax who told him the smuggler wasn't available and briefed him on the pass procedure at Bayonne station, then where to take us and where to leave us. He did wonderfully well under the circumstances - there was no way he could have taken us back to Tours. He put us as close to the frontier as he could.

We were probably fortunate to have been captured by the *Wehrmacht* when and where we were. Had we gone any further the chances were that we would have run into a mine field, or barbed wire, or a trigger happy patrol who, in the dark, would have shot first and asked questions afterwards. We were certainly never briefed in England what to expect on the border of Spain. Then perhaps I expect too much when one recalls that men broke out of POW camps and made their way home with little information on what to expect at the borders of neutral countries. A very good friend of mine, when about to cross the Spanish border, found himself in the middle of a hail of bullets fired by trigger happy German border guards which killed all his companions. At least when that cell door clanged shut on us we were still alive and uninjured. What a pity, getting so near and yet so far - I wonder if we could have got across?

In Paris, many years after the war, Robert took me to a reunion dinner of his Neangaman comrades. After dinner I was introduced as an ex-pilot who used to assist the *Resistance*. To my embarrassment they got to their feet and applauded me. These people who had suffered so much, applauding me who had done so little, it was too much! It was a very emotional moment. Fortunately I had the presence of mind to get to my feet and, clapping my hands together, shouted, 'Non, non! Je vous applaud!' It is still the best utterance in French I have ever made!

CHAPTER THIRTEEN

THE IRON DOORS CLANG SHUT

Es war einmal ein Lattenzaun,
mit zwischenraum hindurchzuschaun.

Der Lattenzaun

There used to be a picket fence,
with space to gaze from hence to thence.

The Picket Fence

Christian Morgenstern - Galenlieder - Gallows Songs

We spent 15 days in a small whitewashed cell in that ancient fortress at Bayonne. A high window was set into extremely thick walls, but we were warned anyone looking through it would get a bullet from the guard outside! The sun streamed through the window casting the shadow of the bars on the white walls. We used this as a sundial by marking the wall when our only meal of the day was due! It always took a long, long time for the shadow to reach that mark!

In one corner there was a brown stone sink, which I first thought was a shower, my first contact with a continental loo! A shower indeed, I must have thought we were staying at the Savoy! The door was solid iron and echoed a dreadful finality when it clanged shut. It had a hole cut in it guarded by a flap outside, a flap that moved aside at odd times of the day and night and an eyeball would peer in to see what we were up to. Occasionally, through this hole, roughly rolled cigarettes with a match would be pushed by our fellow French prisoners. Can you imagine that? They never gave up helping us even behind prison walls. At night we slept in two-tiered bunks that were firmly fixed to the wall.

Each day we were given a bottle of weak lemonade to drink. We were warned not to drink the water from the communal basin outside our cell, where we washed every morning. The soap was harsh and rough, mostly made of sand. After washing we were allowed in a small exercise yard where we would walk for an hour in the warm sun. Our silent perambulations were broken on occasions by the noise and the brief sight of low flying Focke-Wulf 190's or 'wedding ring' Junker Ju 52's mine sweeping nearby estuaries. These activities in the air poignantly reminded me that my flying days were over. I swore I would never keep a bird in a cage after this!

Back in our cell we either dwelt on the words of despair and defiance scratched on the walls, (there were none of comfort!) or listen to Mac's soporific voice telling us of his life on the prairies of Canada. I enjoyed listening to these tales - they lulled me to sleep!

Suddenly we were told we were to leave jail and a jailer produced our civilian clothes and ordered us to wear them over our uniform. I protested, and the guard at my side shifted his rifle butt onto my foot. There was a look of rage on the jailer's face and his huge hand screwed into an enormous fist. There was no doubt where that blow would have fallen had I disobeyed him further. He bellowed at me again to put the civilian clothes over my uniform. It was pointless antagonising him further, so I dressed with as little haste and as much dignity as I dare. Mac, Ernie and Lloyd did the same. We were chained together and handed over to a *Feldwebel* and his escort to take to Paris.

During the journey our *Feldwebel*, a short, plump man of middle age, produced from his wallet photographs of his family and passed them around for us to see. He said he came from the Ruhr and was concerned for their safety. Twice en-route he pulled down the compartment window blinds to prevent us from seeing damage inflicted by the RAF on two marshalling yards; St Pierre des Corps bombed on 10/11th April and Juvisy on the 18/19th April 1944. At Juvisy he was late in pulling the blind down and we had a glimpse of the enormous damage that had been wrought. In particular I remember a number of Tiger tanks, scattered about like so many corks on a rough sea. After a little more than two weeks after the raid only the main line was functioning. There was tremendous damage all around. When I see Juvisy today, I can scarcely believe it ever happened.

In Paris we left the train at Gare D'Austerlitz and when we were walking towards the exit when two nuns came out of the shadows, they were carrying four boxes. Under the watchful eye of our German guards they gave one to each of us and without a word disappeared back into the shadows from whence they came. I turned my box over in my hand and found it to be a French Red Cross parcel. The guards were quite unperturbed, it must have happened many times before.

Outside the station we boarded a bus with barred windows and moved off. During our journey through the streets of Paris I was surprised to see most of the motor traffic was gas driven. The gas was either contained in a huge bag or a tank on the roof, or generated in a small trailer towed behind. In London the few civilian vehicles on the road at that time were driven by petrol or oil which had been shipped across the Atlantic.

Our bus stopped in front of a large gate within a high wall. It was opened only after careful inspection of passes and ourselves. I noticed our *Feldwebel* was receiving quite a number of salutes. I discovered later in the *Wehrmacht* one saluted any one of senior rank to yourself. Pity the poor private! The gate closed silently behind us. We left the bus in a courtyard and were prodded through another door within a door, I felt like Alice going through the looking glass. The building inside took on cathedral-like proportions. Perhaps if I saw it today the visual impact would not be so great, but then it looked huge. We were handed over to another German NCO, an enormous man, almost in direct proportion to the hall in which we were standing! He ordered our chains be taken off and took our Red Cross parcels from us, placing them to one side. He pulled aside my coat to search me. I was totally unprepared for his reaction. 'UNIFORM?! UNIFORM?!' he bellowed. It was a shout of authority, worthy in the best tradition of the British RSM! 'Why are you wearing civilian clothes over your UNIFORM?!' he bellowed. At least that's what I thought he said, although the words he shouted were not in any language I understood. I braced myself for a blow that never came. He hung on to my coat and shook it like an angry dog. I knew the next word, 'Pourquoi?' he queried. 'Because we were told to do so by the *Wehrmacht*,' I answered in words to that effect, my French has never been that good. 'Take them off!' he yelled. This I did, we all did, in much haste I may add. They were taken away and we never saw them again.

The *Feldwebel* who had brought us from Bayonne came up to me, saluted, shook me by the hand, and wished me luck. It was the only friendly gesture I'd had since I had been captured and yet again I was taken by surprise. I have often regretted this incident, since it could have only added to the despair and misery of those watching in the shadows. As he turned away I saw them, a number of people watching our every move, old, young, men, women and children their clothing adorned with a yellow star. Although at the time I recognised the Star of David on their clothing, it was only after the war I realised that they were in that awful prison probably waiting for transportation to the gas chambers. I had been terribly indiscreet and it took a long time for me to forgive myself.

We were led away, stripped, searched and put into a cupboard in which you could only stand or sit with difficulty, there was a small grating at the top of the door. I do not exactly know how long I was there. It was certainly not as long as the Frenchman next door who really scared me by telling me in a fearful whisper that he had been there two days. He said he was a member of the Resistance and feared the worse. I could not comfort him, we were unable to communicate adequately, the language barrier was too wide. I was pleased when, hours later, I was released from that dreadful box and given a shower - I was filthy and my uniform was deloused. Both functions were a joke. All four of us were then locked up for the night in a damp, filthy, flea ridden cell! Mac said he still had a hacksaw blade sewn into his uniform which had escaped detection. We got it out and cut through the nails that fastened the opaque glazed windows which we gingerly opened and cautiously peered out through the bars. We were confronted by an impassable high wall! We tried the blade on the one of the bars and made a deep impression on it (I wonder if it is there today?). It was a stupid thing to do, like using a winkle pin to open an oyster, but that hacksaw was surprisingly efficient!

In the morning I was taken up into the galleries of the prison and put into a clean, light cell - a cell for officers I was told. There were sheets on the bed and the window was flung open wide. Albeit the view overlooked another cell block, but I could see the sky and by putting my face against the bars I could see, to my left, trees and the roofs of houses. I could feel the coolness of the spring breeze gently wafting through the window. There was a table, a chair, a place to wash and an iron bedstead which, when folded against the wall, gave me space in which to perambulate. A ceramic loo with its footprints stood in one corner. In the drawer of the table I found paper, a nail, a tin bowl, a spoon and short handled broom. Before the door was shut they returned my Red Cross parcel and gave me the first of the eight books I was to read in this confined space. I even had privacy in this luxurious apartment for I was alone (was this called solitary confinement I wondered?). What would those poor souls, rotting, bleeding painfully in the darkness of their dungeons below, have given for this?

I had something else too, from my broken down shoes I removed a worn metal tip, razor sharp, which I carefully hid. If the interrogations got too tough I could use it on my wrists - it was a great comfort to know I had a way out (it sounds melodramatic now - but this was quite true!). In reality there were only two interrogations, both of which were to take place in this cell, skilfully carried out by a person dressed in a white shirt, wearing a tie and grey trousers and speaking perfect English. When he left the first time I felt an absolute fool having given my name rank and number in answer to so many of his questions. I hoped he believed the impression that we had worked our way down to Bayonne without much assistance from anyone. A story we had all decided to stick to if we were captured.

When my interrogator made towards the door he turned and asked me if I would like a haircut and a shave. As military officers, he said, we must keep as smart an appearance as circumstances would permit! I was surprised at his offer and readily accepted. My morale rose, so that was it, that was why I was being treated so well, I was in the hands of the military. Within an hour or so a Frenchman arrived in my cell and, under the watchful eye of a guard, he silently cut my hair and shaved my face. It was the first time someone else had shaved me and, in spite of his exaggerated flourishes with his open razor, I enjoyed every luxurious minute of it.

I spent the first week in my newly found luxury stoically trying to rid myself of the fleas I had gathered from that ground floor cell. The lining of my clothing was smothered with them, and my body covered with their madly irritating love bites. They adored me and thankfully kept me very busy. I recorded on the wall in five-barred gates the number of these newly found friends I managed to destroy between my thumbnails. The first day was well into the eighties, the second a little less, until finally I had destroyed them all!

The contents of my Red Cross parcel soon disappeared. For a short while it supplemented my two slices of black bread and acorn coffee in the morning and the bowl of lentil soup served in the early afternoon. Finally I was left with the last item, a tin of sardines and nothing to open it with! As hunger gripped and with the aid of my iron bedstead, I spent many a frustrating hour trying to remove the lid. It defeated me in the end but, to show for my efforts, the tin had more than its fair share of dents in it. I am sure the sardines inside were glad when I stopped! I had expected to be given another parcel to supplement my meagre rations. I was a fool, there were many more in there getting far less than I.

The mid-day or early afternoon meal created an air of expectancy throughout the jail. You could hear the iron wheeled trolley rumbling noisily on its metal track, halting every few minutes at a cell door to dispense lentil soup to its unfortunate inmate. It would rumble its halting journey towards you, at last stopping outside your door, a key would fumble in the lock and the cell door would open. You would go forward, like Oliver Twist, bowl in hand, and into it would be slopped a ladle of the wretched stuff. Once, across the well between the tiers of cells, a brief cameo took place in the entrance of the cell opposite. A man dressed in civilian clothes was protesting to a guard, in English, probably an airman like myself. The guard took no notice at all while he removed his belt and then beat the unfortunate protester unmercifully with it.

There was no doubt I learnt all about 'the writing on the wall' at a young age. Not the advanced graffiti that backward pupils wrote on school toilet walls, but serious stuff that was scratched on cell walls. I searched those walls for something reassuring, a time scale perhaps, to show how much longer I would have to stay alone in this awful place. There was nothing reassuring written on these walls, some of it was down right terrifying. I remember there was a written plea to God for deliverance, a message of despair, if there ever was one. The daily markings of a flying officer and a flight lieutenant showed that they had occupied this room far longer than I wanted to. As my daily scratches grew in number, I reconciled myself that I was going to be incarcerated there as long, if not longer, than they had been. Fortunately this was not so, but I certainly finished high in the frame!

In the evening the prison came alive with the rhythm of morse being tapped on the water pipes. One rap with the broom for a dash, one tap with the spoon for a dot, or the other way round - I don't recall. It was easy to read and I took the letters down with my nail on a square of newspaper which had been provided for other purposes. The following day I would decipher the impressions made by the nail on the paper! The most incredible messages came across that grapevine. The invasion had started said one, British and American Troops had invaded Spain from Gibraltar and were pushing through the Pyrenees to France said another - victory would soon be ours! I often wondered who the author was of those fictitious messages that throbbed through the water system in the early evening. Probably our captors were not only listening but contributing as well!

I was communicating with an American who had his window open in the cell block opposite. We exchanged messages by wagging a piece of paper in morse time in front of our body. We were doing well until one day my cell door was flung open by a raving lunatic of a guard who stormed in and closed and locked the window. Mac next door got a beating to go with it. The window was shut for a number of days - I felt it was the end of the world! How lucky I was! Elsewhere in there were men who had no windows to shut in their cell. No sun to send its rays streaming through bars, casting shadows on the floor.

Occasionally I would hear the shouting and cheering of a crowd and a shrilling whistle controlling a football match. Beyond the walls were people enjoying the normal pursuits of a free life. But again there was that blood freezing undulating sound of the air raid alarm, so unlike our own. The staccato, echoing, crack of anti-aircraft guns, leaving black powder marks high in the clear blue sky. The glinting of silver wings in the sunlight and an American B24 slowly, so slowly, spinning downward to destruction, a mushroom of billowing smoke and debris marking its demise on the ground. In the sky four parachutes billowed out, four who had escaped, perhaps to join me here? Beyond those walls was also the war, the dead and the wounded - I heard and saw it all through my open window.

I recently found this picture of Fresnes Prison in Paris. It was taken prior to WW II but gives some idea of the grim reality of the place. Even when this photograph was taken it looks the perfect setting for the horrors that took place within its walls during 1939/44. I have always considered myself fortunate!

On the wall I had scratched the 32nd stroke of my solitary confinement; during which time I had been outside my cell exercising for one hour only. Two weeks previously I had been given my last book, *'Summer Lightning'* by P.G.Wodehouse. I knew pages of it by heart, how I hated that book, how I loathed that author. Unexpectedly I had a visitor, it was my interrogator. He was still without uniform, wearing a white shirt with a plain tie and grey trousers. I wasn't sure if I was pleased to see him, my morale was low and I hadn't conversed with anyone since his last visit. 'What the hell does he want?' I asked myself. He had a clip board in his hand with some sort of form stuck on it. He pulled the chair away from the table and placed it deliberately in the centre of the cell. Turning the back of it towards me he sat astride it resting the board on the top rung. He motioned me to sit on the bed. 'Now, Flying Officer Clark, we still haven't been able to establish your identify as an officer of the Royal Air Force as you claim to be,' he began,

'It would help you and I if you would answer a few questions. What was your squadron number?' 'Clark, Frederick Bartlett, Flying Officer 135098,' I replied. 'Where was your squadron based?' he went on. 'Clark, Flying Officer 135098,' I replied, 'I'm only required to give my name rank and number,' I said to him in the hope that he would stop, but he went on with his interrogation.

He offered me a cigarette which I foolishly accepted. I had not had one for a month. When I inhaled the smoke my head reeled and my lungs rebelled against this unaccustomed intrusion. I felt ill and highly emotional. I wished he would go away and he obliged. His departure was as unexpected as his arrival. He got up quickly from the chair and in one movement turned it round and slid it under the table. With a slight bow he said dramatically, 'I am wasting my time with you, you will not answer my questions, I am unable to identify you as an officer of the Royal Air Force. At dawn tomorrow you will be shot!' 'But the German Army does not shoot British Officers,' I protested weakly. I was taking an awful lot for granted! He drew himself to attention, clicked his heels and bowed slightly from the waist, turned and went to the door on which he rapped his clip board. The door opened, he marched out, the door clanged shut behind him and a key noisily shot home the bolt. He left me feeling like the man who had fluffed the most important interview of his life!

It was getting dark. The shout must have come from one of the survivors shot down during the raid on Trappes three nights before. 'Are there any English here?' it sang out. I leapt to my feet and put my face to the bars and shouted back, 'Yes, I'm English!' 'How long have you been here?' came echoing back. 'About a month,' I replied. 'Are you RAF?' 'Yes I am, when did you get here?' 'I've just arrived. Did you hear that the Prime Minister announced in Parliament that over 40 RAF Officers have been shot in a POW Camp?' There were now other voices which made it clear if the shouting did not stop the shooting would start. So I never answered that question but sank onto my bed exhausted with fear.

I must have dozed off, I'd had little sleep when a key in the lock and the bolt being drawn on the door of my cell woke me. It was early light, I was ordered out of bed, told to dress and motioned outside onto the landing. I took nothing with me, I had nothing to take. There were four of them outside the door. Steel helmeted, each with a machine pistol held across his chest, they looked grim. Two fell in behind me and two in front. The order to march was given and march we did, passing along a row of green steel doors and down a spiral iron staircase. Their feet ever in step, their jack boots striking the floor in unison. Out through gates that opened silently for us, out into the cool morning air and into a courtyard beyond. This was it, this must be where the execution would take place. By now I could not care - I was weary, so very weary, of being cooped up like a bloody chicken anyway. The two soldiers in front halted and turned inward towards me.

The rear door of the bus was opened and I was motioned inside. From within friendly voices greeted me, I was among my own kind. We were off to a POW camp in Germany they said. The first stage of my apprenticeship was over. Behind me in the depths of Fresnes Prison in a completely dark, wet and clammy dungeon, lay the beaten, starved body of Wg/Cmdr F.F.E.Yeo-Thomas GC, MC. *'The White Rabbit'* and in the north, men were dying on the beaches - it was the morning of 'D' day, the 6th June 1944. I had been fortunate, flying with 138 Squadron and evading capture I expected far harsher treatment.

I cannot remember who was in the bus that took us through the gates of Fresnes, but there certainly were a number of noisy Americans, full of banter and whistling at girls as the bus passed them by! I was unconcerned when we pulled off the road and passed a sign which said in English 'The American Hospital' (at Neuilly-sur-Seine). We stopped at the foot of some steps and waited. Eventually, down them struggled an American airman on crutches, his leg in plaster. He was followed by another, his plastered arm stuck out in front of him like the bough of a tree, both were assisted into the bus.

Lastly, escorted by two nurses, came a lone figure, a short man, dressed in a one piece brown woollen overall. I thought at the time it could have been an electrically heated inner flying suit. His head was bare and where his terrible burns stopped you could trace on his face the outline of a flying helmet. His eye brows and eye lashes had gone, so had most of his nose. The skin on his face was a mixture of red white and black blotches where the suppuration had attempted to heal. His mouth was twisted and his lips thin. It was only when he took his seat in the bus that I noticed his hands, his skeletal fingers were all that remained after the heat of the flames had melted the flesh. The stench from his terrible burns was repulsive. I can see him now, sitting in that bus, strangely quiet, saying nothing, looking at his hands and claw like fingers, continually turning them over from the palms to the back of them and from the back to the palms again. It was miracle he could see at all.

They said he was a ball turret gunner, which accounted for his small stature. One of those brave men who were locked away in a metal and perspex ball beneath a B17 or B24. It required a second person to get them in and out of that turret, the door of which had to be lined up with the hole in the fuselage before he could get out (and get to his parachute). If the hydraulics had failed then the job had to be done manually. At least this is what I was given to understand. The one that sat in the bus had been covered in burning hydraulic fluid. I wondered what efforts of heroism released him from his burning tomb?

We left Gare de l'Est for Germany in the early evening, unaware of the drama unfolding on the beaches to the north. It was the unmistakable rattle of machine guns that woke us. The train jerked spasmodically to a halt, tugging us from our seats where a few moments before we had been asleep. There was another loud burst of firing more determined than the first, our guards jumped to their feet and left the compartment. A door was flung open and amid shouting, soldiers leapt down onto the track. Naively, my first thoughts were that the Resistance had come to rescue us - so perfect the ambush had been. I gingerly put my head out of the door, the others were ready to follow. I was lucky we didn't have a trigger happy guard. He was there in the corridor and grinned at me, indicating with the muzzle of his machine pistol that I should put my head back in. We waited a long time in the darkness for a new locomotive to arrive.

In the early morning we could see from the carriage window that we were approaching a large town. Damaged houses appeared at the line-side, a burnt roof here, a jumble of bricks there, small air raid shelters at the bottom of gardens - evidence of a wounded city. A familiar sight in London, Coventry, Liverpool, Canterbury, Plymouth and many other cities in England during the 'Blitz'. Shunted into sidings beside the track were mobile heavy anti-aircraft guns, their barrels pointing to the sky with their victories painted on them, a white bar with a star for an American aircraft, a roundel for the British.

The train pulled into a platform and we were ordered out. I felt as if I was standing in the middle of a desert, rubble instead of sand forming the dunes. There was hardly a place where one orderly brick stood upon another. The sight was sickening. It must have been the aftermath of two RAF raids on Frankfurt-on-Main in March 1944 where, during the first raid on the night of 18/19th, 55,500 civilians were made homeless. During the second, on the night of 22/23rd, 120,000 were made homeless. Surprisingly, only 1,369 persons were killed. Regrettably the preserved medieval quarter of the town was destroyed. A total of 55 RAF aircraft were lost on these two attacks. So much for statistics. At the time it looked horrific, as had London where I participated as a civilian in the 'Blitz'.

A local train took us into Frankfurt main line station which appeared to be undamaged. As we left the train we were quickly surrounded by a crowd of civilians, one of whom angrily shook a walking stick at us, shouting at us, first in German and then quite clearly in English, 'Terrorfliegers! Luftgangsters! Lynch them! Hang them!' Behind us the wounded Americans were descending with difficulty onto the platform. First the man on crutches, then the man with his arm in plaster and finally the man who was so severely burned. I saw the crowd's attention fix on him, several turned their head away, one woman involuntary put a handkerchief to her eyes. Without a further sound the crowd melted away.

The tram that took us to Oberusel was packed, rocking violently from side to side. Our fellow civilian passengers were sullen and silently belligerent, there were no smiles from us. The Luftwaffe's interrogation centre, Dulag Luft, Oberusel was at the end of the line. The cell they pushed me into was smaller than that at Fresnes. The windows were glazed with opaque glass and shuttered from the outside at night. There was a small hole the size of a cricket ball in the shutters through which a glimmer of light penetrated, otherwise the cell was in total darkness. The toilet was outside and to perform any necessary function one pulled a lever which let down an indicator outside to summon the guard. The indicator when released flopped down with a series of thumps like the echoing sound of a muffled cannon shot. The guards never hurried to this important summons and then watched over us.

The wooden bed was covered with a mattress made of fine woven brown paper and filled with fine wooden strips. To while away the time I pulled strips out of the mattress and wove them into patterns - there was nothing else to do. Beneath the window was a radiator which gave out a great deal of heat. I stripped to my pants and sat on my bed in a pool of perspiration, gasping for breath. A guard opened the door looked in, saw my predicament, apologised, and said he would turn the heat off, which he did! Before long, this time fully clothed, I was shivering in a blanket from the intense cold that surrounded me! It then occurred to me why the walls were made of asbestos!

I spoke to my neighbour whom I saw when our meagre rations were being distributed. He was a pathfinder pilot and said he had been here for two weeks, I wished I had never asked. I would never last two weeks, I fell into a deep depression.

Outside a clock loudly tolled the quarter hour throughout the day and night. I swear that it chimed at odd times since I found myself waiting for a chime that never came or was left with the feeling that it was a short fifteen minutes! Possibly a figment of my now neurotic mind. But that chiming clock was a swine. In my solitude I searched my memory of the film briefing of this place shown at Tempsford some two months ago. 'Nothing like our place at Hyde Park,'[1] the Pongo had boasted. 'We don't let 'em go until they have told everything. If you capture 'em when they're wet and they dry out, chuck a bucket of water over 'em and make 'em wet again, give 'em to us as you find 'em!' He was a callous bastard, going on to tell us of their great success following the interrogation of a Luftwaffe officer captured in the front line in Italy. At first they couldn't make out why he was there, then they found out he'd been sacked from his job at Peenemunde. It was from him they learned that 'V' weapons were being tested there. Maybe he wasn't such a bastard after all, had it not been for the efforts of the likes of him, London might have been reduced to rubble not unlike like the city I had just passed through. He certainly had more time than the *Luftwaffe* to interrogate his captives, there were a lot less of them than there were of us! His methods were[2] certainly milder than either those of the Gestapo or of the today's military interrogator. I hoped that film and briefing had not been reported to *Dulag Luft*!

I was becoming more and more neurotic than ever, although up to this point, not a finger had been laid on me. After three days solitary I was taken out for my first interrogation. He was a smartly dressed, fussy Luftwaffe corporal and waved his arm airily in the direction of a chair in front of his desk. I sat in it. He opened a file in front of him and through gold rimmed spectacles peered at a paper inside. His English, as I was soon to find out, was perfect and accent free. He began by asking me my squadron number and the name of the Squadron Commander. It was the same old routine, name rank and number, my parrot was on trial again. God! How tired I was of all this! At the end of his interrogation I asked him when I might be released and sent to a prisoner of war camp. I said I had been in the hands of the Gestapo for over a month (which I hadn't, but was counting on him not knowing!) 'Gestapo? he queried, he appeared to lose some of his composure. 'A month with the Gestapo?' 'Yes,' I bluffed, 'In Fresnes, Paris.' He closed his file, held it vertically, and rapped it on his desk, the

---

[1] - *No 8 Kensington Palace Gardens - 'The London Cage' - Central Interrogation Centre.*

[2] - *What he didn't tell us was that in the camp where I was going after interrogation I would find two huts full of officer survivors from the last raid on Peenemunde in August 1943. They had been threatened that if they did not destroy the target that night they would go back night after night until the job was properly done!*

interview was over. He pressed a button a guard appeared and escorted me back to my cell.

I spent an uncomfortable night in the pitch dark of my cell, listening to that mad clock chime away the hours, waiting and watching for daylight to appear in that small hole in the shutters. That afternoon I was again taken from my cell and seated in front of that same desk. The same corporal walked into the room and sat himself before me and peered, presumably, at the same file on the desk before him. He said he wasn't going to ask any more questions, I did not believe him. He went on to say that they knew all about me and had been waiting sometime for me to put in an appearance at Dulag Luft. It all sounded rather ominous. He then smugly proceeded to read of a series of facts about my RAF career. My squadron, how long I had been at Tempsford, where I had done Heavy Conversion, OTU, and many other details which could only have come from my personal records. It was all there, typed on a foolscap sheet of paper, from which he was reading. At first I thought of Kit Carson, my wounded navigator, and wondered if those Gestapo pigs at Tours had been to work on him. But it was other information about me that I found most disturbing, information that Kit could not have possibly known. Where did that come from? One of the 300 Irish workmen at Tempsford? Someone at MI6? I don't know.

It was a strange experience, perhaps I talked in my sleep! There could be no doubt in my informant's mind that the information he was giving me was correct. He had only to look at my face, which surely must have betrayed me. I was thankful he made no mention of those missing days when I was in the hands of Loiseau. 'Tomorrow you will be taken to a transit camp,' he said, pushing the button on his desk. 'From there you will be sent to a Luftwaffe POW camp.' He was true to his word, that night the shutters at the window of my cell were left open. The following morning I left for Wetzlar where the transit camp was situated. I could not believe that part of my ordeal was over. At the least I had protected the interest of my French Resistance helpers, but unlike today's POW I was never really put to the test.

At Wetzlar we were under canvas, what a joy it was to walk once more in the open air, feel the wind on one's face and to hold a conversation with someone. My clothing was taken from me on arrival and put into a steam boiler to delouse them. I can still remember the heat left in my uniform when I put it on afterwards. At the same time I was given a shower. From the Red Cross store came a clean shirt, a khaki great coat, some socks and a new pair of boots. I can remember little of the surroundings at Wetzlar except the Leica camera factory was nearby. Its windows were shattered by strafing P47's, they said. The Americans had laid out a soft ball pitch and were continually pitching balls around, yelling and generally making the most of it. There was a black American fighter pilot shot down in Italy, from the 'Fighting 99th,' I think he said. He was recovering from a terrible beating he had been given. He was a great personality, a great morale booster and had a fund of stories, one of which I shall never forget, regrettably far too risque to repeat here. I can see him now, standing on the home base of that makeshift soft ball layout while telling it and the pleasure it gave him when we roared with laughter at the end of it. He also had a fund of R/T stories concerning his black colleagues on his squadron. He was quite a character and the only black USAF pilot I ever met.

There was also an American football player who, before the war, played for the Chicago Bears[3] He said when he got home he was going buy himself a 'poiple shoit' with a 'poiple tie' and a 'poiple car' to match! Judging by the appalling injury to his foot and leg he certainly wasn't going to play the grid iron game again.

Two other characters were an unbelievable duo: one was small, with a bald head, and looked not unlike a clean shaven garden gnome and also looked much too old to be the B17 Navigator he was. In a loud Bronx accented voice he was giving a blow by blow account of all his missions. How he saw the Eiffel Tower poking through low cloud that covered Paris at one time and so on. It wasn't so much what he was telling us, but he was making sure that everyone heard it. His accent and rapid delivery grated the very tip of your nerves. In one corner of the tent four USAF officers were quietly playing bridge. One of them, a captain, impatiently threw his cards face down on the blanket they were using for a table. 'Lootenant,' he called. There was no reaction from our raconteur. 'LOOTENANT!' the captain yelled. The voice hesitated. A third, 'LOOTENANT!!' split the air. There was no doubt now in the mind of the navigator that an officer senior to himself demanded his attention. The voice stopped and he drew himself to attention. 'Take a deep breath, Lootenant,' commanded the captain and the lieutenant obliged, standing rigidly to attention as he did so. The next order was quite remarkable and should be recorded in the annals of military history, 'Now blow it out your arse!' the captain commanded. When the laughter subsided the game of bridge continued - in silence.

On the 10th June 1944 I wrote my first card home from Wetzlar. I have it in front of me as I write. I printed it and it read as follows:-

[3] - *I have an interest in the game and I wonder if he was in New Orleans when they won Super Bowl XX in 1987.*

'My dearest Mum & Dad please don't worry about me I am as fit as a fiddle. Not a scratch. This is not my permanent address will write from there in a few days time. Give my love to Dorothy my next letter will be to her. This is all for now. Cheerio all my love. Freddie.'

It was sent home by air and was the first notice my parents had that I was alive. On 16th June, amid great air activity by gaggles of Me. 109s, a party of us left the camp by tram for the railway station; Ernie, Mac and Lloyd had already gone their separate ways. We were to meet again for a brief few days when the war was drawing to a close. Lt Johnnie Ball RNVR who was torpedoed in the *Ark Royal* as a midshipman was in the party.

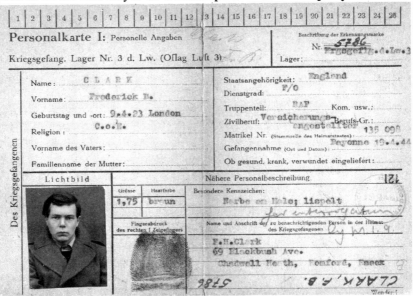

The photo shown on my personal record card at Stalag Luft III was taken when I left Dulag Luft. My hair was cut shortly afterward.

I remember little of that journey to Sagan except the wooden seats of the train were as hard as the black bread and blood sausage we shared with our guards. We left the train the following day. Sagan in those days was in Lower Silesia and the home of Stalag Luft III. We marched through the town and on to a road that eventually passed a hutted area enclosed in a high double barbed wire fence. We went through a guarded gate and into a building in the *Vorlager*, where we were searched, photographed, finger printed and given German identity discs to wear around our neck. My name was called and to my astonishment a brown envelope was produced and opened before me. In it was my silver cigarette case, my wallet, my watch and my pen -eight cigarettes were in the case. I was not allowed to keep the pen because writing implements containing ink were *Verboten* and I was given a receipt for it, which I still have. To my eternal regret the beautiful cigarette case that belonged to my father was stolen after the war.

We were informed we were at Belaria, a camp which was part of the Stalag Luft III complex. The other compounds were in the woods the other side of Sagan. At Belaria there were no trees other than those that lined the road outside the camp! We formed up in threes and the camp's double gate was opened to admit us. To the best of our ability we tried to enter marching in a military manner, halted and awaited for the allocation of our quarters. A hand tapped me on the shoulder causing me to jump and a voice said, 'I've been waiting six bloody months for you to arrive, Nobbie.' I turned and looked into the grinning, chinless, face of Peter Boyle. I had last heard from him 10 months previous. His letter had come from Chipping Warden saying:

Dear Nobby,

I'm cheesed! This is a terrible camp - hard C.O. etc., & dispersal is about twice as hard as Banff! Wimpey IIIs here. Haven't flown yet, ground school at the moment. Mostly a waste of time, but some good gen. Don't know anyone else here. Get my crew, poor buggers, on Sunday.

Excuse for now, on my knees, be good, love to Archie ('Pip')

Yours Peter

P.S. Can you read this?

I had - with difficulty! He was flying his first operational flight in a Lancaster on its way to bomb Frankfurt when they were shot down. He was 'second dicky' to the Squadron Commander and had the most experienced crew on the squadron with him. He alone survived the exploding aircraft, his 'poor buggers' were left behind!

I walked into that camp on the 17th June 1944. The same day the headlines of the official newspaper of the Nazi Party - The *Volkischer Beobachter* - screamed, *'MIT NEUEN SPRENGKORPERN GROSTEN KALIBERS - Gegen London und Sudengland.'*[4] The battle of the V 1's had begun four days earlier and, unbeknown to me, my parent's house in Chadwell Heath already lay in ruins. My father saw the weapon fall, fortunately both my mother and he were unhurt.

After the war I went back to Tours many times to visit Mamie Pincon. We, together with her son Robert, became great friends. (There is a Dorothy in their family, Mamie's Great Grandaughter named after my wife). Mamie, Janine Pincon, died at the age of 84 in 1981, unhappily I was in Israel and could not be contacted. Loiseau, Roger Pincon, died earlier in 1965 aged 67. Ernie Wilkinson, before he died, made a visit to Tours and the Vallee, we were the only two of the 21 airmen that went through Mamie's hands who went back to see her. I made a habit of seeing her every time I visited France.

I have been back on four occasions to the 'Vallee' and to the vineyard where we crashed. They think I was very skilled in keeping the aeroplane out of their village - in fact it was the stringing wires in their vineyard that

[4] - *With new explosive devices (weapons) of large calibre (are used) against London and southern England.*

Mamie Pincon shares a sip of wine from the glass given to me by Maurice Rougebec.

stopped us from toppling over the cliff into it! They have given me over the years, among other things, the rudder bar, the control wheel and a leaflet[5] that had been in my aeroplane. Above all they have given their friendship. It was ten years since I had seen them when I arrived unannounced in spring 1992. What a reunion party that was! After, we climbed the road that led to the top of the cliff and foraged in the tilled soil for pieces of my aeroplane. I was surprised with the amount we found.

I learnt from my first visit in 1959 that the farmer who nightly brought food to the barn was betrayed by his wife who thought he was having a clandestine love affair. As a result of this he and eleven others were executed. His wife was sent to a concentration camp wherein she was tried and executed by her own countrymen.

On a number of occasions I have visited the Cimitiere de la Gaudier in Nantes where Eric Keep and Ron Thompson are now buried side by side. It is a public cemetery and the graves of the 92 airmen and 15 soldiers buried there occupy a small, but well kept corner. There are 77 RAF, 6 RCAF, 4 RAAF, 4 RNZAF and one unidentified RAF airman buried there. Very few of the 107 were over the age of 26 and there is one aged 19. It is a peaceful

---

[5] - *The March 1944 edition, No. F33 of 'Le Courrier De Liair' (Apporte Par La RAF)*

*Fernand Thierry gives me the wheel of 'K'-King. It had
been used to steer a go-cart for ten years!*

and moving place, not large as to overwhelm you with a sense of a great
impersonal tragedy, like one enormous cemetery to the south of Nantes, but
small and intimate, where one wants to linger and quietly mourn each one as
if it were a personal loss. Eric was aged 21 when he died and Ron 22.
Beneath Ron's stone are the words:

'May the winds blow softly on this sweet and hallowed spot.'

Le Cimitiere de la Gaudier, Nantes.

*In the foreground is the grave of Ron Thompson
and next to it that of Eric Keep.*

The occasion of Robert Pincon, Ancienne Deprotee Resistence, Croix de Guerre avec palme, Medaille de la Resistance, Medal of Freedom (USA), receiving the Legion d'Honneur at Chalon-sur-Soane 21st October 1961. Left is Mamie and right Roger.

EPILOGUE

THE 75TH YEAR - TRAINING THE 1993 RAF PILOT

'By hotter winds our firey hearts are fanned.'

Extract from 'Hassan' poem by James Elroy Flecker (1884 -1915)

The Royal Air Force Pilot of today would have first been interviewed, tested and assessed by The Officer and Aircrew Selection Board (OASC) now at Cranwell. In 1992 OASC was transferred from Biggin Hill and consequently this historic RAF station was closed. Unhappily, revenue expected by the Air Staff at MOD for the private development of the vacated site and economies from centralisation have not materialised and it is apparently on the cards that OASC may have to move on from Cranwell because of the lack of space there. The Battle of Britain Memorial Chapel at Biggin Hill remains an active and well used church, supported by the local population. However the regular RAF presence at what was a living monument to one of the great periods of our modern history has been lost forever for what appears to have been nothing more than a bureaucratic exercise in empire building.

Wherever it finally rests, OASC's primary task is to select adults for direct entry to RAF officer training. In addition it selects 16-year-olds for flying scholarships - 30 hours of pilot training at a civilian flying club - or for sponsorship through two years of Six Form studies to 'A' levels which automatically includes a Flying Scholarship. It also selects for the RAF sponsorship scheme through university. The University Cadetship carries with it 3 years of pilot training - up to 120 hours - on BAe Bulldogs of the University Air Squadron.

Sooner or later all those selected by OASC begin training at the Royal Air Force College, Cranwell. They do a 5 month course of ground studies at the department of Initial Officer Training (IOT). Those that succeed at IOT are commissioned and move to their specialist training. Pilots who have not flown a Flying Scholarship or with the University Air Squadron go to PFTS (Preliminary Flying Training School), a unit created to standardise initial flying training. Here they will fly 60 hours on Chipmunks (originally a DH Canada-designed aircraft of which 735 were built for the RAF at Chester!)

From PFTS they graduate to FTS at either Linton-on-Ouse or Cranwell to fly the BAe/Hunting Jet Provost or its 1989 Brazilian replacement, the EMB-312 Tucano. An uprated version for the RAF, built in Belfast by Short Brothers in collaboration with Embraer, is powered by a Garrett TPE331-12B gas turbine engine driving a four-bladed Hartzell propeller - it is a beautiful looking aeroplane. Those with Flying Scholarships or University Air Squadron experience go straight from IOT to FTS. After 9 months and about 100 hours flying the basic course would end and they are rated as a pilot to fly either 'Fast Jet', 'Multi' or 'Rotary'. The Fast Jet stream remain at Linton or Cranwell for a further 60 hours applied flying training on the Jet Provost/Tucano.

The 'Multi' pilots go to METS (Multi-Engine Training Squadron) No 6 Flying Training School at RAF Finningly to fly the BAe Jetstream T.Mk 1, the RAF multi-engine trainer. This twin-engined aircraft is powered by turbo-prop engines built by Turbomeca and was first designed by Handley-Page in 1966, first serving with the RAF in 1976. Here, at METS, after 6 to 8 months and 60 hours flying, the trainee will be awarded his pilot's flying badge. Thence he would go to a Hercules, Nimrod, Tristar or to VC10 (Tanker) OCU (Operational Conversion Unit). A Sentry (AWACS), VC10 Andover or a DH 125 pilot will go direct to a squadron for conversion training.

The Pilot classified as 'Rotary' will train at RAF Shawbury in a two part course using Gazelle and Wessex aircraft. It is planned to replace the Wessex with the Puma in the near future. After 60 hours flying they receive their pilot's wings and if designated a 'Support Helicopter Pilot' they move to either a Chinook or a Puma OCU. If a pilot was to be trained in 'Search and Rescue' duties he will go to RAF Valley.

The 'Fast Jet' pilot continues his training on the BAe Hawk T.Mk 1. at either RAF Chivenor (No 7 FTS) or a RAF Valley (No 4 FTS). Both bases run identical courses of 100 hours flying, comprising conversion to the faster and more complex aircraft followed by training in airborne tactics and combat manoeuvring plus weapon delivery training. At the successful completion of the course the Fast Jet pilot is awarded his wings prior to his posting to an Operational Conversion Unit (OCU).

Assuming our pilot, having graduated, on the Hawk had been selected to fly the Tornado, his first OCU unit would have been TTTE (Trinational Tornado Training Establishment) at Cottesmore. In 1981 it was a 13-week course, four at ground school, 35 hours in the air. There were originally 22 German, 21 RAF and 7 Italian Tornados on the Unit. In 1988, most of the Tornado Units having been formed, the Tornados on this Unit were reduced to 18, 16 and 4 respectively. Up to that time 462/370 Pilot/Navigators for

Germany, 377/333 for the RAF and 109/78 for Italy had been trained.

The RAF crews then proceeded to TWCU (Tornado Weapons Conversion Unit) at Honington. Pilots fly 32 hours (15 hours dual), the navigator flies 29 hours, 15 of which are with an instructor. They are then posted to a squadron, the pilot hours at this time would be approximately 420. Six months later they will be accepted as operational.

The prospective Harrier pilot will first learn to hover in a helicopter before proceeding to Wittering for his OCU. When he arrives at a squadron it will have cost £3M to have trained him! Meanwhile a small number of the Fast Jet stream go from Chivenor/Valley to the Buccaneer or the Jaguar OCU - both at Lossiemouth - for a 50 hour course before joining their squadrons.

At approximately £13M a throw the Tornado is an expensive and exotic piece of hardware. During the Gulf War 6 were lost due to enemy action and one due to an accident. It has been said that during World War II the Handley Page Halifax production aircraft were reputed to have cost £12,500 each![1] The first production delivery took place in July 1980. The first Tornado squadron, No 9, was formed at Honington on 1st June 1982. Having pioneered many new modifications they were finally transferred to Germany in October 1986. They were replaced at Honington in 1990 by No 13 - a reconnaissance squadron flying Tornado GR.Mk1's.

No 13 Squadron, you will recall, was the squadron in which Sgt Albert Stanley and his observer, Air Mechanic Wardlow, were serving when, whilst flying an RE 8 on a reconnaissance sortie in 1917, they died.

---

[1] - Page 49 *'Halifax Second To None' by Victor Bingham - Airlife 1986.*

IN MEMORIAM

During my research I came across the names of many casualties. I thought I would make a list of them. All were itimate friends, or fellow airman with whom I had drunk or rubbed shoulders in the mess, briefing or crew rooms and others, who likewise had died when I was in close proximity. It is a horrifying list, most of them were very young. With very few exceptions all of them were RAFVR.:-

Flt/Sgt Eric V Mathews, pilot of Liberator EW108 of No 358 Sqdn which crashed 7 miles North West of Jessore in India on 25th May 1945. We were great friends at school.

Fg/Off Ron Say, navigator/observer killed in a Wellington at No 20 OTU Lossiemouth. We studied Maths together while waiting for call up.

LAC E.F.W.Charrosin. who died at 31 P.D. Canada. We dined many times together at Lyons Corner House, Marble Arch at his Fathers expense. We were at Hemswell together

Fg/Off Norman Brockhouse and his Navigator were killed flying a Beaufighter at No 54 Night Fighter OTU Charterhall in 1944. (The same unit on which Richard Hillary author of 'The Last Enemy' was killed.) We were together at Hemswell and in South Africa.

The 301 Polish Squadron pilot Sgt. K.Ceglinski and the second pilot Sgt S Kuropatwa who were killed at Hemswell in a Wellington 1c R1641. Crashing on take off and catching fire on the night of 18th August 1941. The remaining members of the crew survived, the navigator being seriously injured.

The Unknown Soldier who died of Meningitis on H.M.T. 'Otranto'.

Lt. D.J.W.Compton, my ab initio flying instructor, at No 7 Air School. Kroonstad South Africa, who died with his crew in Italy on 16th August 1944 whilst flying a Marauder of No 12 Squadron SAAF. Their names appear on the RAF memorial in Malta.

LAC Gordon W Cornish who was killed in an unfortunate flying accident on 17th October 1942, at No 22 Air School (SFTS), Vereeniging, South Africa. His brother Sgt Clifford H Cornish had been killed the week previusly flying a No.229 Squadron Spitfire over Malta. We had been together since Hemswell. I remember how shocked we all were for his family.

Fg/Off B.S.Leuty. killed in 1944 flying a Lancaster of No.12 Sqdn. ('The Shiney Twelfth') He and the names of his crew are carved on the RAF Memorial at Runnymede. A room-mate at 22 Air School.

Fg/Off Nigel St George Pleasance was posted to 138 Squadron on the 18th May 1944 and was lost at sea on the 18th July 1944 when flying Halifax LL387. His target in France was 'SHIPWRIGHT 9'. His crew Flt/Lt H.D.Binns (Nav/B), Sgt Fergus (Nav), Sgt R.L.Lee (Wop/AG), Sgt J.Allison (A/G), Sgt W.L.Dalgleish RCAF (A/G) and Sgt E.R.Hearn (F/E). His and the names of his crew appear on the RAF Memorial at Runnymede. His name appearing opposite to that of Brian Leuty. We were the greatest of friends at 22 Air School and later but I had gone before he arrived on the Squadron.

Flt/Lt. James F.Muir DFC killed with his crew in 1944 whilst flying a Lancaster of No.207 Sqdn. A room-mate of Nigel Pleasance at 22 Air School. A quiet man whom I did not know well.

F/Sgt 'Bill' J.K.Flanagan killed in 1944 at No 1 AD no details. A truly wonderful character and a room-mate at 22 Air School.

The crew of Whitley LA792 which crashed and burned after engine failure 400 yards NW of Kineachy Lodge, Boat of Garten, Inverness on 6.10.43

Fg/Off Dallimore, Sgt Gess, Sgt Kelly, Sgt Cawthorne, Sgt Coster and Sgt Haycock, there were no survivors. 19 OTU Kinloss.

The Crew of Whitley BD 627 who died when it flew into the sea in Spey Bay while on a training flight on 31.10.1943. Killed were Sgt Garner, Sgt Mann, Plt/Off Lynch, Sgt Kincaid. Sgt Jones, the Rear Gunner was picked up in a dinghy. 19 OTU Kinloss.

The following crews who died while I was at 19 OTU Kinloss whose names I have not been able to trace:-

The crew of Whitley LA853 which crashed and burned near Disforth on 27.9.43. There were no survivors.

The three crew lost in the sea having bailed out before Whitley BD386 ditched a half mile off Kirkton Head, Peterhead due to engine failure on training flight on 24.10.43.

A Crew of 69 Course who died whilst on a cross country training flight in an Anson. No details.

And in memory of those crews who survived the most bizarre crashes during my training at 19 OTU !:-

Crew of Whitley Z9422 who ditched in Findhorn Bay after engine failure on take-off from Kinloss at night on 4.10.43.

Crew of Whitley N1369 and that of Anson DJ104 which landed on top of it at Kinloss on night of 19.10.43. N1369 was probably the oldest Whitley on the Unit. Delivered to RAF between 28.8.39 & 23.10.39.
Crew of Whitley EB 386 who landed on top of a hill in the circuit of Kinloss on the night of 25.10.43. with the new O.C. Flying in control.
There is no mention of this incident anywhere in the ORB. It has been completely covered up!

Crew of Whitley LA881 who crashed on take-off on West side of Forres airfield and burned at night of 25.10.43. It was probably the newest Whitley on Unit. Delivered to RAF between 4.2.43 & 22.3.43.
At No.1659 Heavy Conversion Unit RCAF - Topcliffe. On 18th January 1944 Halifax R9386 flown by Fg/Off F.H.Baker lost his Port Outer engine overshot and crashed 3/4-mile south-east of the Airfield. Two of the crew were killed. Minutes later Fg/Off P.Lavellee flying Halifax LW334 flew into a hillside at Black Hambleton, near Osmotherley, Yorks. He was flying in thick fog at a altitude of 1100 feet. There were no survivors.

Overleaf are listed aircrews at No 138 Squadron Tempsford were known to me and were lost:-

On 8th February 1944 Fg/Off G.O.Carroll was flying Halifax LL114 on Target 'JOHN 35' France and 'IAGO 1 /MONTANO 1' Belgium. It crashed at Austras 5 miles west of Grenoble, France. He and the rest of his crew were killed. Fg/Off A.E.Reid RCAF (Nav) F/Sgt J.A.Taylor RCAF (A/B), Sgt R.D.Clement (Wop/AG), Sgt G.S.Woodrow (A/G), Sgt V.W.Radford (A/G), Sgt P.T.Thompson (F/E). They are buried in Austras Communal Cemetery Isere. Dennis Carroll and I first met in South Africa.

Lost on the same night (Target 'JOCKEY 15', France) was Halifax LW275 flown by the 'A' flight Commander Flt/Lt (Act Sqdn/Ldr) T.C.Cooke DFC DFM and his crew Fg/Off R.W.Lewis DFC (Nav) Plt/Off E.Bell (A/B) Fg/Off J.S.Reed (Wop/AG) Fg/Off R.L.Beattie RCAF (A/G) Fg/Off A.B.Whitcombe (A/G) and Fg/Off L.J.Gornall (F/E). Happily all survived.

Posted in on 18/2/44 on 4th March 1944. Fg/Off W.C.Kingsley RCAF pilot of Halifax LL279 on Target 'JOHN 23' France was killed together with 4 other members of his crew. Two others were taken POW. His crew was Fg/Off G.A.Roberts RCAF (Nav), Fg/Off J.E.Wright RCAF (Nav/B), F/Sgt K.F.H.Hart (Wop/AG), Sgt H.W.Bradbury (A/G) Sgt E.F.Gilcash RCAF (A/G) Sgt J.R.Dutton RCAF (F/E). It was their second operational flight.

On 31st March 1944 Flt/Lt B.B.Mill flying Halifax LL287 crashed into the Wester Scheldt, 2 kms West of Hansweet Holland. His target was 'OSRIC 27' in Belgium. He and 4 others of his crew survived. Plt/Off F.Anderson, Flt/Lt E. Francis and F/Sgt E.Bates were lost at sea.

Posted in on 27/1/44 on 1st April 1944 Fg/Off F.B.Clark was pilot of Halifax LL252 on Targets 'ORAGE and PETER 5' which crashed at Vallee de Cousse 13kms North East of Tours, France. He together with Fg/Off R.J.Carson RCAF (Nav) injured, Sgt E Wilkinson (A/G), Sgt D.W.L.Brown RCAF (A/G) and Sgt W.R.McBurney RCAF (F/E) were taken POW. Sgt E.M Keep (A/B) and Sgt R.G.Thompson (Wop/AG) were killed.

Posted to 138 Squadron on 8/2/1944. On 28th April 1944 F/Sgt G.H.Williamson flying Halifax LL356 on Target 'OSRIC 59' in Belgium whilst his body was washed ashore his crew was presumed lost at sea. They were Sgt E.Dootson (Nav), F/Sgt A.J.G Barnes RCAF (A/B), Sgt H.F.Benbow (Wop/AG), F/Sgt E.R.Clayworth RAAF (A/G), Sgt J.E.Smythe RCAF (A/G), Sgt G.P.Croad (F/E).

Posted to Command 138 Squadron on 18/2/44. On 8th May 1944 Sqdn/Ldr (Act Wg/Cmdr) W.M.Russell DFC & Bar flying Halifax LL280 on Target 'CITRONELL 1' France crashed in Kattegat. He and his crew Fg/Off D.Brown DFC (Nav), Fg/Off B.P.McGonagle (A/B), Fg/Off J.A.Armour DFC DFM (Wop/AG), Fg/Off A.F.Bryce (A/G), Fg/Off N.Simister DFM (A/G), and Plt/Off G.Cable DFM (F/E) were all killed. I flew this crew down to Tempsford from 1654 HCU Wigsley.

On the same night Fg/Off H.H.McMullen RAAF and his crew were presumed lost at sea. They were flying Halifax LL192 on Target 'TABLEJAM 46' in Denmark. His crew was Fg/Off L.F.Stannard (Nav), Fg/Off K.J.Murphy RCAF (A/B), Sgt J.B.Stynes (Wop/AG), Sgt A.A.McPherson (A/G), Sgt L.L.J.Smith (A/G) and Sgt R.Boffey (F/E). 'Mac' McMullen and I flew the 'jinx' Tiger Moth to Waterbeach and return. I once flew LL192 on an air test.

On 9th May 1944 Fg/Off H.S.Coldridge and his crew failed to return. I did not know him.

On 17th May 1944 Halifax LK736 - the dreaded 'A' Apple, crashed at Great Barford, Bedford, following engine fire on a training flight Fg/Off V.C.Carter (A/B) Lost his life. I took this aircraft on two operational flights, it was a terrible aeroplane to fly.

On 1st June 1944 W/Off H.F.G.Murray flying Halifax LL276 crashed in Holland. Fg/Off L.J.Solomon (Nav), F/Sgt F.Stead (Wop/AG), Sgt A.P. McCulloch (A/G), Sgt R.Robinson (A/G) and Sgt T.McCluskey (F/E) died with him. F/Sgt L.P.Notton (A/B) and Fg/Off J.Pearcey RCAF (Nav) were taken prisoner. F/Sgt Murray, as he was then, took me on my first operational flight and I flew this aeroplane on an operational flight on 26/2/44.

On 2nd June 1944 Plt/Off D.H.Hayman RAAF was flying Halifax LL289 on Target 'PERCY 7' in France when it crashed killing him and Plt/Off Haynes (an extra crewman), Fg/Off D.Hargreaves (Nav), Plt/Off J.C.Fardon RAAF (A/B), F/Sgt A.H.Dickel (Wop/AG), Sgt D.A.Page (F/E). The two Gunners Plt/Off G.G.Houston and Sgt A Lyall survived. Plt/Off Hayman was a F/Sgt when I first arrived on the Squadron.

On 3rd June 1944 Plt/Off (Act Flt/Lt) T.M.Thomas was flying Halifax LL307 on Targets 'RODERIGO/OSRIC 77' Belgium/Holland when it crashed killing the entire crew. They were Fg/Off D.A.J.Smith (Nav) Fg/Off L.V.Warboys (A/B),F/Sgt E.Nelson (Wop/AG), F/Sgt J.K.R.Vincent (A/G), Sgt J.A.Vick (A/G) and Sgt E.Parry (F/E). 'Tommy' Thomas and I commenced Flying Operations on the same night.

Posted in 18/2/44 (The third crew to be lost who were posted to 138 Squadron on this day.) On the 8th June 1944 Plt/Off A.D.McKay RCAF was flying Halifax LL466 on Target 'DONALD 26' France he and his crew were killed. Sgt W.J.Cheshire (Nav), Fg/Off C.J.Ennis DFC (A/B), Fg/Off K.Bateman (S), Sgt D.W.Drummond (A/G), Sgt E.W.Carlson RCAF (A/G) and Sgt J.R.Ireland (F/E).

On the same night two other aircraft were lost LL307 flown by Plt/Off H.C.Jones and LL306 flown by Fg/Off F.H.Lyne. There was a F/Sgt Jones who started about the same time as I did perhaps this could have been him. Fg/Off Lyne I did not know. 3 aircraft lost, 2 nights after 'D' Day

Sqdn/Ldr Peter E Boyle, who was killed flying a glider, details unknown. We were in South Africa, 14 AFU Fraserburgh and Stalag Luft III together.

Sqdn/Ldr Jack Jagger who lost his life flying a Meteor VIII at Coningsby in 1952. we were great friends in Stalag Luff III. He was my daughter's God Father.

Flt/Lt. Geoff Rice DFC who died of cancer in 1982. He was a founder member of 617 Squadron who flew on the 'Dams Raid' but was forced to return when he hit the sea and lost his bomb. A most modest man and a great friend. We were room-mates in Stalag Luft III.

Sqdn/Ldr Greg Holdcroft SADO (Senior Administration Officer) at Tempsford who died before he wrote that promised book about Tempsford. What a story that would have been. A great friend. Sgt Ernie Wilkinson my Mid-Upper Air Gunner and Dispatcher who died after a long illness, who came to war when he could have stayed at home.

Twelve unknown members of the Resistance in the Chateau-Renault area who died as an indirect result of my crash into the Vallee de Cousse. In particular that brave farmer who brought food to us each evening.

'Loiseau' - Monsieur Roger Pincon (1898-1965) Chevalier de la Legion d'Honneur, Croix de Guerre, Medaille de la Resistance. Also served in the Great War in the French Artillery.

'Mamie' - Madam Janine Pincon (1897-1981) Ancienne Deportee Resistence, Chevalier de la Legion d'Honneur, Croix de Guerre avec palme, Medaille de la Resistance, Medal of Freedom (USA).

There must be others but I have no wish to find out and no further wish to fight the tug at my emotions.

ACKNOWLEDGEMENTS

Mr J.R.Bailey, Managing Director of Bailey Bros & Swinfen Ltd, Chaz Bowyer (Skol), Cecil Lewis, 'Pip' Hagues, Jack Beaumont, John Barson, Norman Franks, Ken Merrick, Jonathan Falconer, P.J.V Elliot, the librarian, and Mr Mungo Chapman of the RAF Museum, Commandant A.E.Smit of the SAAF Museum, Pretoria and Air Commodore A.J.Bell OBE, The staff of the Public Records Office Kew, Air Historical Branch 5 (RAF) of the Ministry of Defence, R. Piper GMBH & Co. KG of Munich.

Sources: *Wings Over France* - Lt. Col. Harold Hartney, *Sagittarius Rising* - Cecil Lewis, *Secret War* - Nigel West, *Galgenlieder und andere Gedichte* - Morgenstern, *Five Years in the RFC* - McCudden, *The First Great Air War* - Richard Townshend Bickers, *Vol I War in the Air* - Raleigh. *Vols II - VI & Appendicies* - H.E Jones, *Tiger Squadron* - Ira Jones, *The First Of The Few* - Denis Winter, *'SOE in France'* M.R.D.Foot. HSMO.

SELECTED READING

WORLD WAR I

Bickers, Ricard Townsend. - The First Great Air War.
- Hodder & Stoughton, 1988.

Bruce, J.M. - British Aeroplanes 1914-18 - Putman, 1957

Clark, Alan. - Aces High - The War in the Air over
the Western Front 1914-18. - George Weidenfeld & Nicholson, 1973.

Hartney, Lt. Col. Harold. E. - Wings Over France.
- Bailey Brothers & Swinfen Ltd, 1974.

Jones DSO MC DFC MM, Wg Cmdr Ira ('Taffy') - Tiger Squadron.
- W.H.Allan, 1954.

Jones, H.A. - The War in the Air Vols 2 to 6.
- Oxford University Press, 1922 to 1932.

Kierman, R.H. - Captain Albert Ball VC DSO ** MC etc.
- The Aviation Book Club, 1939.

Lewis, Cecil. - Sagittarius Rising.
- Heineman : Peter Davies, 1936, 1966, 1982. Re-issued by Greenhill 1993

Livesay, Anthony. - Great Battles of World War I.
- Guild Publishing, 1989.

Mathews, Borlaise. - The Aviation Pocket-Book for 1917
- Crosby Lockwood & Son - 1917.

McCudden VC DSO MC MM etc, Major James Thomas Byford. - Five
Years in the Flying Corps. - The 'Aeroplane' & General Publishing Co Ltd,
1918.

Raleigh, Sir Walter. - The War in the Air Vol. 1.
- Oxford University Press, 1922 to 1932.

Royal Air Force Flying Training Manual Part I - Flying Instruction.
HMSO (Air Publication 129), 1923.

Warner, Phillip. -Passchendaele - Sidgwick & Jackson, 1987.

Whitehouse, Arch. - The Fledgling - Nicholas Vane, 1964

Winter, Denis. - The First of the Few. - Fighter Pilots of the

First World War. - Allan Lane / Penguin Books, 1982.

WORLD WAR II

Bingham, Victor. - Halifax - second to none - Airlife, 1986

Brown, Anthony Cave. - Bodyguard of Lies - W.H.Allen, 1977

Falconer, Jonathan, -RAF Bomber Airfields of World War 2 - Ian Allen
1992

Foot, M.R.D. - SOE in France: an Account of the Work of the British
Special Operations Executive in France, 1940-44. - HMSO, 1966.

Foot, M.R.D. - SOE The Special Operations Executive 1940-46.
- British Broadcasting Corporation, 1984.

Fuller, Jean Overton. - Double Webs.- Putman, 1958.
Jackson, Robert. - The Secret Squadrons. - Robson Books Ltd, 1983.

Jones, Liane. - A Quiet Courage. - Bantam Press, 1990.

Lorain, Pierre. (adapted by David Kahn) - Secret Warfare: the Arms and Techniques of the Resistance. - Orbis Publishing, 1984.

Marshall, Bruce. - The White Rabbit. - Evans, 1952.

Marshall, Robert. - Secret Service Treachery in the Dirty War
- An article published by The Editor of 'The Listener', 1st May 1986.
Marshall, Robert. - All The Kings Men. - Collins, 1988.

Merrick, R.A. - Flights of the Forgotten. - Arms & Armour, 1989.

Merrick, R.A. - Halifax An Illustrated History of a Classic World War II Bomber - Ian Allan 1980

Middlebrook, Martin. & Chris Everitt - The Bomber Command War Diaries.
- Viking / Penguin Books, 1985.

Morgenstern, Christian. - Galgenlieder und Andere Gedichte (Gallows Songs and Other Poems) - R.Piper & Co Munich, 1972.

Roberts, R.N. - The Halifax File.- Air-Britain (Historians) Ltd, 1982.

Roberts, R.N. - The Whitley File.- Air-Britain (Historians) Ltd, 1986

Ruby, Marcel. - F Section SOE. - Lee Cooper / Heineman, 1988.

Various Authors - Action Stations Volumes 1, to 10.
- Patrick Stevens Ltd, 1979 to 1987.

Verity, Hugh. - We landed by Moonlight.- Ian Allen Ltd, 1978.

West, Nigel. - Secret War, The story of SOE, -Hodder & Stoughton, 1992.

OTHER TITLES AND PRINTS AVAILABLE FROM INDEPENDENT BOOKS

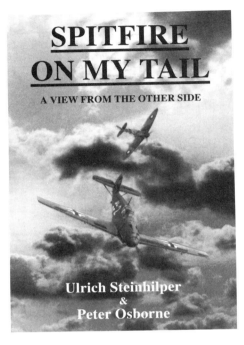

'SPITFIRE ON MY TAIL'

A View From The Other Side

Ulrich Steinhilper & Peter Osborne

Non-fiction   *Illustrated*

ISBN 1 872836 003

Spitfire On My Tail is the detailed account of how one German grew up and joined the *Luftwaffe* as a career officer and airman. It was written by Ulrich Steinhilper who was an *Oberleutnant* with JG 52 (52nd Fighter Wing) based at Coquelles near Calais. He flew over one-hundred and fifty combat missions during the Battle of Britain and saw his *Gruppe* of thirty-six experienced pilots whittled down to just a handful by October.

It is a very personal and human story of the naivety of youth being shaped by the forces of war. Poignant lessons learned by tragic accidents, counterbalanced by anger towards those who saw the war as a means of personal advancement and self aggrandizement.

There is no doubt there is, today, a movement towards a more balanced understanding of events and *SPITFIRE ON MY TAIL*, already being referred to as a classic of the period, presents a rare opportunity for students of this classic air engagement to see The View From The Other Side. In a market where new books on the subject, and many re-issues of classics, offer a bewildering choice *SPITFIRE ON MY TAIL* is in a class of its own.

'SPITFIRE ON MY TAIL': 335 Pages, 84 black & white illustrations, hardback only. Price: £14.95

'TEN MINUTES TO BUFFALO'

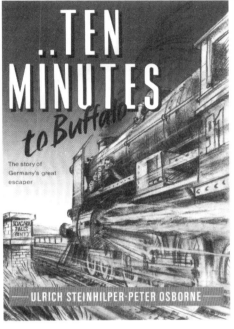

*The Story of Germany's
Great Escaper
Ulrich Steinhilper & Peter Osborne*

Non-Fiction   Illustrated

ISBN 1 872836 01 1

'*Ten Minutes to Buffalo*' is long-awaited sequel to Ulrich Steinhilper's highly successful first book, '*Spitfire On My Tail*'. Unlike the first book, which tells the story of how a young German came to fly in Hitler's Luftwaffe and to fight in the Battle of Britain, '*Ten Minutes to Buffalo*' is a catalogue of courage and determination on the ground. In this way it is set to repeat the successful formula by providing a rare chance to witness how things were for 'The Other Side,' this time behind the barbed wire and in Ulrich Steinhilper's case - all too often outside the wire! It relates a story of remarkable courage and perseverance in the most appalling conditions, braving arctic weather and appalling hardship with one thought in mind - to get home.

From his first camp in England away to the vastness of Canada he and a select few of his fellow officers were to become known as *Die Ausbrecherkönige von Kanada* (the breakout kings from Canada) and Ulrich was to shine among them. His escapes were innovative and even audacious and it was only bad luck that seemed to keep him from a 'homerun'.

Very little has ever been written about the conditions of German officers as prisoners of the Allies and practically nothing of their ingenuity and perseverance in planning and executing escape plans so similar to their counterparts in German hands. This remarkable book is entirely written from original hand-written sheets which date from 1942 and which give it a great immediacy and accuracy. '*TEN MINUTES TO BUFFALO*' 431 Pages, 45 black & white illustrations, hardback only. Price: £14.95

'FULL CIRCLE'

The Long Way Home
From Canada

Ulrich Steinhilper & Peter Osborne

Non-Fiction   *Illustrated*

ISBN 1 872836 02 X

'Full Circle' is the last of three books which record Ulrich Steinhilper's remarkable experiences in the Second World War. From being a front line fighter pilot in the Battle of Britain he becomes a Prisoner of War, but for Ulrich the war is far from over.

In *'Ten Minutes To Buffalo'*, the story of the first three escapes is told and in *'Full Circle'* the story is continued as Ulrich and Hinnerk Waller find themselves back in custody. But that is far from the end of Ulrich's career as an escaper. Nor is it the end of the detailed and fascinating description of life as a POW. Locking up large numbers of bright young men led to the most ingenious schemes to manufacture their own radios, make their own tools and later, on their *Ehrenwort* (word of honour), to rebuild and run a farm.

Ulrich describes in graphic detail his last attempt to get back to Germany, admitting it was the worst mistake he ever made in his life. From documents, hand-written at the time, and from numerous letters and postcards home he accurately reconstructs what it was like to be a prisoner of the Allies and the hardships that brought at the end.

'Full Circle' completes Ulrich Steinhilper's odyssey and with it what is now being described as one of the most important contributions to the broader history of the Second World War to emerge in recent times.

'FULL CIRCLE' 408 Pages, 74 black & white pictures and illustrations, hardback only. Price: £14.95

'Close To The End'

'CLOSE TO THE END'

The print depicts the 27th October 1940 when Sergeant Bill Skinner and A/Flight Lieutenant JC Mungo-Park of 74 Squadron Royal Air Force (The Tigers) attacked Oberleutnant Ulrich Steinhilper (Yellow 2) and Feldwebel Lothar Schieverhöfer (Yellow 4) of 3/JG52. The prints are individually signed by Bill Skinner and by Ulrich Steinhilper and are priced at £19.95. All prints are on heavy acid-free paper and printed in high quality fade-free inks to an image size 300 mm X 600 mm. The signatures are in pencil or ink if preferred.

'BORN LEADER'

'BORN LEADER'

The Story of Guy Gibson DFC & Bar, DSO & Bar, VC.

Alan Cooper

Non-Fiction   *Illustrated*

ISBN 1 872836 03 8

There is little doubt that if asked to name a bomber pilot from the Second World War most people would name Guy Gibson. Not only was he an outstanding pilot but he was to lead the famous Dambusters raid on the night of 16th/17th May 1943. Post-war the film of the operation ensured that Gibson became a household name, even though he had been killed in the latter stages of the war.

'Born Leader' is a detailed account of how circumstances moulded one of the most outstanding pilots of our time, written by Alan Cooper who is recognised as being one of the most knowledgable authors on the subject, having also written: The Men Who Breached The Dams (1982) Beyond the Dams to the Tirpitz (1983) Bombers over Berlin (1985) The Air Battle of the Rhur (1992) The Dam Busters Squadron - 50th Anniversary 617 Squadron [With Foreword by Her Majesty Queen Elizabeth The Queen Mother] (1993).

May 1993 will see the fiftieth anniversary of the Dams Raid and will generate great interest in those who flew the operation. This biography of Gibson will be a must for all.

192 Pages, 44 black & white illustrations, hardback only. Price: £14.95

'BORN LEADER'

The Story of Guy Gibson VC, DFC & Bar, DSO & Bar.
Alan Cooper

SPECIAL EDITION

A special edition of 'Born Leader' is available containing the signatures of at least eight people who either flew on the Dams Raid or were 617 groundcrew on the night of the raid. Added to this the books are also signed by Richard James DFM, who flew with Gibson on night fighters and Richard Todd who played Gibson in the post-war film of the raid; at least ten signatures in all. A complete list is available by return.

The signed editions are individually numbered and limited to 617 copies. **Priced at £24.95**

Each of the copies of this special edition raises £5.00 for charity and to date over £500 has already been donated to charities like The RAF Benevolent Fund Eagle Lodge Appeal and the Cheshire Foundation.

'LAURELS FOR PRINZ WITTGENSTEIN'

Werner Roell

Non-Fiction   *Illustrated*

Due January 1994

'Laurels for Prinz Wittgenstein' is a translation of the acclaimed German title *Blümen für Prinz Wittgenstein*, written by Werner Roell. It is the story of a member of the German aristocracy who was to become the a nightfighting ace as the RAF nightly increased their effort to destroy German industry. A modern day knight, von Wittgenstein was to be awarded the *Ritterkreutz* (Knight's cross of the Iron Cross) for the destruction of eighty-three four-engined bombers in the defence of Germany.

Wittgenstein was to pay the ultimate price for his dedication to what he believed was his duty and whatever one's views on what was ultimately discovered to have been perpetrated in the name of the German people that should not be spoken of in the same place as the bravery of outstanding airmen like 'The Prinz'.

'Laurels for Prinz Wittgenstein' is a rare chance to see the great night air war from the other side and in so doing to see part of what the British airmen faced nightly. In the words of the author, Werner Roell - himself a *Kreutzträger* (holder of the Knight's Cross) - *'If you honour your enemy you honour yourself.'*

Hardback, illustrated

£14.95

SPECIAL EDITION

'LAURELS FOR PRINZ WITTGENSTEIN'

Werner Roell

It is proposed to produce a special signed edition of *'Laurels For Prinz Wittgenstein'* to help raise money for airforce charities. The signed editions will have a specially designed book plate inserted, bearing the original signatures of the two surviving members of Wittgenstein's crew and Werner Roell the author. It hoped to add other Luftwaffe personnel and in particular Ju 88 aircrew to the list, but certainly the three airmen above have already signed. A full list of signatories and their service honours and awards will be available on request in January.

The special editions will retail at £24.95 with at least £5.00 from each sale going to an aircrew related charity.

SPECIAL EDITION PRINTS

'OPERATION CHASTISE' - John Larder

The jacket of *'Born Leader'* is a reproduction from a print of John Larder's painting entitled *'Operation Chastise'*. The actual print size is 26" X 19" with a 3" border. These are available, signed by John Larder at £18.00.

SIGNED EDITION

A high quality print as above, signed by: Squadron Leaders Scott Anderson & Colin Paterson, and John Larder. Also bearing the crests of the Battle of Britain Memorial Flight and of 617 Squadron - The Dambusters. Priced at £25

DAMS EDITION

'Operation Chastise' signed by three air crew who flew on the Dams, four ground crew and 'Chan' Chandler, who flew 97 missions with 617 Squadron including the raid on the Tirpitz. These prints are also signed by the crew of the BBMF Lancaster which flew over the Derwent Dam on the fiftieth anniversary 1993. Limited to 200 copies. Priced at £95

'50 YEARS FLY BY'

A stunning new print by John Larder, to mark the 50th Anniversary of 617 Squadron, Royal Air Force. A Numbered Special edition of **617 copies only** bearing the signatures of original Dambusters plus 1960's Vulcan crew from 617 Squadron and Tornado aircrew who served in the Gulf (twelve signatures in all). Priced at £95.

'VULCAN THUNDER'

The latest print from John Larder depicts the display of the last RAF Vulcan XH558 at Finningly. The prints are individually signed in pencil by John Larder, Flight Lieutenant John Gill, a former Vulcan Pilot and Flight Lieutenant Ted Farrent who was electronics officer on Vulcan, both formerly with 9 Squadron. The prints are priced at £25

FLOWN EDITION

There are also available 200 copies of the print flown from Cranfield to Waddington following the last display flight of XH558, signed by John Larder, Flight Lieutenant John Gill, Flight Lieutenant Ted Farrent and Squadron Leader Vince O'Sullivan who piloted the 617 Squadron Vulcan around the world in 1966.Each print come with a 'flown' certificate and also have an A4 colour reproduction of the navigator's map and notes for the last display at Cranfield. These are priced at £40.00

SPECIAL EDITION

SPECIAL EDITION

The special edition of Vulcan Thunder is limited to 250 copies and is signed by all ten of the crew of XH558 who flew her through her last display season. Priced at £55.00

All prints bear original individual signatures not printed facsimiles. Post and packing is free for all prints, but please add £4.00 for overseas orders. All book orders should have £1.50 added for p & p (£2.00 for overseas). All overseas orders are sent surface mail unless airmail is required, in which case £5.00 should be added.

** INTERNATIONAL VISA CARD PURCHASES WELCOME **

INDEPENDENT BOOKS,

**3,Leaves Green Crescent, Keston, Bromley, BR2 6DN, England
Telephone: Biggin Hill Kent (0959) 573360
Fax 0959 540002**